# U.S.-Mexican Energy Relationships

# U.S.-Mexican Energy Relationships

## Realities and Prospects

Edited by

**Jerry R. Ladman**
Arizona State University

**Deborah J. Baldwin**
University of Arkansas at
Little Rock

**Elihu Bergman**
Americans for Energy
Independence

**LexingtonBooks**
D.C. Heath and Company
Lexington, Massachusetts
Toronto

**Library of Congress Cataloging in Publication Data**

Main entry under title:
    U.S.-Mexican energy relationships.

    Papers presented at a conference co-sponsored by the Americans for
Energy Independence of Washington, D.C., and the Center for Latin
American Studies of Arizona State University, held at Arizona State University
Dec. 13-14, 1979.
    Bibliography: p.
    Includes index.
    1. Petroleum industry and trade—Mexico—Congresses. 2. Energy
industries—United States—Congresses. 3. Mexico—Economic conditions—
1970-    —Congresses. 4. Mexico—Foreign relations—United States—
Congresses. 5. United States—Foreign relations—Mexico—Congresses.
I. Ladman, Jerry R., 1935-    . II. Baldwin, Deborah J. III. Bergman, Elihu.
IV. Americans for Energy Independence. V. Arizona. State University,
Tempe. Center for Latin American Studies.
HD9574.M6U56        338.2'7282'0972        80-8878
ISBN 0-669-04398-2

Published simultaneously in Canada

Printed in the United States of America

Casebound International Standard Book Number: 0-669-04398-2

Paperbound International Standard Book Number: 0-669-04399-0

Library of Congress Catalog Card Number: 80-8878

*To Mary, James, and Liz*

# Contents

# List of Figures

# List of Tables

# Preface and Acknowledgments

This book consists of edited papers, comments, and discussions that were presented at a conference on U.S.-Mexican energy relationships held 13-14 December 1979 at Arizona State University. The conference was co-sponsored by the Americans for Energy Independence of Washington, D.C., and the Center for Latin American Studies of Arizona State University. Elihu Bergman, executive director of Americans for Energy Independence, and Jerry R. Ladman, director of the Center for Latin American Studies, were organizers and cochairpersons of the conference. This volume is in the Energy Policy Series of the Americans for Energy Independence.

The idea for the conference grew out of a concern that, although much was being written to describe the new Mexican petroleum reserves and their potential for adding to U.S. and global supplies, fostering Mexican economic development, and influencing bilateral U.S. and Mexican foreign policy, no attempt was being made to make an authoritative and comprehensive statement on the realities of the situation. Nevertheless, policy was being made and decisions formulated on the basis of existing information. Thus, to fill this hiatus, the idea emerged of a conference as a forum in which a number of recognized experts from Mexico and the United States would gather to present papers and prepared comments as well as to discuss in depth the ideas and issues related to oil. This book makes the resulting information available for policymakers, scholars, and the interested public.

A number of persons should be recognized for their assistance in conducting the conference. The office staffs at Americans for Energy Independence and the Arizona State University Center for Latin American Studies spent many hours in correspondence and preparation. The Arizona State University Office of Conference Services provided considerable assistance in organizing the logistics.

In particular we are very grateful for the financial support provided by a number of national and Phoenix-based organizations that made the conference possible. These contributors are as follows:

The Arizona Bank

Arizona-Mexico Commission

Arizona Public Service Company

Florida Gas Transmission Company

The Ford Foundation

General Electric Corporation

General Host Corporation

Greyhound Leasing and Financial Corporation

Salt River Project

Stone and Webster Engineering Corporation

U.S. Department of Energy

Valley National Bank

Westinghouse Electric Corporation

Finally, we owe special thanks to the office staff of the Center for Latin American Studies, who so willingly typed and retyped the manuscripts for this volume, and to Cynthia Miguélez for the translation of several papers. We also appreciate the indulgence of the contributors, who so willingly accepted the editorial changes necessary for the economy and interest of the volume.

# Introduction

Symbols play a key role in the course of U.S.-Mexican relationships. After a hiatus of four decades, oil has recently reacquired a prominent position as the result of major new discoveries of Mexican petroleum reserves, announced by the government in the mid-1970s. This announcement occurred at a time when Mexico was reevaluating its development strategy, and the United States and the rest of the world were confronting the realities of the limitations, vulnerabilities, and costs of the world oil market. Consequently, Mexican oil became a preeminent factor in U.S.-Mexican bilateral relations because it represented a symbol of means not only to provide Mexico the opportunity for development but also to provide the United States and other nations with an additional source of energy.

The nationalization of the Mexican petroleum industry in 1938 symbolized the end of an era in which foreign interests exercised significant control over Mexican natural resources. It likewise symbolized a new set of conditions for U.S.-Mexican relationships. The action of President Lázaro Cárdenas involved more than an adjustment in economic relationships. When it was issued, the nationalization decree triggered external and internal reactions of significant proportions. The world outside Mexico was forced to reevaluate the premise of its relationship with Mexican private and public sectors. The United States was confronted with the real limitations of its power and influence on Mexican economic development. Nationalization established a new direction for the course of the Mexican Revolution by signaling a revitalization of the revolutionary ideals, first espoused in 1910, that had been unfocused throughout subsequent years. The decree may not have been the ultimate panacea for Mexico, but it remains the ultimate symbol of nationhood.

Nearly four decades later, the symbolic role of oil emerged once more as a critical factor in U.S.-Mexican relationships. The global energy transition of the 1970s created value of great dimensions for the major new petroleum discoveries that were being disclosed with dramatic regularity during the final half of the decade. In terms of U.S. interests, the Mexican asset symbolized a tangible buffer against the economic vulnerabilities of increasing U.S. oil dependence. For Mexico this asset symbolized, contradictorily, both a renewed target for exploitation by the United States and an opportunity to accelerate the reduction of Mexican economic dependence on the United States. Within this symbolic framework emerged some new realities of changing political and economic relationships, for both Mexico and the United States.

The purpose of this book is to explore some of the new realities, including the influence of traditional and contemporary symbols on these realities, and how they will affect U.S.-Mexican bilateral relations. This book consists of papers, prepared comments, and edited discussions presented at a conference held in December 1979. The conference originated from a concern that hope and fantasy were interfering with a realistic assessment of present and prospective relationships between Mexico and the United States, newly dominated by the increasingly critical and transcendental factor of energy. To the extent that a diversion from reality (an escape, if you will) exists, there is an inclination to avoid some of the difficult choices each country ought to be making in its own self-interest. There is also an inclination to employ faulty expectations in the process of making the choices.

The conference was designed to identify and describe present reality, to assess it, and, by so doing, to achieve a clearer understanding of the prospects for the future. A comprehensive format was developed to focus on the wide spectrum of factors that influence U.S.-Mexican relationships. On the Mexican side, the issues involve petroleum reserves, the Mexican National Petroleum Company (PEMEX), opportunities for economic development, and changing political conditions. For the United States, the issues involve the consequences of dependence on oil imports, energy policy, and the impact of Mexican economic development on the U.S. economy. Last, these national concerns and other world events are considered jointly as they influence global relations.

The book is divided into four parts: (1) background; (2) the Mexican perspective; (3) the U.S. perspective; and (4) the changing conditions of Mexico's external relations—U.S., hemispheric, and global. Each part is followed by a summary of the open discussion ending each segment of the conference.

In part I, Williams broadly reviews historical and contemporary bilateral relations with an emphasis on the role of petroleum. His characterization of these relations as historically ambiguous and fragile entities provides a perspective in which to assess the contemporary situation. Puente Leyva traces the economic background and consequences of the current Mexican oil boom through both the Echeverría and López Portillo administrations. He expresses concern about the capabilities and intentions of the Mexican government to use petroleum revenues to resolve its agricultural problems.

Part II, The Mexican Perspective, begins with an optimistic projection by Grossling of the quantity of Mexican petroleum reserves and their location. This assessment is followed by Sepúlveda's discussion of the evolution of the Mexican National Petroleum Company since 1938. The metamorphosis of the company, according to Sepúlveda, involving a transition from an oil company dedicated to social concerns to one striving for economic efficiency, has affected the corporation's relationship with the government as well as its capability to handle the demands of the current oil boom. The chapter by Villarreal discusses the alternatives available to Mexico in efforts to capture the benefits of a greatly expanded petroleum industry. This theme is further elaborated by Randall's chapter in a discussion of the political economy of Mexican petroleum in the context of an inflationary economy.

In part III, the U.S. perspective, Netschert underscores the U.S. need for Mexican petroleum in the near future. However, he recognizes at the same time that this need is likely to conflict with the capacity of the Mexican economy to absorb the related revenue without subjecting itself to serious inflation. These circumstances, on the one hand, determine the complex environment in which to develop mutually satisfactory energy relationships. Goldmuntz argues, on the other hand, that, in the long run, the United States may not be dependent on petroleum imports, given U.S. domestic possibilities for conservation and substitution. The chapter by Reynolds analyzes the probable impacts on the U.S. economy of Mexican economic development resulting from petroleum-related expansion.

Part IV, the changing conditions of Mexico's external relations, focuses on oil as a factor in global political relationships. Pellicer de Brody examines the influence of petroleum in contemporary U.S.-Mexican relations. Ojeda's chapter, which was presented at the conference by Miguel Wionczek, investigates the potential role of oil as a negotiating tool, using as examples the impact of petroleum on Mexico's relations with Israel and the United States. The book concludes with a guide to source materials on contemporary Mexican petroleum.

Several major conclusions are derived from the information and analysis in this volume. Foremost among them is that Mexican oil does not provide the United States with an elixir to facilitate an adjustment to the new energy realities that it is confronting; the evolving U.S.-energy transition will not be fueled by Mexican oil. In developing an effective response to the energy challenge of the 1980s, the United States must deal with domestic capabilities, including coal, nuclear energy, domestic oil and gas, realistic pricing, and efficient use of energy.

For Mexico, the new bonanza is not an elixir that will achieve a quick resolution of issues that have been conditions of Mexican national development since the Revolution, involving agricultural sufficiency, employment, exports, migration, and the patterns of income distribution in Mexican society. Although oil will be an increasingly important factor in bilateral relations, it will not be the dominant factor. Similarly, Mexican oil will not be a dominant factor in the international relationships of the two countries but will remain an ingredient of the relationship, the significance of which will be determined by the success of the U.S. energy transition, the progress of Mexican economic development, and the conditions of global oil dependence. Meanwhile, in the interest of mature relationships and creative policymaking for both countries, Mexican oil is most accurately viewed in a context of reality amid symbols.

# Part I
# Background

# 1

# U.S.-Mexican Energy Relations: Ambiguity and Fragility

*Edward J. Williams*

A certain tentative hesitancy suffuses both form and substance in U.S.-Mexican relations. Calculated insult alternates with insensitive diplomacy, leading to ongoing ambiguity and fragility. The ultimate causes of that precarious uncertainty emanate from a dismal record of historical intercourse in tandem with a series of structural differences compounded by the mind-boggling complexities of contemporary bilateral relations.

It is little wonder that the present energy relationship reflects those omnipresent qualities. Although some positive achievements have been recorded and more are promised, the situation during the 1970s was always precarious, and all evidence points to more of the same for the 1980s. This chapter describes and analyzes the ambiguity and fragility of the bilateral energy relationship during the recent past, the present, and the immediate future.

Ambiguity and fragility are mutually reinforcing concepts. In the case at hand, for example, vacillating uncertainty in Mexico's hydrocarbons policy has implied a sense of concern (or mistrust) in the United States manifest with the potential for insensitive exercises in hegemonic pressure. From the northern side of the Rio Grande, the indecision (or perversity) of U.S. policymakers about the embittered gas-purchase accord catalyzed the fragility of bilateral relations, leading to a serious crisis in U.S.-Mexican relations.

## Historical and Structural Determinants

Providing a detailed history and analysis of the well-known chronology and context of bilateral relations is beyond the ken of this effort, but a sense of the scenario must be offered by way of divining the root causes of the present malaise.[1] It is, in truth, a dreary tale of mutual aggression, insult, and disparagement.

Most of the historical record is common knowledge. In the nineteenth century, the imperialistic expansion of the United States stripped Mexico of more than half of its territory. In the turmoil of the post-1910 internecine struggles in Mexico, the U.S. ambassador connived in the overthrow and eventual assassination of President Francisco Madero and his vice-president,

3

José María Pino Súarez. In the same context, U.S. forces occupied Tampico and, less successfully, launched an invasion into Mexico to punish Pancho Villa. These examples of hegemonic muscle flexing are the most-dramatic explanatory causes of Mexico's ongoing fear and mistrust of the United States, but they are complemented by dozens of other episodes in which the United States forced its will upon its weaker neighbor.

The transgressions of Mexico have been less overwhelming and less frequent, to be sure, but egregious enough to contribute to the fragility of relations. Mexico's flirtation with Imperial Germany in the World War I-period is a case in point.[2] Villa's depredations provide even more-frightening examples of Mexico's excesses. His massacre of Americans in Santa Ysabel, Chihuahua and his subsequent raid on Columbus, New Mexico evoke fear and mistrust on the U.S. side of the border. More recently, the discourteous treatment afforded President Carter during his state visit adds another illustration of Mexico's contribution to the ongoing fragility of bilateral intercourse.

Furthermore, confrontation over petroleum plays a key role in the history of modern U.S.-Mexican relations. From 1917 to 1938 and beyond, the two nations were locked in an ongoing struggle centering on the protection of U.S. petroleum interests in Mexico. The issue revolved around U.S. industry's opposition to the implications of Article 27 of Mexico's 1917 Constitution that declared national ownership of all subsoil wealth. The ongoing controversy reached a crescendo in 1938 when President Lázaro Cárdenas nationalized the industry. The threat of intervention then hung heavy, and a boycott of Mexican oil was imposed, only to be lifted with the coming of World War II. In that sense, Mexican oil nationalism is Mexican nationalism in spades; latter-day visions of nationally produced hydrocarbons being sold to the United States evoke a poignant ambiguity in the minds and hearts of Mexican policymakers.

Should these historical influences be insufficient, the structural context also adds its weight to the ambiguity and fragility of the bilateral equation. It spells a rich and powerful Anglo-Saxon-Protestant nation in juxtaposition to a relatively poor, less-powerful, Latin-Catholic culture. Economic asymmetry features the United States exporting capital and manufactures and importing raw materials and people. The Mexican contribution to the interaction is, of course, exactly opposite. Mexico needs U.S. money and manufactured goods; it must sell its commodities and raw materials, and it is compelled to let its people fend for themselves by migrating to the United States. The psychological quality of the intercourse is also part of the context; sadly enough, ambiguity and fragility always characterize relations between the rich and the poor.

Political asymmetry conjures the same message. The United States has global interests and commitments; Mexico has limited regional concerns.

In the execution of U.S. world strategy, Mexico has played a minor role. This situation adds further indignity to a precarious relationship and catalyzes occasional examples of mutual recrimination. Empathy seldom characterizes interaction between the powerful and the less powerful. Finally, sociocultural differences also contribute to a structure of disparity and becloud effective communication and discourse. Several dichotomies suffice to suggest the disparate qualities and differing characteristics of the two nations: white versus brown, Protestant versus Catholic, Anglo-Saxon versus Latin, materialistic versus humanistic.

In sum, the evidence is all too convincing. As Mexico and the United States have struggled to evolve a semblance of a stable and predictable energy relationship during the 1970s and beyond, they have been encumbered by a challenging context. The historical depredations of old conjure reciprocal fear and mistrust. The structures of bilateral relations compound the problem by contributing more fear interspersed with arrogance and disdain. History and context set a scenario of eroding predictability and stability and of crystallizing ambiguity and fragility.

**Contemporary Determinants and Influences**

As that context of bilateral relations continues to influence the present evolution of energy relations, it is complemented by a series of more-specific features of the scenario emanating from and characterizing the component parts of the relationship. In Mexico, the crux of the matter is the formation and execution of a production and exportation policy. At the highest level of decision making, that policy has been vacillating and unsure. At secondary levels, domestic political opposition and the activities of the Mexican National Petroleum Company (PEMEX) have added to the problems of policy formation.

In the United States, the obvious desire for increasing amounts of Mexican hydrocarbons has led to a more-consistent posture, but enough insensitivity and perversion have crept in to compound the uncertainty of the relationship. Informed by and extrapolating from the respective domestic scenes, the enormous complexity of bilateral relations has occasionally led to petroleum commerce's being dragged into the larger fray, increasing tensions and endangering amity.

*Mexico*

To reiterate, in Mexico changes in production and exportation policy have contributed to uncertainty. Differing economic realities and ever-growing-reserve quotations explain much of the motivation for changing policy posture, but domestic political opposition and managerial and policy deficiencies in PEMEX have also influenced the policymakers.[3]

Although a general commitment to increasing production characterized policy in the 1970s, some reorientation at several levels of policy and practice evolved during the decade. Policy style and rhetoric underwent change, and more-substantial ambiguity appeared with the announcement of 1980 as a production "platform" year. During the Echeverría administration (1970-1976), the milieu was befogged by a situation that juxtaposed conservationist rhetoric with concentrated exploitation. The government's restrictive pronouncements may have reflected internal policy struggles, or they may have been manipulative camouflage, but they seemed to have had little effect on practice. From the outset, PEMEX hurried exploitation and production.

Some of the verbal inconsistency continued with the new regime. On the whole, President López Portillo seemed to promulgate a fairly moderate policy, but his PEMEX chief displayed some contradictory inclinations. The measured presidential position appeared to reflect increasing concern about Mexico's ability to digest the significant new sums of money projected to come from larger production and exportation. As the chaotic Iranian situation became more visible, many Mexicans became increasingly fearful of the destabilizing impact of too much money spent too fast in search of rapid development, although the more-moderate position had carried the day as early as the presentation of the national oil company's annual report in 1978. In the report, Director General Jorge Díaz Serrano announced that the government had established a production platform for 1980. At that time, policy review was to be undertaken with the possibility that production would level off. In the words of the annual report:

> After the production platform of 1980 is attained, Mexico can decide if the same pace of production is to continue, or if it is convenient to increase or reduce it, with the tremendous advantage of having, by then, enough income and ease to project the execution of a master development plan . . .[4]

The Mexican policymakers may decide to taper off production increases beginning in 1980, but the situation is uncertain. A review of export policy and practice illustrates the point. The Mexican government's export policy during the 1970s stated differing projections at various times. The long and the short of the alternative proposals revolved around two contradictory policy recommendations. On the one hand, many people counseled that Mexico minimize its exports. At one time and from some sources, that position focused on the necessity to husband resources for future generations, but a similar stance was also assumed from differing sources who were more concerned with the possible destabilizing influences of too much money.

On the other hand, a strong current of opinion advised that the imperatives of serious economic problems and plentiful reserves compelled the nation to a policy of increasing export earnings. Nationalistic sensitivities and domestic political discretion weighed heavily in favor of conservationist rhetoric, but evolving practice hinted at a less-restrictive policy before 1977. After 1977, the official stance changed to emphasize increasing exports, but the critics continued a rearguard action designed to convince the policymakers of their folly. By late 1978, official export policy did begin to inch back to a rather moderate stance, although the motivations behind the revision were frequently not those published by the critics. The main concern by that time was economic destabilization, not the future needs of the Mexican industrialization process.

The recipient nations of Mexico's petroleum is still another element of policy and reality that is particularly germane to the United States and to this discussion. As in other areas, the trends are in transition and definite patterns are difficult to ascertain. Similar to other aspects of petroleum policy, furthermore, ambition tends to befog practice. During the Echeverría years, policy statements indicated exporting to the Third-World nations. In much the same vein, several early policy statements also reflected the endemic anti-Yankee posture that frequently worms its way into Mexican foreign-policy stances, contributing to the fragility of relations. At the very outset, Echeverría was quick to declare that the United States could expect no special treatment in oil deals. Indeed, he argued against increased sales of any degree because they would strengthen Mexican dependence on the United States.

The posture of the subsequent López Portillo government has evolved friendlier ties with the United States, and pronounced export policy follows suit in declaring the United States as a "natural market" for Mexico's hydrocarbons sales. Even now, however, export diversification continues to be a major plank of policy ambition, but the focus has changed to Brazil, Western Europe, and Japan. That policy flows naturally from a longer tradition of Mexican export ambitions in seeking access to the rich markets of the developed nations and is based on fear of too much dependence on the United States.

The scenario has important significance for hydrocarbon exports to the United States and, concomitantly, U.S.-Mexican relations. As Mexico has pursued a policy of diversifying its export recipients in tandem with its plans for a production platform, a cutback in shipments to the United States looms as a possibility. Without even noting present export contracts with Israel and Spain and future ambitions to sell considerable amounts of petroleum to Brazil and other countries, a recent analysis lends credence to the point. "Even if PEMEX catches up" with production goals, the analysis states, "there must still be doubt about its ability to fulfill the provisional contracts it has with Japan, France, Canada, and Sweden."[5]

Furthermore, that doubt will be compounded if the policymakers are firm in their putative commitment to review production and export policy and taper off increases. In truth, the probable outcome will be a decision to push ahead with ongoing expansion, but that is not quite the point of this discussion and analysis. Rather, the focus here is to describe and explicate the ongoing uncertainty of Mexico's hydrocarbons policy and its contribution to the instability of U.S.-Mexican relations.

To proceed, the delicate characteristics of the scenario on the Mexican side are also illustrated by a description and analysis of two second-level considerations—the influence of the Mexican opposition and the endemic problems of PEMEX. The domestic opposition has fought tooth and nail against increases in production and foreign sales. PEMEX has clouded the picture through inefficiency and inept policy planning and execution.

From the very beginnings of the present oil boom in 1974, governmental petroleum policies and programs have catalyzed opposition. Four specific cases illustrate the point and imply an ongoing sense of frustration among significant sectors in Mexico that are pregnant with potential for contributing to continuing ambiguity in the Mexican petroleum policy.[6] In each case, the opposition mustered measurable support in Mexico, leading to dramatic protest that reverberated onto the larger milieu of national policymaking.

The first case revolved around a policy debate concerning the decision to construct the gas line (the *gasoducto*) from the southern fields in Tabasco-Chiapas to the United States. It pitted the anti-Yankee Left (and some others) against the López Portillo administration and PEMEX. The second imbroglio emanated from the socioeconomic problems and dislocation wrought by large-scale migration to the southern fields. It features a series of complaints, threats, and protests launched by southern peasants, interest-group leaders, municipal officials, and governors against the administration and PEMEX. The third example of dissidence grew out of the administration's initiative to amend Article 27 of the Mexican Constitution. The change was designed to facilitate the condemnation and expropriation of land by PEMEX. It involved a federal deputy and member of the Institutional Revolutionary Party (PRI) against the official party's leadership and the president. Finally, the fourth case exploded in the wake of the blowout of Ixtoc 1 in the Bay of Campeche. It crystallized nagging doubts about PEMEX and particularly called into question the mentorship of Director General Díaz Serrano.[7]

Whatever its vices and virtues, the Mexican political system is certainly not fragile, and the opposition failed to deter the policymakers from their proximate purposes. In each of the specific cases noted, however, the opposition's arguments and protests embarrassed the government and elicited only partial response. At core, the most-important implication was wresting some degree of accountability from a secretive and authoritarian political system.

More to the point of the unpredictable nature of Mexico's hydrocarbons policy and bilateral energy relations, however, the several examples of opposition also implied some degree of real or potential revisions in direction. Along with other circumstances, the Left's critique of the *gasoducto* project contributed to Mexico's firm stance on gas prices and the eventual diminution of the amounts to be sold the United States. The trouble in the southern fields combined with the imbroglio over the amendment of Article 27 to nudge PEMEX to reallocate some human and financial resources in response to popular protest. The Ixtoc-1 fiasco capped all in calling into question PEMEX's crash program for exploitation and production. More particularly, the blowout also jeopardized the policy-making influence of Díaz Serrano, a leader of the expansion group in the nation that seeks further increases in production and exportation.

The future promises more of the same intrinsic ambiguity connected with the scenario. The Mexican polity will be increasingly concerned with the consequences of the new oil. The issues debated will revolve around programs to exploit and export the petroleum. The expenditures of the oil earnings will form the crux of the more-specific political struggles. New coalitions within the PRI may arise from the rearrangement of differing interests as they benefit and/or suffer from the impact of the new wealth. Oil states and oil cities will pack more political punch than in times past. The situation is in flux, in sum, and its fluidity implies a context short on focus and long on influences for change. Change, to pursue the point, connotes a precarious transition destined to increase fragility in the system and ambiguity in production and hydrocarbons policy.

As it was in the 1970s, furthermore, PEMEX may be expected to be both the focus and catalyzer of those unpredictable events. The contributions of PEMEX to the confusion derive from productive inefficiencies and errors in policy planning and execution. The inefficiency of PEMEX may be exaggerated by its critics, but it is real enough to merit notice and will certainly continue into the 1980s.[8]

To some degree tied to the problems of inefficiency, errors in policy planning and execution have pockmarked the oil monopoly's record in the 1970s and its promise to effect the future course of events. In all fairness, building one of the world's largest petroleum operations is a complex undertaking intrinsically fraught with imponderables and understandably bothered by the unexpected. During the 1970s, for example, drilling equipment was difficult to come by, costs of imported petrochemicals skyrocketed, and the PEMEX merchant fleet was found wanting. All of those problems demanded revisions in policy and sabotaged the successful completion of well-laid plans.

The *gasoducto* project was the pristine case in point. In 1977, PEMEX laid out a prospectus for large amounts of relatively quick money to be earned by the scheme. The line was to be completed by 1979, and sales to the United States were programmed to pay for the construction costs in only two-hundred days. The evolution of events proved policy to be ill conceived, and the nation spent large sums of precious capital to finance a losing operation, at least for the time being. As noted previously, the present drive to diversify export sales may also be ill conceived. Unless production is changed, PEMEX may well encounter problems in meeting its obligations.

That scenario of hasty decisions in the context of a crash program determined to increase production also refers back to the influence of the political opposition in Mexico. A certain insensitivity has characterized PEMEX's policymaking and execution, making it an all-too-easy target for its critics. Both the *gasoducto* and Ixtoc-1 episodes illustrate the point. In both instances the oil company was caught red-handed in ill-conceived and poorly planned projects. As the debates raged, the entire hydrocarbons policy was called into question, compelling the decision makers to fabricate ex post facto apologies and endangering the continued viability of the industry.

In sum, the ambiguity of the Mexican hydrocarbons scenario has been clearly exemplified by vacillating policy anent on production and exportation. The official rhetoric has evolved from conservationistic to expansionistic and back to a more-moderate position. As the 1980s begin, official policy is still in flux as the expansionists and conservationists continue their struggle. As the present scenario nears its end, furthermore, President López Portillo's ability to hold the debate in check will diminish and the clash may become more passionate. In the same context, indecision at the top has facilitated constant harassment by the opposition, adding to a nexus of uncertainty pregnant with possibilities for more change in the future. Finally, PEMEX has also muddied the waters—productive inefficiencies have combined with inept policy formation and execution leading to a series of botches designed to discredit the company and endanger the evolution of an effective, long-range hydrocarbons policy.

## United States

With the exception of the inane diplomacy over the gas-purchase deal, ambiguity of bilateral energy relations has been less evident in the United States, but enough inconsistency and insensitivity have evolved to contribute to confusion and add to fragility. Several examples illustrate the change. In addition to the gas-purchase imbroglio, they include the clumsy handling of discussions on environmental pollution in the United States stemming from the Ixtoc-1 blowout, a minicrisis in the matter of continued loans to Mexico emanating from an aborted ruling by the U.S. comptroller of the currency, confusion caused in Mexico by President Jimmy Carter's announcement of a reduction in petroleum imports, and a certain nuance of policy statements coming out of Washington in the 1970s that may be interpreted to have caused doubts about reserve quotations promulgated by Mexican officialdom.

The dreary tale of the gas-purchase negotiations are well known and need no long recitation here.[9] Suffice it to emphasize that the entire episode exemplified the worst of U.S. diplomacy. It manifested culpable inattention to events in Mexico, degenerated to atavistic hegemonic muscle flexing, jeopardized a clearly announced policy in Mexico, and undercut President López Portillo. U.S. insensitivity angered Mexican decision makers and led to unseemly insults during a summit meeting of the two presidents in 1979, thereby crystallizing the endemic fragility of relations and bringing the two nations to the brink of a serious crisis.

Although not quite so egregiously heavy-handed, nor so prolonged, U.S. diplomacy on pollution damages caused by the Ixtoc-1 spill was cast from the same mold. Special Ambassador Robert Krueger set out public demands for damages without the courtesy of previous consultation with Mexican officials. In the process, he evoked the wrath of Mexico's decision makers and sabotaged any possibility of an amiable resolution of the problem. In the same stroke, he also added another increment to Mexico's fear of U.S. pressure and exemplified once again the unpredictable characteristics of U.S. policy.[10]

The other three cases are less well known, but they also served to becloud mutual understanding during the 1970s and lead to a sense of uncertainty about U.S. commitment to evolve a mutually beneficial bilateral energy relationship. In 1978, in the first instance, the U.S. comptroller of the currency moved to limit U.S. private-bank lending to Mexico. The action grew from the comptroller's interpretation of banking regulations specifying that a U.S. bank could lend no more than 10 percent of its loan capital to a "single client." The comptroller defined all borrowers in Mexico as a single client. PEMEX, for example, was not a single client but shared that status with all other borrowers in Mexico. Mexican authorities were quick to protest (along with those from Brazil), and the Carter administration obviously pressured the comptroller of the currency to rescind the ruling.

In mid-1979 President Carter also caused some consternation in Mexico with his announcement for a reduction in U.S. hydrocarbon exports. Although certainly not panic stricken, officials in Mexico were concerned about the policy and sought assurances that the move would not jeopardize future energy relations. The sense of the Mexican posture appeared to indicate that U.S. emissaries should have consulted with Mexican officials before the policy was promulgated. A sense of disappointment and moderate concern, rather than anger, was reflected in the Mexican position.

In a rather diffuse way, finally, the U.S. position on Mexican reserves throughout the 1970s contained a nuance of political maneuvering not calculated to encourage a milieu of trust in Mexico. While Mexico was quoting rather conservative figures on reserves before 1977, U.S. sources were more exuberant. Later, however, the roles were reversed. Quotations out of Mexico waxed increasingly enthusiastic, but sources in the United States began to assume a more-conservative tone. They emphasized the long lead times necessary to bring in production and pointed specifically to the relatively high costs of exploiting the Chicontepec fields. Domestic events in the United States go a way in explaining the change in posture, but the change did cast an aura of doubt on Mexico's quotations—a move hardly designed to encourage trust and cooperation in bilateral energy relations.[11]

The United States, in sum, did its part in the 1970s to becloud and confuse understanding between the two nations. The diplomatic insensitivity surrounding the gas-purchase affair brought the entire relationship to the abyss. The graceless handling of the issue of pollution damage from Ixtoc 1 was hardly more elevated. In the same context, U.S. policymakers also permitted the questioning of ongoing financial assistance to Mexico, failed to come in contact with their Mexican counterparts on U.S. policy, and in a more-general way, encouraged doubt concerning the quantities of Mexico's reserves throughout the decade of the 1970s. Combined with the ambiguity of the scenario coming out of Mexico, those activities added their weight to an uncertain context for bilateral energy relations.

### Complexity of Bilateral Relations

The discussion of the positions and events in Mexico and the United States offers a flavor of the complexity of bilateral relations, but that fact should be crystallized and its import for the energy relationship described and analyzed. Commerce in hydrocarbons between the two neighboring nations, in short, is part of a larger whole. The more broadly conceived panoply of issues at controversy in U.S.-Mexican intercourse obviously influences commerce in oil and gas. Their complexity, on the one hand, offers a scenario pregnant for creative diplomacy as trade-offs and bargains are negotiated. On the other hand, clearly other issues also can become entangled in the energy relationship and catalyze tensions leading to increased ambiguity, threatening the precarious fragility of the bilateral equation.

Articulated linkages appeared as the energy relationship evolved and more are destined to surface as the situation matures. Directly and by implication, Mexico's readiness to ship off large quantities of oil and gas have been tied to the provision of developmental capital, a more-dignified role for Mexico in bilateral interaction, the Colorado River-salinity issue and the so-called tomato war, concerning the access to U.S.-markets for Mexican winter vegetables. Extrapolating from those specific problems, the entire trade relationship is enormously significant, and the sensitive issue of Mexican undocumented workers is equally salient. Beyond those focuses, the possible linkages are almost endless. They include the gamut of issues in bilateral intercourse running from Mexican antiquities to U.S. air routes.

The imbroglios over the *gasoducto* and Ixtoc 1 illustrate the most-specific category of linkages. From the Mexican perspective, the episodes exemplified a frame of mind in U.S. foreign policymaking that has accorded Mexico too little attention and too many slights. The Carter administration has responded institutionally with the creation of the special coordinator for Mexican affairs, but that is only part of the issue. A special coordinator connotes special treatment, prior consultation on matters of significance, and a peculiar sensitivity to Mexico's role as neighbor and, equally cogently, to the nation's place in global affairs. The United States has initiated a response but has not carried it to maturation.

The controversy surrounding Ixtoc 1 also exemplified how the fragility of bilateral relations feeds on long-festering problems. President López Portillo responded to the claim for damages by damning the United States for its inattention to Mexico's petitions for cleaning up irrigation waters coming from the Colorado River. The issue was linked, in quite bombastic terms, to the petroleum relationship, and it will continue to be associated with it. Construction on the desalinization plant is to begin in 1980, but the United States must be ready to hurry its completion in response to Mexico's just claims and in fulfillment of the treaty negotiated in the mid-1970s.

The flap emanating from the comptroller of the currency's aborted ruling implies another linkage. Mexico's developmental ambitions in tandem with the requirements of a burgeoning hydrocarbons industry conjures enormous capital requirements for the time being. The United States, again, has been responsive, but that responsiveness must continue if an ambient of mutual trust is to condition the energy relationship.

Mexico's capital requirements and their significance for commerce in oil and gas are even more-dramatically exemplified by the issue of trade relations. An analysis of the tomato war makes the point in warning that "the delicate negotiations are irrevocably bound to America's eager pursuit of Mexican oil and natural gas . . . "[12] The tomato war, in truth, is only one manifestation of a larger linkage that grows from Mexico's demand for special considerations in the U.S. market. As Mexico moves toward less protectionism with the dismantling of its licensing system and the reduction of some tariffs, pressures will increase for reciprocity from the United States. Mexico's stance on the continued expansion of hydrocarbons production and exportation is bound to be linked to the trade issue.

As is frequently noted, furthermore, U.S. policy on undocumented Mexican workers is a key part of the larger relationship at issue between the two nations. The problem tends to sensitivity in Mexico and the United States, and easy solutions are quite possible, but the nagging omnipresence of the issue continues to lend to the fragility of relations. Mexico, and Mexicans, are poignantly aware of the tie between the energy relationship and the issue of undocumented workers. As the Select Commission on Immigration and Refugee Policy in the United States pursues its work, moreover, it is abundantly clear that the United States is also cognizant of the relationship between U.S. policy on undocumented workers and Mexican policy on oil and gas.

Although this discussion touches upon some major issues of controversy between the neighboring nations, the list is really much longer, and the complexity of relationships is even more baffling than is indicated here. The very complexity of the equation implies fragility, but more to the point of this discussion, it also demonstrates the literally endless possibilities for linkages and for Mexican demands upon the United States.

## Conclusion

This chapter highlighted the themes of ambiguity and fragility in U.S.-Mexican energy relations during the 1970s and predicted more of the same for the future. The fragility of the bilateral relationship emanates from a history of conflict and mutual disdain. The record combines with disparities in wealth, power, and sociocultural systems to impede reciprocal trust and cooperation. In tandem, the two factors contribute to an omnipresent tone of precarious ambiguity in bilateral intercourse.

More directly, the policies, programs, and pronouncements emanating from the two nations have been pockmarked by vacillation and contradiction. In Mexico, official policy has gone from conservationistic to expansionistic and back again. Reflecting and adding to official indecision, the opposition in Mexico is ever critical of official policy and has made occasional inroads with more of the same in the cards. PEMEX, in the process, compounds the ambiguity of the situation by suffusing the scenario with inefficient production, ineffective policy formation and execution, and insensitivity in the political arena. In the United States, a policy encouraging increases in production and exportation in Mexico is contradicted by heavy-handed exercises in hegemonic politics, awkward errors in diplomatic interaction, and unsuccessful coordination of policies and programs germane to Mexican hydrocarbons.

The complexity of the issues at controversy are matched only by their sheer numbers. Some of these issues relate specifically to the energy relationship, but all are potentially linked to it. The 1970s highlighted the crystallization of some of the linkages, the present hints at the addition of more, and the future promises still further linkage as the energy relationship matures. The three elements of the scenario, in sum, conjure a precariously tentative tone in U.S.-Mexican energy relations.

## Notes

1. A good chronological treatment of bilateral relations is found in Karl M. Schmitt, *Mexico and the United States, 1821-1973: Conflict and Coexistence* (New York: John Wiley & Sons, 1974). A radical treatment focusing more on contemporary relations is Peter Baird and Ed Mc-Caughan, *Beyond the Border: Mexico and the U.S. Today* (New York: North American Congress on Latin America, 1979).

2. On the World War I-German connection see Cole Blasier, *The Hovering Giant: U.S. Responses to Revolutionary Change In Latin America* (Pittsburgh, Pa.: University of Pittsburgh Press, 1976), pp. 106-116.

3. Much of this discussion is based upon Edward J. Williams, *The Rebirth of the Mexican Petroleum Industry: Developmental Directions and Policy Implications* (Lexington, Mass.: Lexington Books, D.C. Heath and Company, 1979), pp. 23-24, 43, 47.

4. Petróleos Mexicanos, "Report Delivered by the Director General, 1978," prepublication copy (México, D.F., 1978), p. 5.

5. For the quotation, see "Mexico's Oil Boom Comes Bursting into the Black," *Latin America Economic Report* (17 August 1979):252. See also a report from *Lloyd's Mexican Economic Report* on the reduction of the U.S. share of the Mexican petroleum exports in "Mexico to Cut U.S. Oil Share," *Arizona Daily Wildcat* (University of Arizona), 7 September 1979, p. 3.

6. The first three cases are described and analyzed in Edward J. Williams, "Petroleum Policy and Mexican Domestic Politics: Left Opposition, Regional Dissidence, and Official Apostasy" (Paper presented at the annual meeting of the Southern Economics Association, Washington, D.C., November 1978). Appropriate references to the fourth dispute are listed in the following note.

7. For the most-critical accounts of the Ixtoc-1 debacle, see Lucia Luna, "Por ley, Díaz Serrano deberá responder de los daños, por el Ixtoc," *Proceso* (7 August 1979); Isabel Morales, "Desprecia PEMEX los daños que causa su contaminación;" *Proceso* (2 July 1979); and "La pro-

curaduría, bombero de Díaz Serrano," *Proceso* (30 July 1979). See also "Ixtoc Undermines PEMEX Complacency," *Latin America Economic Report* (5 October 1979):307.

8. For discussions of PEMEX germane to this analysis, see Williams, *Rebirth of the Mexican Petroleum Industry*, pp. 112-19, 147-53; and Richard B. Mancke, *Mexican Oil and Natural Gas* (New York: Praeger, 1978), pp. 127-49.

9. Two good accounts of the *gasoducto* controversy pertaining to U.S. activity are Richard R. Fagen and Henry R. Nau, "Mexican Gas: The Northern Connection," in *Capitalism and the State: In U.S.-Latin American Relations*, ed. Richard R. Fagen (Stanford, Calif.: Stanford University Press, 1979), pp. 382-427; and Judith Gentleman, "Nationalism and Dependency: An Analysis of Their Impact in the U.S.-Mexican Gas Negotiations" (Paper prepared for delivery at the Annual Meeting of the Latin American Studies Association, Pittsburgh, Pa., April 1979). The Gentleman treatment is part of a forthcoming Ph.D. dissertation on the subject being done with the political science department at the State University of New York at Buffalo.

10. See "U.S.-Mexican Gas Talks Hampered by Ixtoc Claim," *Latin America Economic Report* (31 August 1979):265.

11. See Williams, *Rebirth of the Mexican Petroleum Industry*, pp. 17-19.

12. "'Tomato War' Seen Threatening Talks on Mexican Oil," *Journal of Commerce* (7 August 1979) Information Services on Latin America (ISLA), 756.

# 2

# Mexico: Petroleum and Perspectives

*Jesús Puente Leyva*

## Recent Antecedents: The International Framework

In the technical and intellectual circles of the world during the 1960s, many people took for granted the assumption the price of crude oil would decline in the 1980s. It was almost certain that the price would drop from two dollars a barrel to one dollar a barrel and that even this price could be cut if oil-exporting countries decided to compete among themselves by reducing export taxes on crude oil. This vision was not void of objectivity; in the two decades after World War II, the international supply of petroleum was abundant, and at times, excessive. The cost of production was very low, between ten and fifteen cents a barrel in the Middle East, and many people believed that petroleum reserves were sufficient to supply the world for centuries.[1]

Contrary to this expectation, the world has experienced a spectacular increase in petroleum prices that, in the course of the last six years, has multiplied tenfold. This rise began during the dramatic climax of the Yom Kippur War and the oil embargo of October 1973. For the oil-producing countries not only a political but also a rational economic decision caused them to demand the real value of their exportable, nonrenewable natural resources. In the early days of OPEC, analysts from the United States were convinced that OPEC countries would not dare raise their export taxes on crude oil, nor the official price of oil, to the point of maximizing the monopolistic earnings of the organization as a whole. In such circumstances, the global level of production and exportation of oil would be so low that the distribution of oil between the producing countries would create conflicts and make the internal cohesiveness of the cartel precarious.

In 1980 a good part of the political ambiguity and economic uncertainty has disappeared. OPEC, in spite of some internal dissension on pricing policy, has survived. The so-called oil war is certainly a confrontation, but it does not correspond to unilateral, irrational, Islamic-inspired action. Paraphrasing recent political pronouncements, this is not a fight between the "good guys and the bad guys." Rather, "OPEC inherited the market structure built by the cartel that was dominated by the United States and adopted more-rational policies of price and production."[2] Furthermore,

17

economies based on the availability of cheap oil must now adjust to a new reality since the age of cheap energy has ended.[3]

In these terms it is naïve, as well as useless, to accuse the OPEC nations of being villains. More-objective questions must be faced. First, oil-producing countries constitute an authentic monopoly that could try to maximize its overall earnings through joint regulation of the level of production and supply of oil. However, OPEC is not operating as an authentic monopoly, nor as an authentic cartel, given that the current agreed-upon base price for crude oil is lower than the monopoly price that would allow maximum real earnings in the short run for the countries that belong to this organization.[4]

Second, the relevant and objective point that the oil-producing countries confront, whether or not they are members of OPEC, is the current pressure of world demand and the forseeable shortage of energy that will occur starting in the next decade.[5] After 1985 the energy future of the world is hard to predict. It is practically impossible to make political predictions, but technically, that the worldwide supply of oil will be adequate until the middle of the next decade is highly probable, although most people agree that in the last fifteen years of this century a growing gap between supply and demand will occur. This situation will correspond to the difference between the required level of import in the largest consumer countries and the maximum possibility for exports from producing countries. The deficit in the export capacity in the year 2000 probably will equal between one-third and one-fourth of the total needed imports. Even more pressing is the prediction that by 1990 this gap could reach 10 million barrels of crude oil a day.[6] Some people also fear that if petroelum prices do not increase sufficiently to encourage petroleum-energy substitutes, covering these shortages will not be possible.[7] Considering the price of replacing the energy the world now consumes, no one doubts that the price of oil on the international market is still too low.[8]

These factors transcend all countries such as Mexico that are not members of OPEC but that are beginning to play a strategic role in the oil market. This market is brutally sensitive to slight fluctuations in supply. Estimates indicate that a global deficit in supply as small as 2 or 3 percent could provoke an increment in the international price of oil of up to 40 percent.[9] Recent experience suggests this estimate to be low. In May 1979, after the insurrectionist movement in Iran, estimates indicated that the production of crude oil in the free world would reach an average level of 52.6 million barrels a day, and in 1979 an average daily deficit of 2.3 million barrels would be registered. This figure is equivalent to 4.2 percent of the predicted overall demand.[10] In 1980 this deficit has provoked an average increase in the international price of petroleum of 80 percent.[11]

Over the medium-term period the problem is even more serious. The Arab countries have adopted a united conservationist policy that will allow them to maintain a strategic margin of international scarcity, thereby favoring their bargaining position with the "club" of the rich nations—especially the United States. Even though Iran has started to produce crude oil once again, the country is wrought with instability. Whatever the course of events in the future may be, Iran has decided not to return to the high level of production that existed in the times of the Shah (6 million barrels per day in 1977); a maximum amount of 4 million barrels of crude oil a day instead will be produced.[12] Saudi Arabia, the Arab nation most disposed to the interests of the United States, also participates in this strategy, although technical and financial factors are cited as reasons. Whatever the reason, the Saudis will not produce more than 12 million barrles a day in the near future, which is far below the 16 million barrels recently announced as the target level. Furthermore, it is scarcely half of the 25 million barrels a day that Aramco, the Arabian American Oil Company, had proposed to produce at the beginning of this decade.[13]

**The Mexican Oil Situation**

What is the role of Mexico within the world's energy and petroleum future? Certainly Mexico is the country that projects the most-promising, sure, and accessible energy supply for its neighbor to the north. U.S. Central Intelligence Agency (CIA) researchers predict that in the mid-1980s Mexico will be the most-important oil-producing country that is not a member of OPEC. Furthermore, by that date Mexico will produce 3 to 4.5 million barrels of oil a day. This could mean that Mexico could provide up to 3 million barrels a day to its neighbor, covering 25 percent or more of U.S. imports of crude oil.[14] These estimates were made at the beginning of 1977 based on a volume of proved reserves of hydrocarbons of 11.2 billion barrels of crude oil, of which roughly two-thirds were petroleum and the rest was gas. Even if only the current proved reserves of 45 billion barrels of hydrocarbons are accounted for, Mexico probably can produce up to 6 million barrels a day in 1985.[15] Therefore, the CIA predicts that, adding the eventual exportation of gas, Mexico would be the principal provider of energy to the United States by the mid-1980s.

The relevant question, given these predictions, is whether or not Mexico should become an oil superpower. This decision, paradoxically, will depend more on events in the medium term than on the conventional predictions expressed as a political plan in the six-year period of a presidential administration. The decision will depend upon internal factors such as the propensity of the high-income-level social groups to import, the incapacity of the country to produce necessary food and natural resources, the financial necessities of the public sector, and the need to service the foreign debt.

It will also depend upon the investments accumulated in the oil sector such that the total volume of production remains profitable. Finally, although less obvious, it will depend upon the volume of proved reserves of hydrocarbons the country will have in the near future.

In relation to this last point, Mexico faces a political problem. Perhaps it should not claim proved reserves that place it as the sixth-largest producer of oil in the world today and that project it as third largest in the mid-1980s, behind the USSR and Saudi Arabia. This level of reserves is consistent with the projected requirements of the United States and therefore suggests that Mexico should supply its neighbor with its needs. Mexico might be better off to deliberately moderate the growth of these reserves. This moderation would not mean reducing the number of jobs nor limiting the dynamics of exploration but rather applying more-conservative geologic-probability criteria of evaluation. These criteria should be such that, when circumstances make it economically and politically necessary (as happened in the last three years), they could be controlled with inverse flexibility.[16] Such a scheme of estimating proved reserves would lessen external pressures for Mexico to increase production and would permit the country to produce at levels that are more consistent with realistic programs and policies of economic growth and development.

### The Oil Boom of the 1970s: The Energy Relationship between Mexico and the United States

Prior to the early 1970s Mexico faced the prospects of continuing to import increasing amounts of oil. However, during 1972 and 1973 the Mexican government informed the public, with measured objectivity, that PEMEX had found a new area of hydrocarbon production in the state of Chiapas and that these finds, which by then had functioning wells, promised to be important reserves.[17] Convinced of the productive potential of this region, in 1973 the government stated that by mid-1974 the importation of crude oil would be eliminated.[18]

Simultaneously, external pressure on Mexican oil production began. In the United States the new oil fields in the Mexican Southeast were compared to those in the Persian Gulf. The estimated capacity for exploitation was 20 billion barrels or double the proved reserves of Alaska and equivalent to almost ten times current U.S. annual imports of crude oil. The matter acquired sensational overtones thanks to the concerted efforts of the media in the United States. Within the period of a few days in October 1974, the *Wall Street Journal, The New York Times,* the *Washington Post*, and the *Journal of Commerce* all made the estimates public. The Associated Press (AP) transmitted stories, without citing any source, that the fragility of the relationship between the United States and Mexico had "become very obvious" when it was known that the Echeverría government would give the first opportunity to buy the "increased supply of Mexican petroleum" to Cuba and not to the United States.[19]

Much of this publicity occurred a week before the meeting between Presidents Ford and Echeverría on the Sonora-Arizona border. It also took place at the exact point of time in which the United States suffered the harshest consequences of the so-called energy crisis. It was politically expedient for the United States to suggest that very soon, thanks to its neighbors to the south, it would have an accessible oil supply. Aware of the circumstances of the publicity, President Echeverría expressed publicly that Mexico would not permit exaggerations with respect to the new oil discoveries. He felt they had been exaggerated ". . . in order to lower the price and to sway the attitude of the oil-producing countries of the world."[20]

As important as the hydrocarbon resources are, they did not permit the Echeverría administration in the short run to generate the foreign exchange revenues and fiscal means to reestablish a certain external balance and to moderate the public debt. This could not have been done without damaging, as occurred from 1970-1976, the doubling of the productive base of the country in such strategic areas as petroleum, electric energy, steel, petrochemicals, and fertilizers, not to mention advances in the social area.[21] It would be up to President López Portillo, in the difficult atmosphere of devaluation, to recoup a certain economic stability for the country at the expense of the workers and try to establish a new stage of accelerated economic growth based on the imponderable pivot of oil wealth.

Had the Echeverría administration had the current oil resources at its disposal, the outcome of Mexico's policy of accelerated growth might well have been different. Analysts from the Wharton Group have concluded that the fiscal-reform measures of the Echeverría administration would have been unnecessary if it could have counted on future revenue from petroleum and that "taxes applied to PEMEX would have been sufficient" to finance such a program. It seems reasonable to affirm, according to the Wharton analysts, ". . . that if President Echeverría would have been able to count on the petroleum that his successor has, it would have been possible to remove the restrictions on the external sector and he would have been able to achieve an 8 percent rate of economic growth (annually), without having to devaluate drastically."[22]

The advent of the administration of José López Portillo in December 1976 opened the door to a new oil era in which the new fields in the Southwest would reach maturity and the proved reserves of the country would permit exports of petroleum and gas in volumes scarcely forseeable three years earlier. Nevertheless, the nationalistic tradition of Mexico with respect to petroleum made it improbable that, in spite of the revenues required by the country to reestablish an equilibrium in its balance of payments and cover its foreign debt, the new administration would attempt to produce and export hydrocarbons to the limit of international demand. More specifically, that Mexico would try to satisfy the needs of the United States was doubtful.

This is the climate in which, from the beginning, U.S. interest in the supply of energy from Mexico was felt. Both overt and covert pressure was evident from the United States for Mexico to commit itself to an agreement for the exportation of a significant volume of natural gas to the United States as a condition for selling crude oil to that country.[23] This matter became very controversial both in the United States and Mexico. In the United States the controversy involved the White House, Congress, large petroleum companies, and consumers. In essence, the U.S. need of Mexican gas was recognized, but nonetheless an attempt was made to seek a favorable price that would imply a direct subsidy by Mexico to U.S. consumers.

In 1978 the Mexican government made the decision to consume internally all of the gas that the country would produce and thus cancelled the need to export that type of energy. However, after two years of controversy and bargaining, in September 1979 Mexico finally agreed to export gas at an initial level of 300-million cubic feet daily. That agreement was considered by some observers to be strictly symbolic; a political-diplomatic transaction in the face of U.S. pressure preceding the Mexican president's visit to Washington in October 1979.[24] Olga Pellicer de Brody argued that U.S. leaders had accorded a real touchstone importance to the agreement in order to define the tone and cordiality of the relationship between the two countries. She added that, in this context, "the most-convincing factor that the Mexican government had in the process of deciding in favor of the agreement seems to have been an evaluation of the political cost that prolonging the negotiations would have had on resolving other problems with the United States."[25] Basically, what was involved were the areas of conflict that arose as a result of U.S. interest in improving its position in international commerce and in "accelerating the production of Mexican crude oil in order to lessen its dependence on Middle Eastern countries . . . "[26] That is why, concluded Pellicer, it was legitimate ". . . to see the sale of reduced volumes of gas as a tactical reconciliation that would allow an improvement in Mexico's position in other areas of vital interest to both countries."[27]

Whether it was truly a "tactical reconciliation" or whether longer-run forces came into play is questionable. Clearly the United States was satisfied with the agreement. Within a few hours of reaching the agreement, high-level U.S. officials made known their satisfaction at Mexico's agreement to export natural gas at a price that was lower than that established by OPEC.[28]

A few weeks later, PEMEX made an estimate that the level of exportation of gas could reach a volume of 1 billion cubic feet a day within a short period of time. Since then the mediative aspects of the tie between Mexico and the United States due to the gas agreement are unknown. What remains to be seen is whether, instead of the original proposal of exporting excesses of associated gas from the Southeast, Mexico will decide to export nonassociated gas from the Sabinas fields in the northern part of the country.

## Possibilities for Agricultural Development
## Using the Oil Surplus

Mexico faces tremendous opportunities to use the gains or economic surpluses from oil production for purposes of economic growth and development.[29] The central question, therefore, is how will it take advantage of this unique opportunity? The case of agriculture is particularly important. Given the present problems in agriculture, how can the oil revenues be used to increase production, alleviate poverty, and improve income distribution in that sector?

In order to answer this question it is necessary to:

Define with conceptual accuracy and quantitative precision the magnitudes of the so-called oil-surplus, not only in terms of their impact on the balance of payments but also as additional revenues for the public sector;[30]

Specify medium- and long-term goals of production for the agricultural sector;

Establish the potential capacity of the agricultural sector to retain population in the countryside.

It is difficult to quantify the magnitude of the oil surplus. However, clearly it is sufficient to break some of the bottlenecks that limit Mexican development.

By the end of 1980 revenues from oil exports should be close to 10 billion dollars a year. Of these earnings, 50 percent will be tax revenues to be transferred to the government treasury where they may be assigned to finance other sectors and projects. However, most of these revenues will be needed to service the foreign debt, which by 1981-1982 could ascend to 40 billion dollars. Therefore, without a thorough revision of the domestic-pricing structure of hydrocarbons in order to eliminate the enormous subsidy on internal consumption of all types of fuels (the past presidential report estimated the subsidy at 380 billion pesos a year), Mexico will not be able to count on sufficient surpluses to make the necessary transformation of the agricultural sector without sacrificing debt servicing.

With respect to the goals of the agricultural sector, many people are concerned that no medium- and long-term plans exist to overcome the obstacles to production in the sector. In 1977 *A Five-Year Plan for the Agriculture Sector* was elaborated by both the Secretary of Agriculture and Hydraulic Resources and the Secretary of Programming and Budget, but in reality this plan has remained buried under the efforts to prepare the annual plans. The lack of long-range planning is particularly lamentable given the 1979 crisis in the area of basic foods. This crisis took the authorities and the public by surprise especially because, until a few months before, the predictions were that agricultural production could grow 3 or 4 percent in 1979.

Since the end of 1978 rainfall has been higher than normal, and the level of water in the dams was higher than usual. The financial situation of the farmer had improved in 1978, and tranquility existed in the countryside. The prospects for 1979 appeared good. Yet, only a few months would pass before that year was described officially—and almost characterized as a national emergency—as the worst season registered in the country in the last thirty years. In 1979 the production of corn went down by 2 million tons, and the production of beans and sorghum also dropped. More than 2 million tons of grain and oils will have to be imported in 1979-1980 to satisfy national demand. In order to explain the differences between the optimistic prospects and the actual facts, analysts spoke of a highly unorthodox manipulation of agriculture statistics in the period 1977 to 1979. However, they concluded that, in spite of official claims and quantitative information, the country's agricultural base has not been able to respond to the challenge of development in the last twenty years.[31]

The record of the past and the lack of explicit, long-term government commitment to the agricultural sector makes it appear that agricultural production will probably permanently bring up the rear guard. Rural life will deteriorate, there will be more inequality of the distribution of wealth, and there will probably be a growing dependence on foreign supply of foodstuffs and raw materials. As a corollary, there will be an uninterrupted migratory flow toward the urban areas as well as movements of the unemployed toward the United States in search of work.

This is not an unfounded concern. Looking to the future, the most-authentic technical vision of Mexican economic development, the 1979 *National Plan for Industrial Development*, contemplates a macroeconomic framework in which agricultural production maintains a rate of growth less than that of the population. The consequence will be that the per capita production of foodstuffs and raw materials will become even lower. Worse yet, this plan predicts that the importation of agricultural products will consume 35 percent of all the revenue gathered by the exportation of petroleum by the middle of the next decade. Later, this percentage will increase to 50 percent.[32] These figures are based on levels of production of crude oil of 2.25 million barrels a day and the exportation of 1.1 million barrels of oil a day that the López Portillo administration has defined as the Mexican goal.

Nevertheless, the prognosis for the Mexican balance of payments, especially in respect to the export price of crude oil, is totally speculative. The projections of the aforementioned plan assume that the production of crude oil in the medium-length period of 1982-1990 will increase only as needed to satisfy internal demand and that exports will remain at 1.1 million barrels a day. No exportation of natural gas is predicted.

Eight months after this document was made public, the international price of Mexican crude oil increased 75 percent—equivalent to the plan's projected price increases for a nine-year period. Therefore, the plan quite clearly overestimates the weight of agricultural imports as a percentage of the revenue generated by oil exports. Moreover, at the same time the plan ignores the possibility that the agricultural sector could perform worse than in recent years and that Mexico could be faced with absolute declines in the production of food, with the consequent implication of having to import these items, a situation that may lead to a disequilibrium in the balance of payments.

In the face of all this, the projections of the Wharton analysts are particularly relevant. They concluded that over a medium period of time, Mexico cannot afford to stop the growth of its export of hydrocarbons, including natural gas, without also stopping overall economic growth, putting the country's foreign-trade balance in jeopardy, and accumulating an exaggerated foreign debt on behalf of the public sector.[33] They went on to recommend that Mexico should double its exportation of crude oil over the next decade until it reaches 2.25 million barrels a day and that it should export almost 3,000 million cubic feet a day of natural gas.

**What, How, and for Whom to Produce?**

Mexican agriculture is plagued with a number of additional questions. One of these questions is whether the development of the sector should be oriented toward producing for export or basic foodstuffs. The question has been debated in other forums. Suffice it to say here that this author believes for technical and political reasons that the production of foodstuffs should have priority. Self-sufficiency is an economic and social imperative. Without self-sufficiency it is doubtful that long-run agricultural development can come about. This view is strengthened by the evidence that some developed countries plan to use food exports as a lever to be used for the purchase of oil.[34]

Another question is who should be the beneficiaries of agricultural development? Some people would argue that the answer should be determined by market forces. However, this solution may not bring about socially optimal development in agriculture, an especially important consideration in light of the poverty, unemployment, and malnutrition that exists over much of the countryside. For example, the past market-determined patterns have led to a deterioration of the real incomes of the majority of rural inhabitants, and many persons continue to be undernourished.[35]

Unemployment is a major problem in the countryside. Without the aforementioned investment, unemployment is bound to worsen and rural-urban migration will increase. The industrial plan projects, alarmingly, that employment in the agricultural sector will grow only slightly by 1990; out of an estimated increase of 13 million people in the work force between 1978 and 1990, only 373,000 of them are projected for agriculture.

Apparently the best solution will come about only from an ambitious program in the public sector. Public investments need to be undertaken. Oil revenues will help, but most reliance for obtaining the funds for investment will need to come from deep and thorough fiscal reform in order to capture more of the earnings and wealth of individuals and business. If no reform is made, government oil revenues will need to be used to settle the balance-of-payments accounts including the importation of food and luxury items, and tourist expenditures abroad.

## A Course for the Future

Overall prospects for the next decade show that what David Ibarra wrote ten years ago is applicable today: Until now ". . . economic policy (in Mexico) has pursued . . . the objective of attenuating the economic imbalances predominant throughout the country . . . " and that the principal distributive preoccupation has been to ". . . foment savings and investment, transferring earnings from the consumers to those groups that really or supposedly serve the social function of saving or increasing investments."[36]

The conclusion is that whatever is done in the area of oil is irreversible in that, as in no other country, the dynamics of present accumulated investment determine future production. In this sense, the present official commitment of not exceeding a production level of 2.2 million barrels a day until the end of the present six-year administration in 1982 clearly can be maintained. Nevertheless, no one knows to what point the inertia or dynamics of current programs that can be seen by level of proved reserves will make it necessary to significantly increase that level after 1982.

Mexico has made a major investment in exploration for petroleum. It would be uneconomical not to try to recover that cost with production.

Yet the sheer size of the reserves raises the risk of Mexico's becoming a nation that is the oil backyard for the United States. To confront such possibilities, Mexico should maintain a permanent international alliance with the interests and struggles of underdeveloped countries. Mexico should, as indicated in President López Portillo's "Energy Address" presented before the United Nations in 1979, focus more on the current anguish of the underdeveloped world but without impairing the long-term view of the so-called energy transaction. Mexico must also improve the state of its relationship with the Arab world without harming oil-supply commitments to Israel. But most of all, it should leave the door wide open to eventual membership in OPEC. Finally, Mexico should immediately allow itself a "political price" for its hydrocarbons in the context of its bilateral relationship with the United States. After all, selling oil is not the same as selling shrimp or tomatoes.[37]

The answers to today's problems can be found only in the future. Whatever those answers may be, in the course of the development of the petroleum industry, Mexico must take advantage of economic and political opportunities to reorient the basic points that have characterized its plan of development. Moreover, growth for growth's sake generated by the interindustrial ties between oil activity, and pushed by the forces of the market, will result in what Hernando Pacheco has called "wealth without jobs."

The social and political consequences of this inequality are dramatic. Perhaps our intellectual and political vocation as craftsmen of prediction explains why the future is a constant source of anxiety and question marks. Perhaps because, as realistic as we are, we worry and torment ourselves more with what we know and live today than with all that we do not know about the future. Nevertheless, the spirit of this chapter is that reasons exist for fearing that if the inertia and pragmatism of bad politics alienate us, the problems and conflicts of today will seem small compared to what awaits us in the future. After all, if the current political, economic, and social situation in Mexico does not correspond to the dramatic plot of a cowboy movie, it resembles even less the plot of a musical comedy, in which the villains are converted into generous fairy godmothers and the good victims are Cinderellas that always, providentially, but in time, get their just revenge. Without damaging these metaphors, some people benefit from social conflict. Above ideology, still something objectively is called "the struggle of classes." Only in this context can be understood the historical role of the Mexican state, that after all, was born of an authentic revolution.

## Notes

1. See James E. Akins, "The Oil Crisis: This Time the Wolf is Here," *Foreign Affairs* (April 1973); see also Akins, "World Energy Supply: Co-

operation with OPEC or a New War for Resources," in *Energy: International Cooperation or Crisis*, Antonio Ayoub, ed. (Quebec: L'Université Laval, 1979).

2. Alan L. Madian, "Oil is Still too Cheap," *Foreign Policy* (Summer 1979):170.

3. Ibid.

4. See Robert Mabro, *The Dilemma Between Short and Long Term Oil Prices* (Document presented at the Fourth International Colloquy on Oil Economy). This statement is based on the fact that, throughout time, the price on the spot market for short-term contingency deliveries of oil has been generally 50 percent higher (and more) than the official OPEC Price for delivery of contracted crude oil.

5. Estimates indicate that the level of consumption of petroleum in the non-Communist world will go from 45 million barrels a day in 1975 (51 million in 1978) to a level that will fluctuate between 75 and 93 million barrels a day in the year 2000. In these terms, if we accept an intermediate hypothesis, the new brute reserves discovered in the next two decades must equal, at least, the total of the proved reserves in the world today (555,000 million barrels). See Workshop on Alternate Energy Strategies, *Energy: Global Prospects 1985-2000* (New York: McGraw-Hill, 1977); also A.H. Taher, "An Analysis of Petroleum and Energy Scenarios for the Year 2000," in Ayoub, *Energy*, pp. 79-87.

6. World Bank, *World Energy and Petroleum: Supply and Demand Prospect to 1990* (February 1978), p. 7.

7. Ibid., p. 6.

8. Madian, "Oil is Still too Cheap," p. 171.

9. From the opinions of Walter Levy, reputed expert in this field, in "An Oil Crisis: True or False?" *Time*, 23 April 1979.

10. Kevin Done, "Oil Shortages Start to Bite Around the World," *Financial Times* (12 May 1979).

11. The exception is the crude oil in Saudi Arabia, which only increased 42 percent due to the role this country plays as "moderator" of the speculative pressures within OPEC. This role in practice lets the Saudis transfer subsidylike savings to the consumer countries, especially the United States. Such transfers represent, in recent months, an approximate sum of $4.5 million a day ($1.6 billion a year).

12. S. Henderson, "Iran Holds Down Oil Exports," *Financial Times* (30 April 1979).

13. "The Future of Saudi Arabian Oil Production," *Petroleum Intelligence Weekly* (special supplement, 23 April 1979).

14. See U.S. Central Intelligence Agency, *The International Energy Situation: Outlook to 1985* (April 1977); also Sevinc Carlson, "Mexico's

Oil, Trends and Prospects to 1985, mimeographed (Washington, D.C.: Georgetown University, Center for Strategic and International Studies, 1978).

15. Ibid. More-recent CIA evaluations continue to consider that of all the oil-producing countries that do not belong to OPEC, Mexico is the one that has the most-"brilliant prospects" of substantially increasing its oil production. Nevertheless, the projections that the CIA makes are, for now, more conservative in respect to Mexico's possibilities for petroleum export.

16. This is not an absurd recommendation. Non-OPEC oil-producing countries like Norway have adopted a policy of this nature. See Oystein Noreng, "La relación entre la OPEC y los países exportadores que no la integran: ¿amigos o campañeros de ruta?" *Comercio exterior* (August 1979):863.

17. "Opportunamente se informó de los descubrimientos, puntualiza PEMEX," *El día*, 17 October 1974.

18. Ibid.

19. George Geda, "Conjeturas de la AP en un tendencioso comentario," *El día*, 17 October 1974.

20. Improvised comments at the ceremony in memory of the ex-presidents Plutarco Elías Calles and Lázaro Cárdenas at the Monument to the Revolution, 19 October 1974.

21. The emphasis given to the formation of productive capital in this six-year term is worthy of commentary, but most of all it is worth remembering that almost half of the public investment was made in the industrial sector and that of this, almost three-fourths corresponded to the petroleum, petrochemical, electric, and steel industries. See Carlos Tello, *La política económica de México: 1970-76* (Mexico: Fondo de Cultura Económica, 1979), pp. 193-97.

22. This statement could be called naïve as a "hypothesis of what did not happen"; but it is not so naïve if we take the circumstances of that time into account and consider this statement as a "hypothesis of what could have happened." This makes sense when we realize the fact that the big oil fields (Cactus, Sitio Grande, Bagre, Samaria, Cunduacan, Iride, Níspero, and so on) were discovered between 1972 and 1974; that some of them began to produce in 1973; and that in 1975 all of them were producing. The fact is that these fields in the Southeast, that today generate three-fourths of the country's crude oil, in 1975 produced about half of it and in 1976 about 60 percent. From 1973 to 1976, Mexico's petroleum production rose an average of 20 percent annually, which has not happened since the oil expropriation in 1938. See Abel Beltrán del Río and Enríquez P. Sánchez, "Mexican Oil Policy: Its Prospective Macroeconomic Impact, 1979-1990,"

mimeographed (Philadelphia: University of Pennsylvania, Wharton EFA, 25 October 1979), pp. 17 and 34; and Sevinc Carlson, "Mexico's Oil," p. 5.

23. This was the explicit position of Senators Kennedy and Church. See Congressional Research Service, *Mexico's Oil and Gas Policy: An Analysis* (Washington, D.C.: Government Printing Office, 1979).

24. The negotiations were opened again at the beginning of 1979 as a result of President Carter's visit to Mexico's president in February. See J. Puente Leyva, "Venturas y desventuras de Carter en México," *Sabado*, suplemento semanal de *Uno más uno*, 28 April 1979.

25. Olga Pellicer de Brody, "El acuerdo para la venta de gas a E.U., una conciliación necesaria," *Proceso*, 22 October 1979.

26. Ibid.

27. Ibid.

28. Statements made by Lee Goldman, secretary of Auxiliary Energy for Policy and Evaluation. Warren Christopher, undersecretary of State recognized that ". . . if the agreement had been made two years earlier, the price would not be $3.625, as was finally agreed upon, but rather $5 for a thousand cubic feet. . . ." *Excélsior*, 22 September 1979, report by Fausto Fernández Ponte, correspondent in Washington. Also *El acuerdo sobre gas, triunfo de Carter, dicen en E.U.* in *Uno más uno*, 22 September 1979.

29. This analysis leaves out the industrial sector given that its future (not like in the agriculture industry) is practically "guaranteed" in the wide context of the *National Plan for Industrial Development* and its explicit schedule for fiscal-stimulus investment, for subsidizing prices for energy and petrochemical depreciation, and for subsidizing employment of workers—not to mention the stimulation of the market itself consequent to the increased elasticity of demand that characterizes manufactured products.

30. It is important to point out that until now, studies on this subject have emphasized the effects of the oil boom on the balance of payments (on account) but not its implications for generating domestic savings nor its effect on the balance and budgetary structure of the public sector. See Alejandro Vásquez Enríquez and Giseles Pérez Moreno, "El petróleo, la balanza de pagos y el crecimiento económico," *Economía mexicana* (Mexico: CIDE/March 1979), pp. 51-63.

31. See report by Carlos Cantón Zelina, *Desplome en la producción de alimentos básicos marino, Excélsior* (November 1979); "Sector agropecuaria: se esperan mayores cosechas," in *Examen de la situación económica de México* (Mexico: Banco Nacional de México, January 1979), pp. 35-43; and Arturo Warman, "Estadísticas agrícolas: el milagro de los panes," *Uno más uno*, 2 and 3 December 1979.

32. Secretary of Patrimony and Industrial Fomentation, *Plan nacional de desarrollo industrial, 1979-1982*, 2 vols. (Mexico: SEPAFIN, 1979).

33. del Río and Sanchez, "Mexican Oil Policy."

34. Some statistics should be mentioned here. In the last decade and up to the beginning of this one, per capita agricultural production in developed countries grew almost 20 percent, while it remained constant in the developing countries. During this decade almost two-thirds of the world's exportation of wheat and fodder grains came from the United States and Canada. The importance of the United States is even greater in the case of certain products in high demand like soy beans. Ninety percent of the worldwide export of this product in the last two decades came from the United States. None of this is due to the market or its automatic response. It is due instead to a strategy of national-security and international political negotiations by the United States, and this strategy is clearly seen in the multiple types of support, including subsidies, that agriculture enjoys in that country. See W. Schneider, *Food, Foreign Policy and Raw Materials* (New York: Crane, Rusaark and Col, 1976), p. 122.

35. An interesting note here is that at the same time the production of basic foodstuffs for the population has plummeted, Mexico is celebrating the successes of certain export products. Interesting, too, is that in the face of the deterioration of the minimum salary (in real terms) that affects the great masses of workers in the country, the secretary of Agriculture and Hydraulic Resources says, "The people should pay real prices and thus alleviate the anguishing situation of thousands of producers." One of the problems, a real one, is the problem of prices to the producer and another, even more-real, problem is the extremely low productivity of the majority of Mexico's farmers who sow small plots of land seasonally and are subject to the rip-offs of middlemen, lack of credit, lack of improved seeds, no fertilizers, and as always, no water. See Zelina, "Desplome en la Produccion."

36. David Ibarra, "Mercados, desarrollo y politica económica: perspectivas de la economía de México," in David Ibarra, ed. *El Perfil de México en 1980*, vol. 1, (Mexico: Siglo XXI, 1978), p. 119.

37. Concretely, within or outside of the General Agreement on Trade and Tariff (GATT), Mexico should demand a formally drawn up ad-hoc agreement of reciprocal supply of commercial, technological, and financial material from the United States and other developed countries in return for a sure supply of hydrocarbons. In the face of the recurring protectionist obstacles that confront its exportation of oil, Mexico should announce that it will not sell petroleum to those countries that impose obstacles and barriers that are against its best interests.

# Discussion Summary

Sidney Leveson introduced the discussion session with a call for "a complete understanding of what is important to Mexico" and an agreement with Mexico and the United States "from which everyone benefits." The discussion that followed attempted to first, identify the concerns of Mexico and second, clarify aspects of a mutually beneficial agreement. Agricultural production, Mexican political stability, oil prices, and oil production levels were several of the topics that emerged from the frame of reference outlined by Leveson.

The discussion began in reference to the chapter by Puente Leyva and the question of why Mexico has no apparent plan to use oil revenues to create a substantial infrastructure for agriculture, while it does intend to invest $100 billion in industry each year. Puente Leyva agreed that prospects for sufficient foodstuffs in the coming years were pessimistic if one analyzed the National Industrial Development Plan prepared by the Mexican Ministry of Economic Development. However, he commented further that the government has made efforts to improve agricultural production especially in the areas of irrigation and dam construction. In his view, the agricultural problems that Mexico faces are not of production but of orientation. Much of the agricultural and livestock production in Mexico is presently export oriented. In past years the agricultural-export orientation was important to earn foreign exchange, but today agricultural exports give rise to relatively insignificant revenues in the shadow of oil exports. Therefore, reorientation in agriculture toward the production of grain and other basic foodstuffs could ameliorate Mexican agricultural deficiencies. The national industrial plan, Puente Leyva emphasized, must reflect a concern for the more-traditional sectors of the economy if this reorientation is to be realized.

Among those aspects of a mutually beneficial agreement for oil is the U.S. concern for a secure source of oil. Leveson referred to this concern when he presented the possibility of Cuban interference in Mexican affairs. His greater concern, however, was for the political stability of Mexico in the wake of the changes the oil boom would create.

Leveson suggested that material benefits from the oil boom would probably take thirty-five years to filter throughout the entire society, despite the tremendous progress being made at present. Leveson views this time as the risk to political stability. Furthermore, his opinion is that the lower the level of oil production, the longer the filtering process will take. Thus, political stability would be increased in proportion to production. Leveson remarked that this was the difficult choice that Mexico faced and that only Mexico could make it.

Wionczek disagreed with the view that Cuban interference would necessarily be a reflection of political instability within Mexico. He suggested, however, that if Cuban intervention in Mexico is a matter of concern for the United States, U.S. pressure on Mexico to increase oil production would likely have a detrimental effect in this regard.

Villarreal introduced the final point of this session when he questioned Leveson's comment that the price of Mexican gas is too high for the United States at a marginal price of $100 per barrel and that the United States should negotiate for increased Mexican production. In Villarreal's view, Mexico recognizes that it has a limited capacity to absorb foreign exchange for domestic savings and growth and that this capacity would dictate the optimal level of production and, indirectly, the price of gas. The price of the oil produced in Mexico, he implied, should also include a premium based on the international concern over an oil crisis and the relative stability that Mexico offers the uneasy importer of oil.

Leveson agreed that, as circumstances are today, Mexico should be paid a premium for its secure supplies of oil. He disregarded, however, that the price of Mexican oil should also depend on the availability of alternative-energy sources, as had been implied by other conference participants. The distinction between the shadow price and the market price of oil is a result, in great part, of the inconsistency of U.S. policy, according to Leveson. He concluded that, although a security premium should be paid, it should not be formulated in a manner that would exacerbate U.S.-policy inconsistencies.

# Part II
# The Mexican Perspective

# 3 Possible Dimensions of Mexican Petroleum

*Bernardo F. Grossling*

This chapter summarizes what is known about the petroleum resources of Mexico. It covers both what has been ascertained with certainty and what may only be implied or inferred from geologic observations. The foremost concern is the possible magnitude of the petroleum resources of the Reforma-Campeche Province that were discovered in 1972 and indicated in figure 3-1.

At the outset a bit of clarification as to semantics and purpose should be introduced. Petroleum is a natural resource that is both difficult and costly to find in the ground. Inferences as to the remaining amounts of oil and gas have to be cast in probabilistic terms, but this is difficult and much room is left for confusion, dissent, and misinterpretation. The petroleum that is known with great certainty to be in the ground and economically recoverable is called *reserves*. The undiscovered petroleum, which is presumed to be both recoverable and economical, is termed *resources*. Shortly after the discovery of a new petroleum province, often much uncertainty and speculation result as to its true dimensions. When the petroleum province appears to be large and its discovery has been made in the midst of an energy crisis, the scenario becomes even more sensitive. This is what happened with the Reforma-Campeche Province.

For several years I have been interested in the petroleum prospects of southeastern Mexico, where the Reforma-Campeche Province lies, and have studied this area as part of a general inquiry into the possible magnitude of world petroleum resources.[1] With the advent in 1973 of what is now called the energy crisis, my interest expanded to the broad range of the various energy resources. Besides petroleum, I have already made an extensive study of world coal resources and am now working in nuclear energy and biomass for energy. Therefore, my perspective of this particular find is worldwide, in the context of a crisis of major proportions. Quite clearly mankind has reached a stage of great interdependence, not only in the immediate present but also probably far into the future.

I have been described as an optimist in energy matters, but rather my approach has been to take a positive stance and try to find ways out of this crisis. In order to do that, the positive must be emphasized. Investment decisions follow positive considerations, whereas negative decisions lead only to inaction, stalemate, or frustration.

Note: The location of the initial (1972) Reforma discovery is within the small square.

**Figure 3-1.** Orientation Map of Mexico

Petroleum has a peculiar and difficult-to-ascertain distribution, resulting from its origin in processes that take place in sedimentary pods in the earth. The petroleum-prospective sedimentary areas of Mexico consist of about 690,000 square kilometers onshore and about 440,000 square kilometers in the continental shelves down to the 200-meter-depth line. The bulk of these prospective areas extends along the Gulf coastal plain from Chihuahua and Coahuila in the northeast to the Yucatan Peninsula in the southeast. Also, a significant area lies in the western part of Baja California—namely, the Sebastian Vizcaino and Iray Purisima Basins. Currently, only the continental shelf down to the 200-meter depth is the focus of petroleum exploration, but in the Gulf Region clues indicate that the deeper continental slope, and even the abyssal deep, may be petroleum productive. Along the main eastern sedimentary area, Mexico's Gulf region, a number of subsidiary depressions have led to local basins—Sonora, Coahuila, Burgos, Tampico (old and new Golden Lane), Veracruz, Salina del Istmo, Macuspana, and Reforma-Campeche.

## The Reforma-Campeche Petroleum Province

The Reforma-Campeche area encompasses the Gulf coastal plain of southeastern Mexico, the Yucatan Peninsula, and the Campeche Bank.

It extends southwestward to the front of the folded belt of the Mexican geosyncline. In southern Mexico the Campeche Bank lies in front of the Chiapas Massif. Some facts that have been established about the area are as follows:

Petroleum production that had been established in the area prior to May 1972 came only from Tertiary-age (less than 65 million years old) rocks. The underlying sedimentary section had not been drilled, and its nature could only be inferred from geologic observations along the folded belt of the Sierra Madre and from regional geophysical surveys.

Mexican geologists were well aware of the petroleum potential that the deep and older sedimentary section could have. The Tertiary section had been drilled to depths of about 2,000 to 2,500 meters, yet regional seismic surveys indicated that the total sedimentary section could much surpass 10 kilometers in thickness. Refer to figure 3-2 for seismic-structure information.

PEMEX, in May 1972, completed two wells—Cactus-1 and Sitio Grande-1—in the Reforma area and found a petroleum-productive Upper-Cretaceous to Lower-Cretaceous carbonate section (65 to 136 million years old). The discovery wells tested initially about 2,000 barrels per day, which was far surpassed by subsequent wells.

PEMEX subsequently forcefully pursued the exploration in the surrounding Reforma area onshore and then offshore into the Campeche Bank. By the end of 1978, PEMEX had discovered 45 to 50 Cretaceous fields onshore and about 4 offshore.

Reforma fields have areas of about 45 to 150 square kilometers, but in the Campeche Bank the fields appear to be about three times larger. The oil columns are exceptionally large. They are reported to average 500 meters in thickness. One oil column appears to surpass 2,000 meters in thickness.

Drilling depths range from about 3½ to 5 kilometers.

Mexico's petroleum reserves, as a result of the new find, have increased from a level of about 2.8 billion barrels of proved hydrocarbon reserves in 1972 to a level of 40 billion barrels of proved reserves, plus 41 billion barrels of probable reserves by the end of 1978. More than 90 percent of these proved reserves are in the Reforma-Campeche area. Note that PEMEX designates as probable reserves the amount of recoverable petroleum in the fields already discovered, in excess of the proved reserves, when the full size of these fields from geology and geophysics is taken into account. The hydrocarbon reserves consist of the oil reserves plus the oil equivalent of the gas reserves.

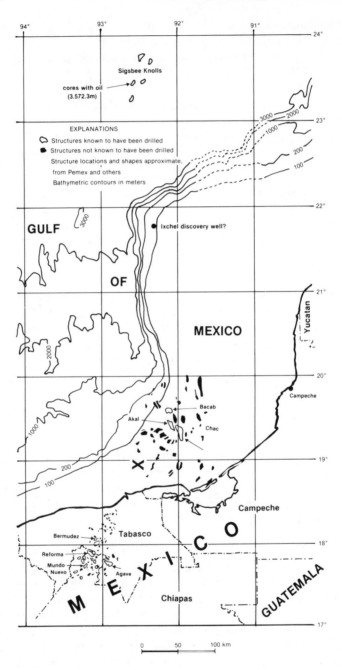

**Figure 3-2.** Reforma-Campeche Seismic Structures

In the first quarter of 1979, Mexican oil production was about 1.8 million barrels per day, of which 500,000 barrels per day were exported. Production is expected to reach a level of 2.25 million barrels per day in 1980. The average 1978 gas production of the Reforma-Campeche Province was $2.9 \times 10^9$ cubic feet per day.

These figures only correspond to reserves that are already located. How much petroleum may be found in this new province? A more-complete perspective of the productive trend can be obtained by projecting the production potential of the Middle-Cretaceous reef, or reefs, that have been traced seismically from Reforma to Veracruz and from Reforma to Ixchel and to the Catoche Tongue areas. Figure 3-3 sketches five ways in which the petroleum potential may be projected. Until now there have been two patches of fields—one onshore and another offshore. First, one would expect that other fields would be found when the areas that enclose the two patches of discovered fields are fully explored and developed. Second, between the patches is an undrilled area of marshes and shallow waters that also offers potential. Third, the productive trend may extend north to the

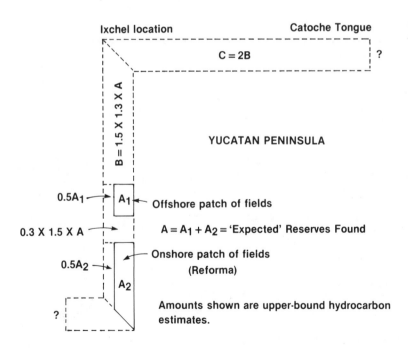

Source: Compiled by B.F. Grossling.

**Figure 3-3.** Conceptual Hydrocarbon-Resources Projection Model for Reforma-Campeche Province

northwest tip of the Campeche Bank (roughly the Ixchel location) and then east to the Catoche Tongue area. Fourth, the productive trend may extend east from the Ixchel area to the Catoche Tongue area along the north flank of the Campeche Bank. Fifth, the productive trend may extend west of Reforma in the direction of Veracruz.

The more speculative of these projections are the last two. The pessimist would argue that the productive trend may not continue along the reef, trend, neither north nor west, and the optimist would argue that more-prolific segments of the reef may yet be found.

With these caveats, table 3-1 presents an optimistic upper-bound estimate of the amount of economically recoverable hydrocarbons in the Reforma-Campeche Province.

## Summary and Conclusions

Upon examining the evidence, the estimated magnitude of the recoverable hydrocarbon resources of the Reforma-Campeche Province appears to be quite high. The following points summarize the prospects:

**Table 3-1**
**An Optimistic Upper-Bound Estimate of the Reforma-Campeche Province Reserves**

| | | $10^9$ barrels |
|---|---|---|
| *Reserves in the two patches of fields* | | |
| Proved reserves | | 40 |
| Probable reserves | $40 \times 0.8$ | 32 |
| (0.8 = probability) | | |
| Total reserves, "expected" value A | | 72 |
| | | |
| *Growth factors* | | |
| Growth by filling in the onshore and offshore patches already developed (A factor of 1.5) | | |
| Growth by filling in the area between the onshore and offshore patches (A factor of 1.3) | | |
| Growth of Ixchel location (A factor of 2) | | |
| Growth to Catoche Tongue (A factor of 2) | | |
| Sum of factors = 7.8 | | |
| | | |
| *Product of factors times reserves A* | $7.8 \times 72$ | 562 |
| Additional expected growth westward from Reforma toward Veracruz. | | 70 |
| *Grand total of projected resources* | | about 630 |

Source: Calculations by the author.

These resources almost certainly will surpass 100 billion ($10^9$) barrels, and with a subjective probability of 1 in 10, they could be as high as 700 billion barrels. A probability of 1 in 10 is very significant; events that may occur with such a probability ought to be at least considered in contingency planning.

It seems intellectually hazardous to project beyond the 700-billion-barrel figure at this time. As of yet no sufficiently realistic model for petroleum-resources assessment of the Reforma-Campeche Province seems to have been formulated that would permit assessing events with probabilities smaller than, say, 10 percent. However, this also means that further surprises on the up side are possible. As the emphasis of our inquiry is on how large these resources could reasonably be, we do not delve here into how small they could be.

The petroleum resources of Mexico are obviously larger than those of the Reforma-Campeche Province. The estimates given here do not fully take into account the possible contribution of the other sedimentary basins of Mexico, onshore and offshore.

## Note

1. See, for example, B.F. Grossling, "Window on Oil—A Survey of the World Petroleum Sources," *Financial Times Ltd.*, 1979; *Brief on Reforma-Campeche's (Mexico) Petroleum Potential Opportunities and Challenges for the United States: U.S. Geological Survey.* Open File Report, no. 79-237, December 1978; "The Reforma-Campeche News Media Record," November 1978, as appendix to above; "World Coal Resources," *Financial Times Ltd.*, 1979; and B.F. Grossling and D.T. Nielsen, "The Geologic Setting of the Reforma-Campeche Petroleum Province," to be published by U.S. Geological Survey.

# 4 PEMEX in a Dependent Society

*Isidro Sepúlveda*

Recent studies have attempted to establish a theoretical relationship between the stages of dependent development, particular state-domination forms, and the general political orientation of state enterprises.[1] The argument proffered is that when societies enter a stage of import-substitution industrialization, they typically have a populist form of government that establishes the necessary protection devices. However, when the easy phase of import substitution has passed and difficulties for further expansion set in, a more-centralized and authoritarian government comes to power.[2] Public enterprises will be affected by this change as the authoritarian-populist government exercises more control over them and may cause the enterprises to assume broader social responsibilities that only can be undertaken at the sacrifice of the economic efficiency of the enterprise.

When the nation passes into the next stage of development, export-oriented industrialization, the degree of government intervention in state enterprises must necessarily diminish as the enterprises become more subject to world-market forces and thus must operate on the criterion of economic efficiency in order to survive. The result is more autonomy for the public enterprises.

This chapter analyzes the Mexican National Petroleum Company (PEMEX) and its relationship with the government and civil society. The relationships in the import-substitution-industrialization period of 1938-1973 are briefly reviewed. Emphasis is placed on the relationships in the export-oriented period since 1977. This orientation provides an understanding of the present-day operations of PEMEX as well as a good basis for a prognostication about future state-PEMEX relations and the ability of PEMEX to administer Mexico's booming oil industry.

## PEMEX and Import-Substitution Industrialization

*Organization and Administration of the
Oil Industry*

Since the 1920s, a group of legal dispositions established by the Mexican government set out to prepare public administration to take control of the petroleum industry in 1938 when it was nationalized. In 1925 the Mexican government created an agency called Control of the Management of National Petroleum (CAPN) that engaged in two different sets of activities: (1) the production and refining of crude in competition with private capital and (2) the regulation of the domestic price of petroleum products. Simultaneously, the government issued policy guidelines requiring the oil companies to train Mexican personnel.[3] Later, in 1931, the labor law was enacted, and it specified that at least 90 percent of the workers in any establishment should be Mexican, that the immigration of foreign nationals was to be regulated, and that enterprises were also to be required by law to train Mexicans in order that they could replace any imported technicians by the termination of the contract.[4]

In 1934 the functions of CAPN were taken over by a semiprivate agency, Mexican Petroleum, S.A., which was more commonly known by the name "Petromex." This company had three functions: (1) to regulate the national-petroleum and petroleum-products markets; (2) to assure a supply of petroleum to meet national needs; and (3), the most-important function, to train Mexican personnel in the technical aspects of the industry. During the Cárdenas regime, the government felt a need for a more-effective control of this industry, and at that time the General Administration of National Petroleum (AGPN) was created as a direct dependency of the executive branch.

When nationalization was declared, on 19 March 1938, Mexico's immediate task was to maintain production in the fields vacated by foreign operators. The Mexican technicians who had been trained by CAPN, Petromex, and AGPN and the Mexican nationals who had been employed by the expropriated companies, together with a few independent American drillers, constituted the nucleus of persons that made possible the continued operations in the industry. Note, however, that much of the equipment was outdated or in poor condition. A month after expropriation, production levels declined by almost 50 percent. However, less than a year later they had returned to their original level.

The industry that the government took over was a hodgepodge of different plants, equipment, and structures, and was not a rational, integrated system. Management, for example, had been carried out by a score of parallel organizations that competed with each other. These organizations presented too much duplication of effort from the standpoint of centralized organization and therefore had to be molded into a coordinated and unified structure. Thus, on 7 June 1938, President Cárdenas created two agencies: PEMEX and the Mexican National Petroleum Distributing Company. PEMEX was responsible for handling all phases of the industry up to, but not including, marketing; the distributing company took over from that point.

The intitial structure in which labor was permitted to participate in the management of the companies did not work. The diffusion of responsibility led to duplication of effort and waste of expenditures. Worse still, it proved impossible to control the power of the local labor unions. By early 1940 the strain between PEMEX and the distributing company on the one hand and between labor and the government on the other were so debilitating that Cárdenas, in 1940, abolished the distributing company and ordered its assets and functions to be transferred to PEMEX. PEMEX has continued to be structured along those lines established by that reorganization.

## PEMEX and the Government

Mexican public enterprises, exemplified by PEMEX, were conceived along the lines of a capitalistic, market-oriented corporation similar to others appearing in the United States and Europe during the Great Depression. The privileges and responsibilities (and perhaps some of the confusion) that PEMEX has confronted are similar to those shared by its foreign counterparts. A great uncertainty exists as to whether or not PEMEX should be operated as a business concern, even though Mexican courts have ruled that it must pay taxes as does a private business. This ambiguity arises from two conflicting forces: the philosophical assumption that public enterprise is not profit-oriented and the economic reality that oil industries are almost by nature highly profitable businesses.[5]

From 1938 to 1952 PEMEX's principal function was not that of profit, but rather to fulfill social ends. Its administrator, however, voiced a concern that the organization should be self-supporting and thus went on to make it work with this objective in mind. Since 1940 the industry has been handled by an eleven-member board of directors with representation of five members appointed by the government and six appointed by the Mexican Petroleum Workers Union (STPRM). Government appointees are from the secretary of treasury and public credit and the secretary of the national patrimony.

Through the board of directors, PEMEX controls its budget and elaborates policies of production and exploration. However, through the Mexican president and his appointees, the government has exercised considerable influence on the operations of the organization. Although the executive board includes the secretary of patrimony, the under secretary of natural resoures, and two representatives from the treasury, countervailing forces still operate to influence the policy of the enterprise. This is due to the heterogeneous composition of the board that provides mechanisms for the confrontation of various positions and interests. Also, the president only intervenes when major problems arise.

*Internal Organization of PEMEX*

**Management and Labor Relations**. After nationalization, management's main objective to maintain a unified organization, and the tenacity of the union in dispersing authority into small work units, resulted in a lack of control over various expenditures as well as over the hiring of personnel.[6] This situation was only worked out when PEMEX and the distributing company were unified into one company. Using the reorganization of PEMEX as an excuse, Cárdenas squelched the disorder with the union, putting to rest the possibility that the industry might ever come under union management.[7] The dispute was finally ended, and management established effective control over the local administrative councils (working units) that, up to that time, had been dominated by workers.

Labor and management disputes became so serious that the Federal Board of Conciliation and Arbitration intervened in 1940. The results of the arbitration were ambiguous but were interpreted as largely favorable to the union. Because of this decision, which questioned the legitimacy of the board, another law was enacted on 3 April 1942 that expressly reaffirmed the powers of the board. These powers authorized the board to appoint certain key positions and, in addition, to approve certain kinds of operations with only the concurrence of three of the federal government representatives. These powers also could not be delegated. Even so, effective control by the administrators was not decisively wrested away from the union until the first collective contract was signed in May 1942.[8]

Management and labor relations throughout the history of the enterprise have not been easy. Notwithstanding the passage of some legislation favorable to management, STPRM has always enjoyed a unique position vis-à-vis PEMEX. In the forty-one years of the existence of the enterprise, the major source of conflict probably has been the union's ideological approach regarding what PEMEX should be as public enterprise. At a more-micropolitical level labor has insisted that PEMEX should be exclusively devoted to promoting social welfare, specifically the welfare of its workers. STPRM's workers are among the highest paid. Moreover, they enjoy substantial subsidies in the areas of education, medical services, housing, and recreation. Another indication of the power the union has wielded has been the nepotism practiced in the industry—more than half of all workers hired by PEMEX in 1975 are thought to have been related to other PEMEX employees.

**Technical Personnel**. With the necessity of rapid expansion, more Mexican technicians had to be trained. Promoting a program of technical education, therefore, was one of management's primary concerns. The technical-education program involved a number of facets. Incentives were offered to students so that they could acquire specialized training in various engineering fields. Management also endeavored to keep PEMEX's technical personnel constantly informed of new processes and techniques that were being developed outside the country. Groups of engineers were sent to other countries, especially the United States, for the purpose of studying the most-modern technical advances.

The program was a success. It built up a select body of Mexican experts capable of undertaking all activities of the enterprise with confidence and instructing the new generations. Since that time, PEMEX has developed its own academic-training network in Mexico, the United States, and France.

During the years following the nationalization of the industry, a number of problems have arisen between the new, young technicians and long-time workers. This conflict became particularly serious when new technicians were appointed to represent the administration. At this early stage, the senior workers were favored by the administration because of their participation in the struggle for nationalization. However, the administration also had to give support to the new technicians in order to maintain a certain hierarchical structure within the industry.

PEMEX's professionalization and modernization have been expanding through the years. As early as 1942 the industry created its own coordinating department of technical studies. Among other activities, this department has been in charge of creating and developing technical programs as well as approving numerous investments. Connected with it is a department of new projects that is in charge of the development of the engineering aspects of operations. By 1960, the Mexican Petroleum Institute had been created to administer research and development in the petroleum field.

*PEMEX's Development: 1938-1973*

This section holds as a first working hypothesis that PEMEX has been successful in carrying out the functions assigned to it in the process of import-substitution industrialization. A second hypothesis is that PEMEX's fundamental problem has been the subordination of its interests as an economic entity to the administrator state as a consequence of the role it has played in subsidizing the nation's process of industrialization. This phenomenon brought about a tendency toward the company's politicization that in time would culminate not only in confusion of basic priorities of the oil industry but also in repeated management and production crises. Finally, we point out that the specific crisis in regard to inefficiency, lack of productivity, and so forth that characterizes PEMEX at this stage are not to be considered an isolated phenomenon, but rather should be understood as the result of import-substitution development strategy and the need of a specific political reorientation that the model presents.

1973 was a year of crisis for PEMEX. At that time the national petroleum industry became incapable of meeting internal demand, and the country became a net importer of crude oil. The sudden need to import crude oil was due to poor planning in the industry, especially in the exploration and production phases. What was happening to PEMEX? Antonio Bermúdez wrote in 1976: "The principal reason for the crisis of 1973 was that PEMEX was going through a period of misplaced priorities."[9]

At the macropolitical level, PEMEX's principal function has been to supply the national hydrocarbons market at modest prices. At the same time serious problems were brewing within the organization with respect to its relationship with the government and with its functioning as an economic entity. The sacrifice of its interest as an economic unit has been a high cost for PEMEX. Apparently from the point of view of the industry, at least, this sacrifice was a mistake.

The decline of PEMEX was caused by problems generated in three areas: (1) the relations of the corporation with the administrator state, (2) the policies developed for its functioning, and (3) the application of these policies in its day-to-day operations. PEMEX's problems reveal the contradictions of a dependent and underdeveloped country in the process of modernization.

PEMEX was a vulnerable institution from the beginning. Neither its aims nor its functions were specified clearly. The act that organized PEMEX indicates that PEMEX has a social, not a profit-oriented, function. Notwithstanding this fact, it has to pay taxes, be self-financing, and provide income. In this manner, the government must interpret what policy shall be used to manage the corporation—be it a statist policy or that of a normal business.

Between 1938 and 1952 PEMEX traversed a period of extraordinary growth and strengthening. Between 1958 and 1973 the organization underwent a severe decline and, ultimately, a crisis resulted. What factors explain this particular development of the petroleum industry? Of course, many factors determined this pattern of growth and decline. They can be summarized, however, by noting that PEMEX experienced two different orientations in these periods. In the 1938-1953 period the industry was managed according to privatist policies. These policies are defined to include those considerations that normally operate in private enterprise—that is, profitability, efficiency, cost-effectiveness, and productivity. At the same time, an effective decentralization is maintained in practice, resulting in a relatively autonomous decision-making process.

During the 1958-1973 period, the concerns of PEMEX management were more-socially oriented, away from a concern for profit. Moreover, the corporation lost its autonomy, and the decision-making process became politicized, thus causing frequent confusion of the priorities of the industry with the social or political concerns of society.

As noted earlier, these two views, the privatist and the politicized, become the dominant forces at different points in the historical-political development of Mexico. The privatist model predominated during a period of extraordinary economic growth generated in part by World War II and the process of import-substitution industrialization. The politicized model predominated in the final years of the 1950s and in the 1960s, a period characterized by increasing economic problems and the beginning of a new stage, export substitution, during which increased subsidies to industry are necessary in order that its products will be competitive in the world market. Moreover, this period witnessed growing pressures fomented by rising expectations that were generated by the modernization process.

The years 1938-1952 have been often called PEMEX's "Golden Age." Petroleum production tripled, refining capacity quadrupled, and distributive systems made considerable advances. Proved reserves were doubled, rising from $2.4 to $4.3 billion. This rapid growth can be explained by the respect accorded to the decentralized nature of the enterprise.[10] This decentralization permitted PEMEX to make its own decisions and to fix its priorities according to market principles and within flexible planning systems of the government. During this entire period, the state did not attempt to control either the price of oil or its derivatives; PEMEX was left alone to determine pricing policy according to the notion of "remunerative price."[11]

During the administration of Ruiz Cortinez (1952-1958), problems emerged that lead to the next stage of decline. Shortly after Ruiz Cortinez became president, PEMEX management asked the president to permit a price increase due to inflation. Oil prices had remained fixed since 1946, while the annual rate of inflation had been between 10 and 12 percent until 1949 and had increased to an average of 16 percent in the following years.

In 1954, the peso was devaluated by 60 percent with respect to the dollar. PEMEX had ordered large quantities of materials from foreign enterprises for the construction of three refining plants, and it renewed its request for a price increase. The president repeated his denial.[12] The reason given by Ruiz Cortinez for his refusal to grant a price increase was that ". . . the role of PEMEX was not one of profit but of social service." This position had serious implications upon the financial situation of the enterprise. It served also as a precedent for later presidential administrations.

Apparently Ruiz Cortinez had two major reasons for his response to PEMEX: one economic and the other political. The economic reasons were that Ruiz Cortinez may have been motivated by the difficulty of Mexican prices to compete in the world market and by the need to subsidize the costs of production for the industrial plant through the supply of low-cost hydrocarbons.[13] This reasoning had some problems. However, the remunerative price subsidized the economy. Refusal by the government to revise the remunerative price in accordance with the rate of inflation can be explained by the political reason: the support of the STPRM given to one of the candidates opposing Ruiz Cortinez during the presidential campaign and the lack of cooperation by the administration to make the union abandon its position.

This negative experience with the union, and indirectly with the administration of the enterprise, likely influenced the president's decision to deny the request for a price increase. The immediate effects of his decision were to seriously restrain the rate of growth of the Mexican petroleum industry. The importation of petroleum derivatives and natural gas and gasoline to supply the northern part of the country increased significantly. The U.S. price for these products was almost twice the price at which PEMEX sold them in the domestic market, and as a consequence costs rose. The financial situation of PEMEX deteriorated and funds were not available to meet its obligations. Payments of taxes were delayed and the company had to borrow. Toward the end of Ruiz Cortinez's term in 1958, the organization was caught in a vicious circle of credit that seriously increased operational costs.[14] In the meantime, PEMEX religiously continued to supply internal demand.

By the late 1950s, government policy in dealing with workers was by means of cooptation—that is, the labor union was granted 50 percent of the industry's contracts. This practice became generalized in subsequent years, with the union's obtaining substantial concessions from PEMEX management. This gave rise to a marked tendency of politicization of relations between management and the union. If the motivation for management decision is political, a disciplined and productive atmosphere is difficult to maintain. The relations among various groups within the corporation deteriorated since an environment of competition, rather than cooperation, was encouraged. Management standards also declined significantly, and corruption went out of control. In general terms, all of these processes can be expressed as a single phenomenon: The orientation of PEMEX moved toward a politicized model of public enterprise.

Conversely, pricing policy was a constant throughout the 1952-1973 period with the sole exception of López Mateos's term (1958-1964), during which time a return to the application of the remunerative price occurred. PEMEX thus became a public corporation dedicated to the task of supporting the development of other economic sectors.

In the process PEMEX became subordinated to the administrative state. The price freeze imposed upon the enterprise detached it from the mechanisms of the market and connected it to the plans and stimuli that emanate from a planning system incapable of leading the particular development of the oil industry. Since the price of petroleum no longer covered operational costs, the enterprise was forced to rely upon credit, principally from public funds, and to a lesser degree, from international sources. Since it could no longer pay its taxes with earnings, it was forced to do so on credit. The kinds of considerations that guided the corporation were no longer those of return on investment and efficiency. The resulting loss of autonomy caused confusion regarding the priorities of the organization. Bermúdez expressed it best when he argued, "One witnesses a period, from 1964 to 1973, during which the confusion of priorities make it lose sight of its principal function, that is, to maintain an equilibrium in reserves, production, and national demand."[15]

This loss of autonomy can be elaborated further. The corporation's interest, that of seeking the expansion of proved reserves, was subordinated to the broader interest of supplying hydrocarbons at low costs. This development runs contrary to the way the industry operates—that is, production normally depends on exploration and the expansion of reserves, not the other way around. In this manner the planning considerations of the government ran roughshod over the natural petroleum cycle.

PEMEX entered the 1970s with a number of serious problems including overstaffing, an overpaid labor force, and nepotism. Nepotism operated at various levels. Not only did PEMEX employees secure jobs for their relatives in the industry but also the managers and leaders of the union secured lucrative contracts for their friends.

As a public enterprise, and the first non-Communist national oil company at that, PEMEX has to deal with some basic problems. The question that needs to be posted is whether the problems of corruption or incompetence are the result of the specific nature of operation of the enterprise or if they are inherent in the nature of a public corporation per se. All organizations, and especially those in the public sector, suffer from incompetence and corruption. The question is one of degree. These concerns can become dangerous when the public enterprise gives greater weight to its social than to its economic goals. Public corporations in other countries have shown that when cost efficiency is emphasized, the level of efficiency increases and many of these problems are avoided.

## PEMEX and Export-Oriented Growth

### Oil Discoveries and the Crisis of 1976

Oil discoveries in the southern Mexican states of Chiapas and Tabasco surprised most oil-industry observers. Thus, on 5 February 1975 the *Wall Street Journal* expressed that "astute observers in and out of Mexico wouldn't be surprised if oil reserves in the Reforma regional eventually prove to total at least 2 billion and possibly 4 billion barrels or more."[16] This cautious optimism began to change in 1976 as PEMEX released frequent and substantial upward revisions of Reforma's probable petroleum reserves.

April 1977, PEMEX Director General Jorge Díaz Serrano was reported as stating that lower-bound estimates of the sum of proved, probable, and potential petroleum reserves in the Reforma area would exceed 60 billion barrels.[17] Moreover, additional large petroleum reserves were known to lie beneath the adjacent offshore waters of the Campeche Sound. Subsequent discoveries support the inference that PEMEX's April 1977 projections were indeed conservative.

Recent exploratory drilling has proved to be successful. On 1 September 1978, President López Portillo reported to the nation that Mexico's potential reserves of petroleum had risen to 200 billion barrels. One month later other discoveries were made in an area known as Chicontepec in the central coastal plain. However, the potential of this area is highly problematic and remains an open question. So far, it is only known that it has the potential of 110 billion barrels and, in places, gas reserves of 40,000 cubic feet. PEMEX says that by itself it will take thirteen years to drill the 16,000 wells necessary to fully develop the 1,275 square mile Chicontepec-field area. This means an average spacing of some 50 acres per well. Wells are expected to average about 60 barrels per day meaning that it will take 87 Chicontepec wells to produce what one Reforma well will deliver. Oil from Chicontepec is heavy, about 18-23 API, which requires sophisticated technology that Mexico does not have at this moment. This problem suggests that Chicontepec will not be in full-scale production for some time.[18]

Whatever the case may be, the oil discoveries in Mexico are enormous, possibly between 70 and 80 billion barrels of petroleum.[19] Nevertheless, the new discoveries also have presented Mexican leaders with some gnawing questions: What kinds of political options does Mexico have for exploiting this resource? What kinds of organizational changes does PEMEX require in order to maximize its efficiency and administrative capacity?

After the financial crisis of 1976, the only possible option was an increase in the exportation of crude. For at least three decades Mexico had been regarded as a less-developed country firmly on the path of modernization. The peso was relatively stable, no bank failures had occurred since 1937, the annual rate of real economic growth had averaged 6 percent over forty years, and by the end of the 1960s the per capita gross national product had risen to $1,200. These macroeconomic indicators masked, however, a parallel deterioration in other spheres of Mexican life.

By 1970, with the inauguration of the Echeverría administration, Mexico's development strategies were in a state of crisis. The economy had demonstrated its incapacity to solve a number of pressing problems including the imbalance between the generation of jobs and the growth of the population, an increasingly unequal distribution of income, and an inability to abandon the import-substitution model for one emphasizing the export of manufactured goods. The adherence to an import-substitution strategy caused a number of problems including an intensification of the capital and technological dependency, an increase in the commercial-trade-balance deficit, an alarming reduction in net tourist expenditures, and an increase in foreign debt.[20]

In the political sphere the nation was suffering from the effects of the confrontation of 1968. The populist alliance had been undermined, and the political system was losing its legitimacy with some strategic sectors of society. Moreover, the system had apparently lost its ability to maintain a semblance of unity through the incorporation and articulation of the demands of important new social groups.

This unfavorable state of affairs was exacerbated by the confluence of two events. One of these was the global recession resulting from the 1973-1974 OPEC oil embargo, with its attendant depression in the international trade of commodities. The other event occurred on the domestic front. President Echeverría set in motion an ambitious social and economic program that antagonized the business sector and jeopardized its position at home and abroad. At the national level the aims of these reforms were to do something about Mexico's deep-seated unemployment problem and its unequal distribution of income. At the international level Echeverría's program represented a move away from an exaggerated emphasis on bilateral relations with the United States and toward the formation of regional political and economic alliances with other Latin American countries.

Ignoring the world recession, the government continued to increase federal spending to push the economy. Since Mexico's exports to recession-ridden countries were falling, the country's balance of trade fell sharply, and government borrowing increased from $6.5 billion in 1973 to more than $10 billion in 1974. By 1976 the government's external debt exceeded $20 billion, and inflation was running 60 percent annually.[21]

While these events were unfolding, the Echeverría administration proceeded with its reforms, making a number of enemies in the process. On all fronts the economy seemed to be grinding inexorably toward a crisis. On 31 August 1976, in a move that caught many people by surprise, the peso was devaluated for the first time in twenty-two years. Panic ensued. Four billion dollars were taken out of the country for deposits or investment in the United States. Domestic investment dropped and unemployment rose. These were hard times for people at the bottom of the economic scale. Twelve days before leaving office, Echeverría expropriated tens of thousands of acres of prime land in the state of Sonora, divided the land into small parcels, and turned the parcels over to the peasants. Talk of a military coup was heard for the first time in recent memory.[22]

The crisis of 1976 demonstrated in a dramatic way the weakness of the import-substitution model of industrialization. It also showed the government the need to achieve a new political compromise with the business sector. This renegotiation implied the redefinition of the nature of the Mexican government itself and of its relations with civil society. The only available escape route apparently was to export oil.

The crisis of the import-substitution model of industrialization is a common phenomenon in Latin America. Indeed, the crisis of 1976 was called the *South Americanization* of the Mexican economy. The industrial apparatus created by this model presents two problems. The first problem is that as the industrialization process advances, it creates a complex dependency upon foreign technology and capital goods. The second problem is that the model creates an industry primarily oriented toward the domestic market. Often the only mechanism available to finance industrialization is via foreign credit or foreign investment. After the passage of time this situation creates a structural disequilibrium in the foreign sector of the economy that moves the country toward stagnation, rising unemployment, and extraordinarily high levels of inflation.

The crisis also made clear that an internal political-bargaining process needed to be effectuated in order to modify the terms of the political contract that had defined the nature of the relationship between government and civil society. In effect, the government had to renegotiate a national-industrialization program with the most-important economic groups in Mexico and abroad. It also had to increase the capitalization process, diminish the dependence of industry on foreign capital and technology, raise the level of efficiency of the national industry, and strengthen those exports with which Mexico had a comparative advantage. The cost imposed by this type of negotiation upon the state has been the sacrifice of its populist relationship with the civilian sector and the acceptance of a more-visible alliance with national and international capital.

The outlines of this new model can be briefly summarized. Financing the industrialization process was, of course, the central problem. By 1976 Mexico had practically exhausted its international line of credit and debilitated the confidence of national financing institutions. The financial problem could, therefore, only be resolved by export earnings. The most-available, useful, and remunerative resource available in 1976 was crude oil. The plan thus involved the export orientation of the industry and the construction of refineries and the industrial base for exporting petrochemical products in the future.

An immediate change was evidently necessary when López Portillo took office. The approach of this administration differs from the previous one in several important respects. In general terms, Mexico will not seek structural changes internally or externally. Its main objective will be the stabilization of the country's economic and political systems. Economically, López Portillo has attempted to boost business confidence. He has pledged a long-term commitment to cooperate with private enterprise. Meanwhile, in the short term the government's interventionist role is still considered crucial, at least until the economy recovers. During this time, the government hopes to win the private sector over in order to encourage it to increase total investment. The public sector will limit its investments to petroleum, petrochemicals, steel, and capital goods in industry. The choice of this administration's theme, "the alliance for production," is an indication of its economic policy and its relationship with business groups.

López Portillo has also brought a different style to his relationship with civil society. The state stops applying reformist policies of the populist type, such as the agrarian reform, the expansion of social services, the Mexicanization of industry, and so on in exchange for the direct cooperation of international capitalism; not very different from the Brazilian case of "secondary-associate development" as described by Cardoso.[23]

Unquestionably, the severity of Mexico's recent economic problems has shaped the current policy on oil exports. The major concern in the adoption of Mexico's new role as an oil-exporting country has been the structural constraints that the current situation imposes upon the volume of exports. Oil is the key to economic recovery; it is also the key to the new model of development. The ambitiousness of Mexico's oil program can be seen in the scale of the investment made. The Mexican government has authorized PEMEX to spend $6.3 billion of the $10.8 billion earmarked for all Mexican industry in 1978. In accordance with the oil program for 1977-1982 PEMEX's goals are as follows:

To drill 1,324 wildcat and 2,152 development wells;

To increase production from less than 1 million barrels to 2.2 million barrels per day;

To increase exports of crude oil from 200,000 barrels to 1.1 million barrels per day and to increase exports of refined petroleum from virtually nothing in 1977 to 300,000 barrels per day;

To make Mexico self-sufficient in petrochemicals by tripling petrochemical capacity to 18.6 million tons;

To construct a 48-inch natural-gas pipeline from Tabasco to Monterrey with a branch to the U.S.-Mexican border.

At the time these goals were announced, they were considered ambitious. Yet due to the enormous reserves of oil found at Reforma-

Campeche, and more recently, Chicontepec, it soon became apparent that the targets for production and export of crude oil could be exceeded easily. In March 1978, PEMEX revealed that it expected to reach its export and production targets, originally set for 1982, by 1980. Given the new responsibilities assigned to PEMEX and its ever-growing reserves in southeastern Mexico, it should be producing between 3 and 5 millions of barrels by the middle 1980s.

*PEMEX's Constraints and Possibilities for Change*

The finances of any institution are revealing about its objectives and form of administration. In the present context finances refer to three aspects of the economic status of an institution: (1) the availability of capital, (2) the income produced by remunerative prices, and (3) the relationship between the institution's resources and its debts. This conceptualization of finances is applicable to public corporations. In PEMEX's case, however, the finances of the organization not only reveal the quality and orientation of its administration but also the nature of its relationship with the state.

In the case of the finances of the Mexican oil industry, the remunerative price is a crucial variable since it must rely upon its own income for operations. This industry at present exploits a nonrenewable resource that requires a large investment in order to be marketed. Moreover, plans are being developed to expand the oil supplied to the world market, which is experiencing extraordinary growth. For these reasons the Mexican industry requires substantial income flows that will permit it to finance its own growth.

The financial equilibrium of a public corporation like PEMEX depends upon a number of factors. One important consideration is its internal administration, which is treated later on. The other major consideration is its relationship with the financial institutions of the state—specifically, the determination of the price of petroleum and its products and the tax structure.

The pernicious effects on the industry introduced by the price freeze of the 1950s began to be corrected in 1973. On December 7 of that year the National Tripartite Commission, composed of government, business, and labor representatives, decided that the much-needed price increase in petroleum products would be postponed no longer. The existing four types of gasoline being produced were reduced to two, and changes were introduced in the distributive system employed by PEMEX in order to reduce costs. Gasoline prices increased by 75 percent in one jump; other products' prices rose by an average of 60 percent.[24]

This increase, however, was not enough to compensate for the neglect the industry had suffered during two decades. Less than a year later, in October 1974, a determination was made that even with the previous increase the price was not remunerative. A new increase of 50 percent was authorized; for that reason these figures translate to an overall increase of 162 percent in the price of gasoline and 150 percent in the price of other petroleum products over the pre-1973 levels.[25]

The tax structure was also unfavorable to PEMEX during the 1950s and 1960s. After 1966 PEMEX paid a 21 percent tax on its income. This onerous tax constituted a serious obstale to the development of the enterprise. This problem also began to be corrected in 1973. The same meeting of the National Tripartite Commission readjusted the tax rate so that PEMEX only had to pay taxes equal to 12 percent of its income. Later, when prices were readjusted in October 1974, a new tax of 14 percent was levied upon the consumption of gasoline. This new tax was not levied on, nor was it collected by PEMEX.[26]

López Portillo brought about changes that gave the industry a new orientation that would place emphasis on production and leave aside the social objectives.[27] In 1977 the statutes governing PEMEX were modified. The legislation specifically mentions that the enterprise would be governed by "income-producing" and "efficiency" considerations.[28] The legislation is silent on matters relating to PEMEX's social function.

The change in the philosophy of the corporation was mirrored by changes in hiring policies and internal organization. Early in 1976 the hierarchical structure of the enterprise was expanded so that the number of personnel categories increased from twenty-four to forty-eight. Promotion policies were changed. Whereas previously seniority and connections seemed to be the principal criteria for job advancement, the new policy emphasized merit and competence. Whereas patronage and seniority as factors influencing employment had abounded before, in 1977 a new category of professional workers was created by which especially competent persons could ascend to higher administrative posts.[29]

Another type of change has been in the area of management-labor relations. Since 1975 a tendency has been to change the relationship of power between the union and the corporation. This has occurred on two fronts. On the one hand, the corporation has grown markedly as a result of its expansion into new fields, and the process has incorporated new workers whose ideology and experience have been different from the older workers who have been long-standing members of the union. On the other hand, the administration has openly taken measures to diminish the power of the union.

For a long time STPRM has been an organization that has not undergone change. Prior to 1975, in fact, many people said that a single group within the union, the generation of 1938, had controlled the union for three decades. Influenced by this group, the union had presented obstacles in the path of changes sought by management. Every attempt by management to reorganize PEMEX met with failure. Moreover, during the 1950s when the enterprise sought to negotiate a number of contracts with foreign companies for the purpose of carrying out exploration, the union obstinately refused to go along.[30]

The new discoveries of the last few years have provoked dissension. The workers employed in the new fields have emerged as a decisive force within the union. Historically the power and influence of the STPRM has been concentrated in Ciudad Madero, Poza Rica, Minatitlan, and the Federal District. In these places, with the exception of the Federal District, the STPRM is the most-important force in labor, social, and political matters. The Ciudad Madero, Poza Rica, and Minatitlan areas comprise the "triangle." Key leadership positions in the union commonly are filled from persons from these three areas. . . . However, the recent discoveries of the petroleum reserves in Chiapas, Tabasco, and Campeche has posed a threat to the stability of the triangle.[31] While this represents an important change in the balance of power within the union, note that even in the area of the triangle events were occurring that diminished the power of the generation of 1938. In these three areas new groups within the union emerged to challenge the traditional leadership.[32]

At the same time the traditional leadership was being challenged from within, it appears also to have been attacked from without. News reports indicated that violent actions between 1975 and 1977, perhaps of a conspiratorial nature, purged the union of those persons that opposed the new program PEMEX was erecting.[33] Our concern is not whether these printed reports are true, but what cannot be denied is that the union has been transformed into an organization that wholeheartedly supports PEMEX's program. For example, the secretary general of the union, Oscar Torres Pancardo, indicated that STPRM is committed to and is working with PEMEX to raise this year's production by some 500,000 barrels, moreover, to work toward raising productivity in petroleum-producing zones. He says ". . . there are no more politicians in the union nor in the company . . .", and worker's efforts are directed to more work and production.[34] This position by a leader of the STPRM is a far cry from the rhetoric of the generation of 1938.

Besides the kinds of activity mentioned previously, the administration has taken overt steps to contain the power of the union. Among these steps the most-important one has probably been that those contracts that the union has negotiated with private businesses have come to be regulated by a special office not under the union's control.[35] Moreover, a trend has appeared to increase the power of middle-level personnel such as technicians and professionals. In fact, some indications exist that the board of directors of PEMEX could be restructured to include representation by these middle-level groups.[36]

In summary, the projected expansion of PEMEX has been the motor behind a drastic reorganization of the enterprise, which has modified or broken the institutional constraints preventing PEMEX from acting as a business. This privatist reorientation is not very different from other public corporations in Latin America.

### Constraints and Foreign Involvement

Because the bulk of PEMEX's drilling has been onshore, Mexico's industrial infrastructure has been geared toward the manufacture of capital goods and services to supply this type of enterprise. However, Mexico's largest petroleum reserves seem likely to be offshore in the Gulf of Campeche. The shift to substantial offshore production will create strong new pressures for PEMEX to purchase the necessary equipment and technical expertise from foreign manufacturers.[37] Rapid expansion of Mexico's offshore-oil production will also be hindered by a shortage of skilled labor. Substantial reliance on foreign equipment and technicians seems inevitable if PEMEX is to carry out offshore production.

The lack of national technological development is likely to constitute another bottleneck for expanding oil operations. Thus, PEMEX probably will seek foreign technology through licensing agreements.[38] Given PEMEX's historical shortage of cash, how will it finance the rapid development of the new fields? This question is crucial, particularly when considering that the six-year plan projects a fivefold increase in the level of investment as compared to the previous six-year period.

The present administration is confronted with the problem of determining how much foreign involvement is politically feasible. Inviting foreign-service companies to participate in the development of Mexico's oil on a large scale would be the quickest way for Mexico to raise its productive capacity. This course of action, however, does not seem to be politically feasible. In the words of President López Portillo:

> Our Constitution reserves the exploitation of hydrocarbons for the nation. It is our obligation to ensure that this provision, which has given our country such substantial benefits, remains in force always.[39]

Faced with enormous demands for oil revenues and strong domestic opposition to foreign participation, the López Portillo government has followed a delicate middle course in developing Mexico's oil. PEMEX will continue to be fully responsible for running Mexico's oil industry, but foreign contractors will be hired on a project basis to break specific bottlenecks.

Compared to other developing countries, Mexico has long had a well-developed indigenous oil-field-supply industry. However, the scale of the industry has been more in keeping with the small oil fields PEMEX was developing prior to the giant Reforma discoveries. Thus, in order to meet its development plans, PEMEX has been compelled to purchase large quantities of drilling equipment, production machinery, pipeline steel, valves, turbines, bits, and compressors from the big multinational oil-field-equipment firms.

PEMEX's expansion project in the years 1976-1982 is expected to cost about $15 billion, of which $9 billion must be acquired from abroad. The obvious question is, given the contraction of such enormous debts, might the organization's financial equilibrium be seriously compromised and the growth of PEMEX be undermined? Since the foreign-banking establishment probably will provide the majority of the investment funds, what proportion of the profits will PEMEX obtain, and what will be the conditions imposed upon the production and export process? According to recent estimates, the $15 billion that should be invested from 1976 to 1982 will return about $40 billion in accumulated profits to PEMEX, of which almost half will be in foreign currency. Many unknowns exist in this estimation process. A plausible suggestion seems to be, however, that if the international-banking establishment provides the $9 billion for investment, it probably will expect to receive roughly one-third of the accumulated financial profits. Mexico will be left with the remainder, and if it is entirely invested in post-1982 oil development, it will almost surely free PEMEX from its chronic dependence on foreign capital or at least from the government.

Regarding the issues of foreign participation and external conditions imposed upon the production and export process, note that even before Mexico had sought those loans, it had been a dependent country and had to act according to an international position of limited options. Notwithstanding this unfavorable situation, the model developed by PEMEX for foreign participation would probably not aggravate or change these conditions in a significant way. As long as credit sources are diversified and the technical and technological constraints are specified by contract and negotiated among as many different firms as possible, Mexico's sovereignty should not be compromised.

The alternatives examined in this chapter for overcoming PEMEX's constraints are indicative of the direction that PEMEX is taking as a public enterprise. Two trends are evident. First, because of its size, its monopolistic control of the hydrocarbons market, and its projected growth, PEMEX will increase its bargaining power with the state. Second, the readoption of privatist concerns such as cost-effectiveness will make the enterprise respond more forcefully to the stimulus provided by the market. PEMEX's position in this regard is at a point of transition. Whereas before it had depended upon the national market, much of its incentives and stimulus will now come from satisfying international demand. This will also probably strengthen PEMEX's autonomy in relation to the state and will also provide the enterprise with a new clientele that will become an important consideration in the decision-making process of the enterprise. Thus, PEMEX likely will extend its contracts with foreign credit, technology, and technical assistance. Moreover, since PEMEX appears to have redirected its priorities in such a way that profitability is basic to its operations, the enterprise's finances might be expected to remain at equilibrium.[40]

## Conclusions

After the nationalization of the oil industry in 1938, PEMEX was a public enterprise that quickly became oriented toward social and import-substitution-industrialization objectives. Economic criteria of efficiency were sacrificed in order to provide subsidies to expand the industrial sector through inexpensive petroleum. Thus PEMEX was relegated to carry out the broader objectives of a more-authoritarian-populistic state. In the process it became inefficient, subject to considerable influence by the oil-workers' union, and developed serious financial problems.

The discovery of the huge oil reserves and the 1976 crisis were pivotal points in redirecting the relationship between PEMEX and the state as Mexico embarked on a path of using petroleum to lead a period of export-oriented expansion. PEMEX apparently has been assigned the responsibility to lead this growth through the exportation of hydrocarbons. Subject to international market forces, PEMEX must now place much more emphasis on economic efficiency—that is, it must become more privatist and less politicized in orientation.

In this context it is important to examine the political arrangements that might accompany the new growth project and the nature of the articulation of interests between the state and civil society. Review of the priorities, means, and goals that brought about the 1976 crisis has resulted in a modification of political arrangements in Mexico that will tend to operate as the political and institutional basis for the new order. At a macropolitical level a stricter definition of alliances at the top of the power structure is noticeable. In order for the new model of export-oriented growth to be successful, the state will have to seek, in a more-systematic manner, cooperation from enterpreneurial groups, either national or international, that will strengthen its export orientation. Review of economic objectives demanded by the new model significantly modifies the nature and relationships between the state and the modern and dynamic entrepreneurial groups that are capable of participating in foreign markets. The state's capacity to maintain this alliance without detriment to its power vis-à-vis the private sector would seem to be based on its capacity to organize its own productive apparatus under the criteria of productivity, profitability, and technological rationality, as well as by its political influence to maintain interests of local entrepreneurial sectors separated from international interests. Under these conditions the nature of the state becomes involved with using technological and efficiency criteria as important factors in making decisions and the appointments of political personnel.

Authoritarian-technocratic models have become a mode for governments in Latin America to replace the import-substitution model. The sociopolitical cost that has resulted is the sacrifice of the populist-bargaining characteristics of Latin American states that have been so prevalent in the last four decades. One might question if Mexico will tend to imitate the same model. Apparently no answer is available to this question yet, and it is difficult at this time to predict one. This difficulty lies in two phenomena. First, Mexico is the only country in the region in which populism is characterized by political bargaining. Second, the export-oriented model demands a more-technocratic and corporatist state. However, this model does not mean that the process for this stage should be accompanied by greater civil or military authoritarianism.

An example of this model can be found in Venezuela, where its reorganization of production, in contrast to Brazil, Argentina, and Chile, has been accompanied by a release in the authoritarian mechanisms of domination of the state's central apparatus and the use of more-representative and participative forms in the articulation of private-sector interests. Mexico could be cited as another example in which change to the export-oriented model is accompanied by an opening of the political system. The econonic capacity enables the state to decrease the imperfections that come with the import-substitution model. In other words, the way in which Venezuela and Mexico face reorientation of their productive apparatus, and their effects in the political environment, within a panorama of oil prosperity allows for a political arrangement to be settled with a certain degree of priority in time and flexibility.

It is important to point out that the new model requires a new articulation of interests in Mexico. The Institutional Revolutionary Party (PRI), which traditionally holds the alliance of populist interests, probably will incorporate significant changes in the composition of groups and the creation of goals and priorities in order to support the new model. The traditionally idealistic agrarian flag of the already weakened peasant sector has experienced a loss of significant influence. The National Confederation of Popular Organizations (CNOP) appears to be one of the greatest keys in bringing about the new economic strategy. Indeed, arguments can be presented that within this sector of the party, professionals grouped in associations and colleges would tend to emerge as the predominant force, thus becoming a crucial element of political support for the process of externally oriented growth. Considering the members of those organizations are mainly public officials, who by themselves constitute an economic and political elite with similar social background, wages, and institutional loyalties, Mexico apparently is witnessing the emergence of a new leading sector that is not very different from the "state bourgeoisie" that Cardoso found in Brazil.

Equally important is the new power structure of labor-management organizations that support the export-oriented model. A significant number of labor organizations are linked to the PRI through the Confederation of Mexican Workers (CTM). The effective articulation of interests within the labor movement has emerged at the same time that technical cadres have been promoted to leading positions within state enterprises.

The export-oriented model that is beginning to take form represents a political definition that favors private-sector economic activity because it has the most financial and operative feasibility to enter external markets. Thus, it is not surprising that private-sector entrepreneurs have supported these changes and PEMEX's expansion. The government has opened the petrochemical industry for private participation and has promised a reinvestment of earnings proceeding from oil to private economic activity.

This new coalition of interests represents the basis for support for the export model and appears to be defined within a type of technocratic authoritarianism in which the government controls the decision-making processes in the country. Such control means that the production apparatus of the state is oriented toward privatist criteria. A sense of identity has been established between public corporatism and most dynamic local enterprise. Populist bargaining has yielded to the new hegemonic groups that strengthen technological and efficiency considerations in political decisions, especially within the middle-class professional and labor sectors.

In conclusion, PEMEX is a central element in the new Mexican economic-development strategy and is on the vanguard of changes that can be expected in public enterprises and the political structure of that country. A rearrangement of the relationship between PEMEX and the state is in its formative stage. The resultant relationship could foster authoritarian aspects of the state or more-extensive political participation. The latter would guard against the extreme aspects of the former. In this regard, the Mexican model could become a different entity from the South American technocratic authoritarianism for the following two reasons: first, because it could retain the nature of an inclusionist system; and second, because of the possibility of economic success, in the course of time, it can become a real force pointing to democratization.

**Notes**

1. Guillermo O'Donnell, *Modernization and Bureaucratic Authoritarianism* (Berkeley: University of California Press, 1972); and O'Donnell, "Corporatism and the Question of the State," in *Authoritarianism and Corporatism in Latin America*, ed. J.W. Malloy (Pittsburgh, Pa.: University of Pittsburgh Press, 1977), pp. 23-47. See also F.H. Cardoso, "Las contradicciones del desarrollo asociado," *Desarrollo económico* 14, no. 53 (April 1974); and Anibal Quijano, "Imperialismo y capitalismo de estado," *Sociedad y política* 1, (1972).

2. Fernando Henrique Cardoso, "Associated-Dependent Development: Theoretical and Practical Implications," in *Authoritarian Brazil: Origins, Policies and Future*, ed. Alfred Stepan (New Haven, Conn.: Yale University Press, 1976. For the case of Chile see Orlando Latelier, "The Chicago Boys in Chile," *The Nation* (August 1976).

3. See L. Richard Powell, "The Mexican Petroleum Industry since the Exportation" (Ph.D. diss., UCLA Department of Economics, 1952), p. 70.

4. Ibid., p. 73.

5. According to the economic philosophy at the time, public enterprises were not viewed as profitable enterprises. See Jesús Silva Herzog, *Petroleo mexicano* (Mexico: Fondo de Cultura Económica, 1941), pp. 79-80.

6. Silva Herzog, *Petroleo mexicano*, pp. 302-04.

7. Ibid., pp. 268-85.

8. Antonio Bermúdez, *La política petrolera mexicana* (Mexico: Editorial Joaquín Moritz, 1976); Silva Herzog, *Petroleo mexicano*, pp. 290-95; and Powell, "Mexican Petoleum Industry," pp. 287-90.

9. Bermúdez, *La política petrolera*, p. 78.

10. Miguel Alemán Valdez, *México la política del petróleo* (Mexico: 1979), p. 350.

11. Remunerative price is lower than the market price. The remunerative price is what will reimburse PEMEX for the value of the crude, the costs of production, and the investments it has to make for the development of the enterprise.

12. Bermúdez, *La política petrolera*, p. 55.

13. Competitive problems of Mexican products were due to the end of the Korean boom and the protectionist policy applied by the United States to countries like Mexico that had refused to become members of GATT.

14. Antonio Bermúdez, *The Mexican National Patroleum Industry* (Stanford, Calif.: Stanford University, Institute of Hispanic American Studies, 1963), pp. 110-32.

15. Bermúdez, *La política petrolera*, pp. 68-70.

16. As cited in Richard B. Mancke, *Mexican Oil and Natural Gas: Political, Strategic and Economic Implications* (New York: Praeger, 1979), p. 1.

17. Ibid. See also "PEMEX Has New Chiapas Tabasco Finds," *Oil and Gas Journal*, 2 May 1977, p. 120.

18. T.J. Stewart-Gordon, "Mexico Oil, Myth, Fact and Realities," *World Oil* 188:35-41.

19. Ibid.

20. See Olga Pellicer de Brody, "Mexico in the 1970s and Its Relations with the U.S.," in *U.S. Relations to Latin America*, ed. J. Cotler and R. Fagen (Stanford, Calif.: Stanford University Press, 1974), pp. 314-333.

21. Clark W. Reynold, "Why Mexico's Stabilizing Development Was Actually Stabilizing" (Testimony presented to the Joint Economic Committee on Inter-American Economic Relations, Washington, D.C., 1977).

22. Richard Fagen, "The U.S. Mexican Relations," *Foreign Affairs* 55:685-700.

23. Cardoso, "Associated-Dependent Development," pp. 195-220; and Pellicer de Brody, "Mexico in the 1970s."

24. *Comerico exterior* (January 1974):50.

25. *Comerico exterior* (December 1974):894.

26. *Comerico exterior* (January 1974):15.

27. José López Portillo, "Conferencia de Prensa del Presidente de los Estados Unidos Mexicanos," *Excélsior*, 7 May 1978.

28. *Informe del Director General Jorge Díaz Serrano* (Mexico, D.F.: Petróleos Mexicanos, 18 March 1977).

29. Interview.

30. Bermúdez, *Mexican Petroleum Industry*, p. 145.

31. Juan Felipe Leal and José Waldenberg, "Es Sindicalismo mexicano, Aspectos Organizativos," *Cuadernos políticos* (January-March 1976):50-51.

32. See Miguel Angel Granados Chapa, "Contra cacicazgos sindicales," *Excélsior*, 17 June 1977, p. 4-A; *Excélsior*, 26 September 1977, p. 1-A; and *Excélsior*, 16 January 1978, p. 6-A.

33. *Excélsior*, 5 March 1976, p. 4-A; *Excélsior*, 28 June 1976, p. 6-A; *Excélsior*, 18 January 1978; and *Excélsior*, 16 January 1978, p. 6-A.

34. *Excélsior*, 27 January 1978, p. 17.

35. Interview.

36. Interview.

37. Mancke, *Mexican Oil and Natural Gas*, p. 85.

38. Ibid. See also Laurence Whitehead, "Petroleo y bienstar," *Foro internacional*, 18 (April-June 1978):662-64.

39. José López Portillo y Pacheco, "Informe de gobierno, 1977," *Comercio exterior* (September 1977):337.

40. In the case of Brazilian and French public enterprises, such considerations of cost-effectiveness have assured a self-sustained growth and an efficient operation. Indeed, these two aspects are indispensable for each other. See Wener Bear, Richard Newfarmer, and Thomas Trebat, *On State Capitalism in Brazil: Some New Issues and Questions* (Austin, Tex.: University of Texas, Institute of Latin American Studies, 1976), p. 14.

# 5 Petroleum and Mexican Economic Growth and Development in the 1980s

*René Villarreal*

Since the 1940s the Mexican economy can be characterized as having followed a strategy of import-substitution-industrialization development. This strategy produced a permanent and growing external imbalance such that the availability of foreign exchange became a critical constraint that fixed the limits of growth. External financing, however, permitted a relaxation of this restriction and a continuation of the process of rapid growth and industrialization. Nevertheless, the mechanism of increasing the foreign debt to adjust the imbalance was not sustainable, as evidenced by the 1976 crisis that led to devaluation.

The influx of foreign exchange that can be generated by new petroleum exports introduces an important qualitative change in macroeconomic conditions in the 1980s. The average annual growth rate of gross domestic product (GDP) could rise to 8 or 10 percent in the next few years over the average levels of 6 to 6.5 percent of the past several decades. Whereas previously the critical constraint to growth was the gap between the need for and the supply of foreign exchange, in the new era of petroleum exports the problem will be an insufficient amount of savings from the new income, thereby creating strong inflationary forces. Thus, the capacity of the economy to productively absorb petrodollars will depend upon the speed with which a net oil-export dollar can be transformed into a net domestic-savings dollar.

Petroleum provides the potential for converting Mexico into a high-level industrial power by the year 2000. The expected growth rates will permit a greater absorption of the working force but not necessarily a lesser concentration of income. This may be the case even though at the outset the growth rates appear to offer favorable opportunities for income redistribution.

In the 1980s Mexico will continue to confront the challenge of guaranteeing independent development of a mixed economy in the face of the growth of transnational capitalism. Mexico will have to work within the framework of a new strategy of industrialization and foreign trade and new policies on foreign investment and technology transfer. The country will need to avoid falling into the trap of monoproduct exportation and dependence on foreign capital and technology. It should try to avoid being classified internationally as a petroleum economy rather than as an

69

industrial economy with petroleum. Indeed, Mexico's singular advantage, in contrast to the other new oil powers, is that it will reach its peak of petroleum production after almost four decades of strong economic growth that has permitted the creation of an industrial base. Petroleum affords Mexico the historic opportunity of converting itself, over the next twenty years, into a highly industrialized country in which the basic problems of development, unemployment, and poverty are solved. However, this opportunity could be missed if the petroleum income is not transformed into a source of productive and permanent wealth but rather is wasted on the importation of consumer goods that will be of practically no benefit to the system as a whole or to future generations.

This chapter analyzes the utilization of petroleum as a lever for growth and development in Mexico. First, macroeconomic factors and policies are examined. Second, strategies for independent, self-sustained development of industrialization are discussed.

## Petroleum as a Lever for Growth

### Constraints

Three key constraints to growth exist in a developing economy: (1) external restrictions or a foreign-exchange gap, (2) internal restrictions or a savings-investment gap, and (3) within the latter, a fiscal gap. Empirical evidence is presented in figure 5-1 and table 5-1 to show which of these constraints has historically limited Mexican economic growth. From the late 1940s to 1980 the critical constraint that determined the limits of economic growth was the availability of foreign exchange. Foreign borrowing was used as a principal mechanism to adjust the external imbalance, but the accumulated foreign debt continued to grow and could not be sustained. From 1961 to 1976 the foreign debt went from 1.26 to 4.47 percent of GDP.

The savings-investment gap was not critical in this period since internal savings steadily increased from 15 percent of GDP in 1961 to 18 percent in 1976. As for the fiscal imbalance, during the 1960s the government's budgetary deficit fluctuated between 0.4 and 1.5 percent of GDP, but in the 1970s it fluctuated between 1.6 to 8.1 percent. The latter figures reflect the high levels of spending in that decade relative to the weak tax base of the Mexican economy. This high spending, in combination with public enterprise's policy of subsidizing the whole economy through price controls and tariffs, contributed to the lack of public savings.

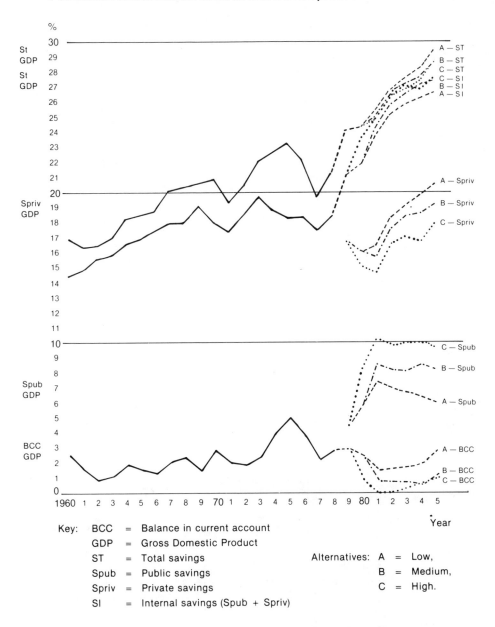

Key:  BCC  = Balance in current account
      GDP  = Gross Domestic Product
      ST   = Total savings                    Alternatives:  A = Low,
      Spub = Public savings                                  B = Medium,
      Spriv = Private savings                                C = High.
      SI   = Internal savings (Spub + Spriv)

Source: Simulation based on the model of Fernando Clavijo and Octavio Gómez, "Parámetros interdependencias en economía mexicana: un análsis econometrico," *El trimestre económico*, 46 (2), no. 182, (1979).

**Figure 5-1.** Savings and Current-Account Balance

**Table 5-1**
**Indicators of Internal and External Equilibrium**

| Year | Current-Account Balance (BCC) (millions of dollars) | Percentage | | | | | | | |
|---|---|---|---|---|---|---|---|---|---|
| | | BCC/GDP | BCC/Exports | Exports + Imports/GDP | Fiscal Deficit/GDP | Total Savings/GDP | Public and Private Savings/GDP | Inflation | GDP Rate of Growth |
| 1960 | − 300.5 | 2.49 | 21.91 | 15.98 | 1.5 | 16.9 | 14.41 | 4.9 | 7.52 |
| 1961 | − 195.3 | 1.49 | 13.35 | 14.86 | 0.5 | 16.3 | 14.81 | 3.4 | 4.92 |
| 1962 | − 120.2 | 0.85 | 7.57 | 14.50 | 0.4 | 16.4 | 15.55 | 3 | 4.67 |
| 1963 | − 170.2 | 1.08 | 9.95 | 13.87 | 0.6 | 16.9 | 15.82 | 3.1 | 7.98 |
| 1964 | − 351.9 | 1.90 | 19.04 | 13.58 | 1.3 | 18.2 | 16.30 | 5.6 | 11.96 |
| 1965 | − 314.4 | 1.55 | 15.78 | 13.25 | 2.2 | 18.4 | 16.85 | 4 | 6.48 |
| 1966 | − 296.1 | 1.32 | 13.52 | 12.34 | 0.5 | 18.7 | 17.38 | 4 | 6.93 |
| 1967 | − 506.3 | 2.06 | 22.85 | 11.63 | 0.9 | 20 | 17.94 | 2.9 | 6.26 |
| 1968 | − 632.2 | 2.33 | 25.15 | 11.57 | 0.8 | 20.3 | 17.97 | 2.4 | 8.13 |
| 1969 | − 472.7 | 1.49 | 15.88 | 11.53 | 1.3 | 20.5 | 19.01 | 3.9 | 6.32 |
| 1970 | − 945.9 | 2.82 | 32.25 | 10.76 | 1.6 | 20.8 | 17.94 | 4.5 | 6.92 |
| 1971 | − 726.4 | 2 | 22.94 | 9.48 | 1.8 | 19.3 | 17.30 | 4.5 | 3.43 |
| 1972 | − 761.5 | 1.85 | 20.04 | 10.69 | 3.5 | 20.4 | 18.55 | 5.6 | 7.26 |
| 1973 | − 1,175.4 | 2.37 | 24.34 | 11.86 | 6 | 22 | 19.63 | 12.4 | 7.59 |
| 1974 | − 2,558.1 | 3.92 | 40.33 | 13.67 | 6 | 22.6 | 18.68 | 24 | 5.90 |
| 1975 | − 3,693 | 5.01 | 58.57 | 11.93 | 8.1 | 23.2 | 18.19 | 16.6 | 4.08 |
| 1976 | − 3,068.2 | 3.85 | 41.63 | 11.74 | 7.5 | 22.1 | 18.25 | 21.6 | 2.12 |
| 1977 | − 1,623.2 | 2.18 | 19.42 | 13.89 | 5.6 | 19.6 | 17.42 | 32 | 3.26 |
| 1978 | − 2,611.1 | 2.82 | 24.23 | 15.11 | 5.8 | 21.2 | 18.38 | 17.3 | 7.04 |

Sources: Banco de México, S.A., "Cincuenta años de banco central," (México, D.F.: Fondo de Cultura Económica, 1977); *Indicadores económicos* (monthly review), various issues; *Informes anuales* (monthly review), various issues; Secretaría de Programación y Presupuesto, *Cuenta de la hacienda publica federal*; and Nacional Financiera, S.A., "Statistics on the Mexican Economy" (México, D.F., 1977).

*Petroleum's Potential*

Present production and exportation levels of petroleum, plus the future possibilities for expansion due to extensive hydrocarbon reserves, introduce important qualitative changes in the economy that will heavily influence development strategy and policies. Petroleum exports in the 1980s will generate enough foreign exchange to eliminate external factors as a principal constraint to sustained economic growth. If the economy were to grow at the traditional level of 6 percent, Mexico probably would have a surplus in the current account of the balance of payments. In fact, enough foreign-exchange earnings should come from petroleum to support annual GDP growth rates of between 8 and 10 percent before encountering an external constraint. Petroleum clearly alleviates the external constraints to high and sustained rates of growth. The question that arises immediately is: What will the new macroeconomic constraints to development in Mexico be in the 1980s?

The new constraints on growth will come, not fron external imbalance, but rather from internal imbalance—specifically, factors that will create pressures for high and sustained levels of inflation. The savings-investment gap will replace the foreign-exchange gap as the principal constraint to growth. The reason is that a net oil-export dollar does not mean a net direct-savings dollar for the national economy. An oil-export dollar ceteris paribus is worth 58 cents of government fiscal revenue, which can be used for current expenditures or put into savings for public investment. The remaining 42 cents are not necessarily net savings for the Mexican National Petroleum Company PEMEX. Expressed another way, a net oil-export dollar represents a dollar decrease in the foreign-exchange gap but does not necessarily represent a dollar decrease in the savings-investment gap.[1] Therefore, the macroeconomic strategy of the 1980s should focus on, and give emphasis to, a policy of encouraging savings and rationalizing spending in both the public and private sectors.

The fact that income from petroleum erases the external imbalance and reduces the savings-investment and fiscal imbalances will allow the government greater freedom in the use of monetary, fiscal, and commercial policies. Taxes on oil then could be destined to finance an important part of the fiscal deficit without having to revert to the traditional means of internal, inflationary financing or to an increased foreign debt. Therefore, monetary policy could be separated from fiscal policy, enhancing the flexibility of both.

*Simulation*

To illustrate and answer, even though only partially and superficially, the questions about (1) the magnitude of the changes in the foreign-exchange gap, (2) the magnitude of the savings-investment gap and, (3) the macroeconomic policies and strategies possible in the 1980s, an econometric model was simulated for the Mexican economy.[2] The model includes three alternatives determined by three hypothetical levels of petroleum production and exportation (low, medium, and high). This simulation is neither predictive nor normative in nature since it does not attempt to identify what the optimum rate of growth for the GDP would be nor what the optimum extraction and exportation rate for petroleum should be. Its function instead is to illustrate the nature of Mexico's macroeconomic problems in the 1980s and to indicate the appropriate direction and magnitude of macroeconomic policy.

The three alternatives considered are determined by the levels of production and exportation of petroleum over the period 1980-1985. The oil-production level in 1979 was an average of 1.5 million barrels a day, and the exportation level was 0.6 million barrels a day. As shown in table 5-2, in the low alternative the levels of production and exportation reached by 1985 are 3.3 and 1.8 million barrels a day respectively. In the medium alternative the levels are 4.2 and 2.6 million barrels a day respectively, and the high alternative shows 4.7 and 3.1 million barrels a day respectively. All alternatives provide for the satisfaction of internal demand first and the exportation of any surplus second.

The basic assumptions of the model are shown in table 5-3. An important assumption is fixing a fairly conservative price for oil at $26 a barrel in 1980 with $2 increases each year until 1985. The reason for the assumption is based on the model's objective to observe the macroeconomic impact of an increase in the volume of production and exportation of petroleum and not the exchange rate. Additionally, as was in effect in 1979, the model includes an ad valorem tax of 51 percent on the value of oil exports.

Another assumption is that the public sector will continue to subsidize the Mexican private sector through policies of relatively low prices for their products and services compared to international prices. PEMEX's prices will have virtually no increase, and the rest of the public enterprises will have much-lower increases than in the whole of the economy. The purpose of this assumption is to allow an evaluation of the impact of this type of policy on internal constraints to growth. ⏸

The model's estimates demonstrate, as shown in table 5-4 and figure 5-1, how external constraints, as seen in the deficit in the current account of the balance of payments as a proportion of GDP, begins to lessen slightly as the levels of oil production and exportation increase. This is especially the case for the medium and high alternatives, for which this coefficient is reduced from almost 3 percent in 1979 to 1 percent in 1985.[3] Nevertheless, parallel to the reduction in the foreign-exchange gap is the appearance of the new restriction on growth—the savings gap. Therefore, while the share

**Table 5-2**
**Alternate Scenarios of Petroleum Production and Exportation, 1979-1985**

| Scenarios | | 1979 | 1980 | 1981 | 1982 | 1983 | 1984 | 1985 |
|---|---|---|---|---|---|---|---|---|
| Levels of alternative production (millions of barrels per day) | A | 1.5 | 1.82 | 2.32 | 2.57 | 2.81 | 3.1 | 3.3 |
| | B | 1.5 | 1.80 | 2.54 | 2.85 | 3.20 | 3.7 | 4.2 |
| | C | 1.5 | 2.20 | 2.90 | 3.20 | 3.70 | 4.2 | 4.7 |
| Exportation of petroleum (millions of barrels per day) | A | 0.6 | 0.82 | 1.24 | 1.4 | 1.5 | 1.6 | 1.8 |
| | B | 0.6 | 0.80 | 1.40 | 1.7 | 1.9 | 2.3 | 2.6 |
| | C | 0.6 | 1.20 | 1.80 | 2.0 | 2.4 | 2.8 | 3.1 |
| Price of petroleum (U.S. dollars per barrel) | | $19.70 | $26.00 | $28.00 | $30.00 | $32.00 | $34.00 | $36.00 |

Key: A = low alternative,
B = medium alternative,
C = high alternative.

**Table 5-3**
**Basic Hypothesis of the Simulation Model**

| Parameters | 1979 | 1980 | 1981 | 1982 | 1983 | 1984 | 1985 |
|---|---|---|---|---|---|---|---|
| | | | | *Percentage Rate of Growth* | | | |
| Public consumption | 13 | 12 | 11 | 10 | 8 | 9 | 9 |
| Public investment | 14 | 15 | 15 | 12 | 12 | 12 | 12 |
| Wages | 18 | 18 | 18 | 16 | 16 | 16 | 16 |
| International prices | 11 | 11 | 10 | 9 | 8 | 8.5 | 9 |
| Index of implicit prices of imports | 14 | 12.5 | 10 | 9 | 9 | 9 | 9 |
| Index of public enterprises' prices including PEMEX | 11 | 2.25 | 2.25 | 2.25 | 4.5 | 4.5 | 4.5 |
| Index of public enterprises' prices without PEMEX | 12 | 5 | 5 | 5 | 10 | 10 | 10 |
| | | | | *Mexican Pesos per U.S. Dollar* | | | |
| Fixed rate of exchange | 23.00 | 23.00 | 23.00 | 23.00 | 23.00 | 23.00 | 23.00 |

**Table 5-4**
**Results of the Simulation**
*(percent)*

| Rates or Ratios | | 1979 | 1980 | 1981 | 1982 | 1983 | 1984 | 1985 |
|---|---|---|---|---|---|---|---|---|
| Rate of growth of the real | | | | | | | | |
| GDP | A | 7.9 | 8.1 | 8.9 | 7.6 | 6 | 7.1 | 6.6 |
| | B | 7.9 | 8.1 | 9.9 | 7.8 | 6.1 | 8 | 7.1 |
| | C | 7.9 | 8.9 | 10 | 8.2 | 7 | 8 | 8 |
| Rate of inflation | A | 18.7 | 21.7 | 20 | 16.7 | 14 | 13.5 | 14 |
| | B | 18.7 | 21.8 | 20.7 | 16.9 | 14.1 | 13.8 | 14 |
| | C | 18.7 | 22.5 | 21.5 | 17.5 | 14.3 | 13.9 | 14.2 |
| Current-account balance/ | | | | | | | | |
| GDP | A | 2.9 | 2.4 | 1.5 | 1.6 | 1.7 | 2.0 | 2.8 |
| | B | 2.9 | 2.4 | 1.8 | 0.7 | 0.7 | 0.5 | 1.2 |
| | C | 2.9 | 0.8 | 0 | 0 | 0.3 | 0.6 | 0 |
| Total savings/GDP | A | 24 | 24.2 | 25.3 | 26.7 | 27.4 | 28.1 | 29.3 |
| | B | 24 | 24.2 | 25 | 26.4 | 27.1 | 27.5 | 28.5 |
| | C | 24 | 24.2 | 24.8 | 26.2 | 26.7 | 27.3 | 28.5 |
| Public savings/GDP | A | 4.4 | 5.8 | 7.4 | 6.9 | 6.7 | 6.4 | 6 |
| | B | 4.4 | 5.8 | 8.5 | 8.2 | 8.1 | 8.5 | 8.2 |
| | C | 4.4 | 8.3 | 10.2 | 9.8 | 10 | 10 | 9.6 |
| Private savings/GDP | A | 16.7 | 16 | 16.4 | 18.2 | 19 | 19.7 | 20.5 |
| | B | 16.7 | 16 | 15.7 | 17.5 | 18.3 | 18.5 | 19.1 |
| | C | 16.7 | 15.1 | 14.6 | 16.4 | 17 | 16.7 | 17.9 |
| Budgetary fiscal deficit/ | | | | | | | | |
| GDP | A | 7.8 | 6.7 | 5.5 | 5.9 | 6.8 | 7.3 | 7.9 |
| | B | 7.8 | 6.7 | 4.1 | 4.4 | 4.7 | 4.7 | 5.1 |
| | C | 7.8 | 4.2 | 2.2 | 2.7 | 2.4 | 2.4 | 3.4 |
| Exports + Imports/GDP | A | 24.2 | 24.8 | 24.9 | 25 | 24.8 | 24.6 | 24.5 |
| | B | 24.2 | 24.8 | 25.7 | 25.9 | 25.9 | 26.1 | 26.1 |
| | C | 24.2 | 25.7 | 27.6 | 27.9 | 28 | 28.5 | 28.8 |
| Imports/(GDP + M) | A | 10.9 | 11 | 10.8 | 11.1 | 11.1 | 11.2 | 11.4 |
| | B | 10.9 | 11 | 10.7 | 11.2 | 11.2 | 11.2 | 11.4 |
| | C | 10.9 | 11.1 | 11.2 | 11.6 | 11.7 | 12.2 | 12.5 |

Source: Simulation based on the model of Fernando Clavijo and Octavio Gómez, "Parámetros interdependencias en economía mexicana: un análisis econometrico," *El trimestre económico*, 46(2), no. 182, (1979).

Key: A = Low hypothesis,
     B = Middle hypothesis,
     C = High hypothesis.

of total savings in GDP (which ex post facto is equal to the share of total investments) rises 4.5 percent from 24 percent in 1979 to 28.5 percent in 1985 in the medium and high alternatives, the domestic-savings coefficient has to increase at a faster rate. For example, it must rise from 21.1 percent in 1979 to 27.3 and 27.5 percent in 1985—that is, 6 and 6.5 points for the two alternatives respectively. In other words, as the economy grows and oil is exported in the 1980s, income will be generated, but that income will have to be converted into effective domestic savings for Mexico to be able to productively take advantage of these resources and supposed oil excesses. A dollar of income from oil exports is not, nor does it automatically become, a dollar of domestic savings, and if it does not it generates inflationary pressure.

The decrease of the foreign-exchange gap in this context is like a two-edged knife. On one side the external constraint to growth is lessened, but on the other side it implies a decrease in external savings' share as a source for financing total investments (its share in the GDP decreases from 3 to 1 percent). If an attempt is made to meet the objective of reaching a high level of annual economic growth of between 8 and 10 percent, a concerted effort will have to be made to increase internal savings' share of the GDP, from 21 to 27.5 percent.

Consequently, to productively take advantage of petroleum income, policies in the 1980s will have to face the challenge of increasing the proportion saved out of a growing GDP, or viewed from the opposite side, the level of consumption in relation to national production will have to be reduced. The required effort will have to be made in both the public and private sectors. The private sector's sacrifice will be relatively less, but still significant, given the difficulty of changing existing consumer patterns in the Mexican economy. In 1979 private savings as a percentage of GDP was 16.7 percent. In accordance with the high- and low-alternative models, it would be 17.9 and 20.5 percent respectively in 1985.

According to the high- and medium-alternative models, the public savings as a percentage of GDP should double from 4.4 percent in 1979 to between 8.5 and 10 percent respectively in 1984. These figures indicate that the biggest effort in the process of generating internal savings should come from the public sector. Assuming that public enterprises will continue to subsidize the private sector, the current deficit of the public sector, without PEMEX, would reach close to 4 percent of the GDP.

It is vitally important to point out that in this manner almost all of the savings generated by PEMEX would be used to subsidize other public enterprises. The consequences are obvious. On the one hand, the channeling of oil resources to subsidize other public companies would lessen the government's possibilities for action in other areas of the economy. On the other hand, the public sector's savings should be obtained by an increase in taxes and thereby double the government's and Federal District's savings.

Given the magnitude of the effort that must be made in public and private savings and investment in the next few years the question is: What should the direction of macroeconomic policy be?

*Macroeconomic Policy*

With the shift from external to internal constraints to growth, macroeconomic policy must be reoriented to handle Mexico's problems in the 1980s. The new macroeconomic policy will face three needs in order to productively absorb the influx of foreign currency from petroleum sales: (1) to steadily increase annual rates of growth of GDP from 6 percent to between 8 and 10 percent, (2) to increase the share of internal savings in national income from 21 percent to levels between 27 and 28 percent, and (3) to maintain the annual rate of inflation at less than 15 percent.

In the face of this macroeconomic situation, the traditional antiinflationary policy of aggregate-demand management should change to reflect the new conditions. Expansionist aggregate-demand policy should be adopted in order to guarantee sustained average annual rates of growth of GDP of 8 to 10 percent. However, the policy should also be selective in order to guarantee that, as aggregate demand increases, the share of consumer spending in GDP should decrease to guarantee an increase in total internal savings. Nevertheless, this measure will not be enough to guarantee only moderate rates of inflation.

The new antiinflationary policy should have a structuralist focus and be principally a policy of selective supply. First, it should be designed to eliminate the bottlenecks that stop the full utilization of existing resources. Second, it should increase the productive capacity through growth in both public and private investments. Third, it should allow an increase in the supply of imports but without stopping the efficient substitution of imports and without surpassing the financeable limits of the deficit in the balance of payments. In other words, the antiinflationary policy from the supply side of the question requires a policy of stimulation of production and investment and a gradual increase in foreign trade.

The results of the simulation show that an increase in petroleum production and exportation is paralleled by an opening up of the economy to foreign trade. As shown in table 5-4, the index of foreign trade (exports plus imports as a percentage of GDP) is 24.2 percent in 1979, and it rises to 24.5, 26.1, and 28.8 percent by 1985 for the low-, medium-, and high-alternative models respectively. Also, the share of imports in the total supply in the high-alternative model increases from 10.9 percent in 1979 to 12.5 percent in 1985. When this phenomenon occurs, the inflation in all of the scenarios is reduced from 18.7 to 14 percent over the same period. By the end of this five-year period, the policy of selective regulation of aggregate demand must be able to reduce consumer spendings' share of GDP from 76 percent in 1979 to almost 70 percent in 1985 or to increase total savings from 24 percent to almost 30 percent.

Policies to stimulate savings will be of the utmost importance in the 1980s. In the case of the private sector, the principal obstacle will be changing the traditional patterns of consumption of the middle- and upper-income groups. Public-sector savings must be doubled. Public enterprises will be of vital importance in making this increase happen. Public enterprises should favor a process to substitute the importation of capital goods and to regulate and orient private investment through a program of purchases from the public sector. The public sector should strengthen its finances by increasing efficiency in spending, continuing the permanent adjustment of prices of public enterprises, and no less important, strengthening the tax system. If internal savings are not increased, the risk is run of having a situation in which the foreign-exchange earnings generated by petroleum serve no other purpose than to finance consumer-spending patterns that would obstruct Mexico's future development.

## Petroleum as a Lever for Development

The basic objectives of the sectorial strategy of development refer to employment, income redistribution, balanced regional development, and independence from foreign capital. The nature of development would undoubtedly make necessary a global treatment of a sectorial strategy, which would exceed the limits of this chapter. However, it is important to point out the potential petroleum bears in aiding to solve these problems by creating a permanent wealth.

### A More-Just Society

Once the external constraint to growth has disappeared, sustained economic growth will certainly be achieved at annual average rates of 8 or 10 percent. Holding the sectorial composition of GDP and the factor intensity in production constant, estimates have indicated that demand for labor could grow 4 or 4.2 percent annually, which is a similar rate to that of the growth of the labor supply. For this reason, even if unemployment persists to some extent, it will not constitute a major problem in the future. Therefore, the main concern in the labor market will be that of coupling skilled-labor requirements for production to the prevailing abilities of the labor force.

Nonetheless, to foresee the income-distribution pattern in the 1980s is difficult. In the face of accelerated growth, income redistribution is not assured. However, an aggressive distribution policy from the state would be expected, provided it would dispose of a greater amount of resources than it did in the past. In raising the standards of living and welfare in Mexico, the government must distribute the new wealth derived from petroleum. Within a basic needs program, an important step has been given in the implementation of the Mexican Food System (SAM), whose main concern is to attain self-sufficiency in producing foodstuffs for minimum-nourishment levels, in which the government shares the risks of production.[4] Thus, a more-just distribution of income will depend upon a political decision and not a lack of wealth itself.

*Industrialization*

In the long run Mexico can not rely on petroleum as a permanent source of wealth. Oil is a nonrenewable resource and therefore is only a temporary means for satisfying Mexican needs. In order to build a permanent basis for wealth, measures should be taken to develop viable production sectors in the Mexican economy. This chapter discusses the reasons and strategies for industrial-sector development. Within this sector should be two basic plans: (1) import substitution and (2) export diversification and promotion.

**Import Substitution.** Substitution of imports should include two programs: first, the rationalization of protectionism of existing industrial plants in order to raise their efficiency and competitiveness, and second, the aggressive development of a capital-goods industry. The program for the rationalization of protectionism that the López Portillo government has formulated in the first three years of his term is one of the most-important aspects of the new model for development. In its first stage, 1977-1979, this policy has had considerable success. The principal factor in this success was that Mexico adopted a position of gradual, rather than instantaneous, liberalization of trade, thus allowing industries to make progressive adjustments to competition.

Yet considerable protection still remains. About 60 percent of the total value of imports are subject to prior permission. The second stage of the program is yet to be developed but will consist of further reductions in protectionism. Given Mexico's current industrial structure, in which large national and foreign corporations coexist with small- and medium-sized industries, this stage will require a collateral program that will allow the latter to compete and survive in the presence of the foreign competition that will appear when protectionist policies are abolished.

In the 1980s the substitution for capital-goods imports should come about within a framework of strict selectivity, specialization, and competitiveness in order to ensure the success of these industries. The creation of a capital-goods industry requires that various elements of protection and stimulation policy come into play, given the technological and production characteristics of such an industry and the international oligopolistic competition that exists in the field.

The development of Mexico's capital-goods industry in the next ten years will require a program of fiscal, financial, and price subsidies given the technological complexity and lengthy periods of investment recovery prevalent in this type of industry. One study recommends that public-sector purchases should be utilized as an instrument of protection and stimulation for the capital-goods industry.[5]

**Export Substitution**. Mexico has decided to utilize petroleum as a lever for its development. However, for reasons of sovereignty, national security, and independence in economic policies, Mexico should not become an economy based solely on the export of hydrocarbons. In the long run Mexico will undoubtedly have exhausted its oil. Therefore, in the meantime it should diversify its export base by means of developing industrial exports. This development should occur at a rate such that industrial goods constitute the principal components of Mexican exports by the year 2000.

*Role of Foreign Capital*

In contrast with the past, the new petroleum revenues mean that Mexico will not need to depend on the foreign financing of its external sector. This situation will not only present the use of a more-flexible policy on foreign debt but also the reorientation of criteria for foreign investment. By the year 2000 Mexican industry will be characterized by either of two modalities. One of these is transnational capitalism in which the dynamic export industry and the capital-goods industry are in the hands of foreign companies. The other modality is national capitalism in a mixed economy in which, on the basis of financial self-determination derived from petroleum income, the transfer of technology from foreign sources is given priority over direct foreign investment. The latter is the mode to which Mexico should aspire.

**Petroleum as an Instrument for International
Negotiation**

Hitherto Mexico's foreign trade has been realized in a bilateral framework, fundamentally with the United States. In the future, however, petroleum will provide the opportunity to diversify Mexico's flow of foreign trade and investment. This diversification is necessary and convenient not only in terms of independent development and growth but also because the United States is faced with one of the worst crises in its history.

The future perspectives of the U.S. economy are not optimistic. These include low increases in productivity, loss of competitiveness, growing dependency on oil imports, and lack of international confidence in the dollar. In this context Mexico emerges as an important element to be considered in the implementation of foreign economic policies in the United States. Mexico represents an important oil supplier outside OPEC. Thus, for Mexico to sell the maximum of its production of hydrocarbons to the United States is advantageous. Furthermore, if Mexico were integrated in a common market or GATT, the United States could substantially increase its exports to the Mexican market.

Two important effects for the United States would arise from these Mexican purchases: on the one hand, its energy deficits could be reduced, and on the other hand, confidence in the dollar in international markets would be increased. Thus exists the interest in integrating both economies. U.S. interests in Mexico are far beyond a simple trade in commodities. If U.S. foreign investment in Mexico were intensified, the United States could postpone industrial reconversion in certain strategic fields such as oil-intensive industries, retarding the evolution of the so-called product cycle. In this respect President López Portillo has stated the inconvenience of such integration in a common market, in a traditional sense, because Mexico would permanently be destined to be an exporter of primary products.

Bear in mind that Mexico should diversify its foreign trade, investment, and sources of technology in order to attain greater economic stability and, more importantly, sound independent development. In diversifying its commercial and financial international relations, Mexico should pass from a monodependent scheme to an interdependent one. The optimum will depend on the economic complementarities and comparative advantages of both countries. Whatever the case, the attitudes and strategies adopted in U.S.-Mexican relations in the forthcoming years will undoubtedly be decisive.

Mexico presently provides a valuable support for the numerous problems confronting the U.S. economy. However, whatever attitude the United States adopts should reflect the new international role Mexico has acquired under the oil. Recent statements from the U.S. ambassador to Mexico seem to recognize the new international status of Mexico as illustrated by the following: 1) sales of foodstuffs for an indefinite period of time have been guaranteed, 2) the decision of not entering GATT has been accepted, 3) President López Portillo's world energy program has been encouraged, and 4) the intention of diversifying Mexican commercial relations abroad has been supported.[6]

Thus, the potential for petroleum as an instrument for international negotiation does exist. In order to convert petroleum into a real and effective policy instrument, not only is it necessary to definitely define Mexico's international role in the 1980s but also to employ its capacity for firm negotiation in international forums.

**Conclusions**

Petroleum, as a nonrenewable resource, is only a temporary wealth. Yet it provides the potential for creating considerable permanent wealth in

Mexico over the next two decades. Mexico presently suffers from many of the problems characteristic of underdeveloped countries such as shortages of food, education, and health services; high levels of unemployment and underemployment; and considerable urban and rural poverty. If the temporary wealth of oil is used judiciously, Mexico can look forward to accelerated growth with relative stability such that by the year 2000 most of these problems can be alleviated considerably.

The year 1980 could be a turning point toward a new Mexican-development model that would permit the country to become an industrial power by the end of the century. For this industrialization to come about, Mexico will need to initiate a reform of the industrial sector based on the development of a more-efficient and competitive consumer and an intermediate-goods-manufacturing industry by means of progressively lowering the level of protection, a capital-goods industry, and a manufactured-goods-export industry. Such a reform would enable the industrial sector to become the engine of growth for the economy and would gradually permit the country to decrease its dependence on petroleum and other primary products as sources of income, employment, and foreign exchange.

Petroleum changes Mexico's requirements for foreign capital. Previously, extreme reliance was placed on foreign direct investment and financing, but in the future more importance will be assigned to the transfer of technology necessary for industrialization.

The challenge facing Mexico is to choose and carry out the appropriate strategy to transform the temporary wealth of oil into a permanent wealth of a developed economy. Gerardo Bueño warns:

> The experiences of other oil-exporting countries do not give cause for optimism. Besides the benefits there have been costs that must not be ignored when formulating an economic strategy based in good part on petroleum exports. The great challenge is to substitute a realistic economic policy for one that includes price and wage pressures, inefficient use of resources, channelization of subsidies to energy consumption, encouragement of imports and discouragement of exports, and the chronic overevaluation of the exchange rate that can be handled by petroleum resources. The most-important conclusion . . . is that the dynamic impulses of oil exports . . . have generally tended to run out quickly.[7]

Recall, however, that Mexico is different from most other new oil-exporting countries. It is becoming a petroleum power after more than four decades of industrial experience, which has formed a base of fiscal, human, and technical capital that can take good advantage of the opportunities presented by petroleum—for example, the launching of a strong industrial sector that will eventually replace oil as the engine of growth. Moreover, Mexico has demonstrated its capacity for political stability.

Despite these favorable factors, realistic economic policies, as set forth previously, alone will not be sufficient to bring the benefits of petroleum to Mexico. The past has shown that political stability in Mexico has been laced with considerable inequity and imbalance for the benefit of a small part of the population. To avoid a continuation of this situation, the government must make the political decision that will guarantee that petroleum will be used as a real lever for social and economic development for the well-being of the majority of Mexicans, and then it must apply the appropriate policy measures.

**Notes**

1. In a framework of general equilibrium, it would be necessary to raise the supposed level of ceteris paribus and see the indirect and complete effect of a net increase of one dollar made from petroleum exports.

2. This model is based on Fernando Clavijo and Octavio Gomez's model published as "Parámetros interdependencias en economía mexicana: un análisis econométrico," *El trimestre económico* 182 (1979).

3. As could be observed in the high hypothesis in two years (1981 and 1982), a position of equilibrium in the balance of federal funds is reached, and only in one year (1983) is there a small surplus. This happens because of the supposition that in this hypothesis the income elasticity of imports is increased. The reason is that Mexico is neither trying to have a surplus in the balance of payments, with an increment in oil production and exportation, nor is it trying to grow at the traditional rate of 6 percent but increasing to 8 percent. Nevertheless, clearly the external restriction on growth has not yet decreased.

4. Editor's note: This section was prepared after the conference. SAM was announced by the Mexican government 18 March 1980.

5. Nacional Financiera, S.A.—ONUDI, México: Una estrategia para desarrollar la industria de bienes de capital (Mexico: 1977).

6. *Novedades*, "Nos garantiza E.U. laventa de alimentos," 5 June 1980, p. 1. Editor's note: This section was prepared after the conference. Mexico's decision to not enter GATT was announced on 18 March 1980.

7. Gerardo M. Bueño, "Desarrollo y petróleo: la experiencia de los paises exportadores," *El trimestre económico* 186 (1979). Reprinted with permission from Instituto Mexicano del Petroleo.

# 6

# The Political Economy of Mexican Oil, 1976-1979

*Laura Randall*

Traditionally, economists analyze growth rates, while political economists examine the composition of growth, the distribution of its costs and benefits, and its complex effects on the nation. The political economy of Mexican oil is a very broad topic and one that can be understood only when placed in the context of the Mexican government's strategy for economic development.

At the end of 1976, Mexico was a country with serious economic problems and considerable internal dissension. Rapid population growth, massive foreign debt, net oil and food imports, continuing but inconclusive invasions of land by peasants, and two devaluations led to a decline in the Mexican private sector's confidence in the administration. Rumors of political assassinations and a possible coup against the government abounded. Mexican labor and capital poured into the United States. Today the U.S. popular press mainly views Mexico as a source of oil, both productive and polluting, and accepts the government's figures on declining birth rates, greatly eased foreign-debt position, increased foreign trade and investment, and somewhat increased Mexican-business confidence.

The turnaround in foreign perceptions of Mexico results from Mexican-oil production, oil wealth, and careful management of information. Mexican-oil production virtually doubled from 1976 to 1979, and it will reach an estimated 1.7 million barrels a day by the end of 1980. Exports rose from 86,400 barrels to 672,200 barrels per day from 1976 to 1979. The corresponding share of export income was 13.1 percent in 1976 and almost 50 percent in 1979. Similarly, as shown in table 6-1, PEMEX accounts for increasing and substantial shares of government investment, foreign credit granted, and tax payments to the government, as well as an increase of public debt and in the service of foreign debt.

The extent of oil wealth cannot be known until oil is produced. Earlier estimates suggested that Mexico had 200 billion barrels of potential reserves, a figure that may be somewhat reduced when the dry holes recently drilled near Ixtoc 1 are taken into account. Of these reserves, 50 billion barrels are likely to be recoverable with present technology and costs, and 28 billion barrels are oil and condensates. At present rates of production, Mexico will run out of oil early in the twenty-first century.[1] For this reason, the use of oil as the focus of Mexico's development strategy and the

**Table 6-1**
**Data for PEMEX, 1976-1979**

| Item | 1976 | 1977 | 1978 | 1979 |
|---|---|---|---|---|
| Share of federal government investment in public enterprise (percent) | 26.2 | 35.1 | 43.6 | — |
| Share of public foreign debt (percent) | 11.3 | 13.3 | 17.1 | — |
| Share of service of public foreign debt (percent) | 37.1 | 21 | 17.6 | — |
| Share of foreign credit granted (percent) | 12.7 | 37.1 | 52.7 | — |
| Share of increase of public foreign debt (percent) | 11.8 | 18.6 | 40.7 | — |
| Share of exports (percent) | 13.1 | 24.8 | 31.5 | almost 50 |
| Share of imports (percent) | 3.6 | 3.8 | 3.8 | — |
| Oil and manufactured derivatives as share of GDP (percent)[a] | 1.9 | 2.3 | 2.5 | — |
| Tax payments to federal government (billion pesos) | 7.8 | 18.3 | 28.3 | — |
| Public-sector expenditure as share of GDP (percent) | 39.4 | 43.6 | 44.1 | — |
| Tax payments as share of GDP (percent) | 0.6 | 1.1 | 1.3 | — |
| Goal of production of crude and liquids (thousand barrels per day) | 944.1 | 1,066.3 | 1,474.7 | 1,710.1 |
| Actual production of crude and liquids (thousand barrels per day) | 894.2 | 1,085.6 | 1,329.6 | 1,660.6 |
| Goal of exports of crude (thousand barrels per day) | 86.4 | 153.0 | 428.9 | 672.2 |
| Actual exports of crude (thousand barrels per day) | 94.4 | 202.0 | 365.1 | 612 |

Budget, 1979

| | | |
|---|---|---|
| Income (billion pesos) | 162 | |
| Percent distribution | | |
| Exports | 54.3 | |
| Domestic sales | 42.6 | |
| Other | 3.1 | |
| Total | 100 | |
| | | |
| Expenses (billion pesos) | 220 | |
| Percent distribution | | |
| Investment | 33.2 | |
| Operations | 30.5 | |
| Taxes | 21.8 | |
| Debt | 14.5 | |
| Total | 100 | |

Sources: José López Portillo, *Tercer informe presidencial, Anexos* (Mexico, 1979); Roberto R. Gutiérrez, "La balanza petrolera de México, 1970-1982," *Comercio exterior* 29, no. 8 (August 1979); Ted Wett and Shannon L. Matheny, Jr., "Mexico," *Oil and Gas Journal* 77, no. 34, (20 August 1979).

[a]These items are sold at less than world price so the contribution of oil and its manufactured products are understated. See pp. 98-100 for details.

rate at which the oil is used up are areas of particular interest, that can be understood in the context of the development strategy.

When López Portillo took office in 1976, he was faced with the choice of either creating business confidence and simultaneously attracting both Mexican funds that had been sent abroad as well as new foreign investment or closing the economy to foreign influence by limiting the flow of capital abroad, increasing favoritism for Mexican over foreign suppliers, and where necessary, either increasing credit to private business to keep it afloat or taking over business to maintain employment. The former course was chosen. As a result, the short-run objectives of the government were to create confidence, contain inflation, and plan for structural modification of the economy. In the medium term, the government hopes to increase the complexity of the economic structure, to shift the location of economic development by building up less-developed areas within Mexico and limiting the growth of the metropolitan area, and to reduce unemployment. Long-run-development goals have been announced, but they may not be binding as President López Portillo's term of office ends in 1982. The policies of his successor of course are not yet known.

The program to restore confidence in the Mexican government encompasses political, administrative, and economic reforms designed to broaden participation both in the electoral process and economic decision making. Plans to restore confidence in the heavily indebted economy necessarily required export promotion, above all, of oil.

## Theories of Inflation

The devaluation of 1976 was followed by an increase in oil production, inflation, and unemployment. An analysis of inflation serves to illustrate the political economy of how Mexico coped with this serious problem.

The government's plans to contain inflation were much more complex than were those to create confidence, and understanding these plans requires a brief review of the theories of the causes of inflation. The government probably considered five theories of inflation that have been developed over time to try to understand its causes. In this section the theories are presented, and in the following section the government's actions to reduce inflation are presented. A statistical estimate of the importance of each factor to explaining Mexican inflation is not undertaken here since the complex situation requires the use of several variables for which only limited information is available. The resulting statistical estimates thus would be of limited reliability.

*Excess Supply of Money*

The first theory of inflation is that increases in prices result from too much money chasing too few goods. Proponents of this theory believe that in the short run, the rate at which money is spent is roughly constant, and the ability of the economy to increase the supply of goods is quite limited. The only result that either increased government spending, or increased provision of credit through the banking system, can have is to increase prices. The remedy for inflation is therefore to limit increases in the money supply. The government is only partly able to do so, in part because of its continuing deficit that requires the creation of funds to finance the government. The government nonetheless reduced the rate of increase of the money supply from 31.4 percent in 1976 to 26.4 percent in 1977. Its rate of expansion rose to 31.6 percent in 1978. These rates of monetary expansion are higher than those for 1970-1976.

The government is also trying to limit inflation by increasing the Bank of Mexico's instruments of control over the supply of money. During the past year, treasury bills (called *Ce Tes*) were created, which enables the bank to carry out open-market operations and reduce the money supply.[2]

*Structural Bottlenecks*

The second theory of inflation is that prices rise because producers are not able to increase output rapidly in response to price signals. Bottlenecks in the supply of labor, raw materials, semiprocessed inputs, capital goods, transport and distribution, and imported components all are blamed for slow growth. Similarly, all arrangements deviating from theoretically pure competition along classical lines are blamed for limits to output. These limits include unions, featherbedding, and rules regarding job security and overtime; monopolies and cartels indulging in restrictive business practices; and transnational corporations restricting access to technology and allegedly indulging in practices of dubious legality. Most, but not all, of these problems can only be solved in the medium and long run. The government, however, has moved to eliminate one supply bottleneck by abolishing the requirement for prior import licenses for 1,500 items. This move reduced the share of imported articles for which such licenses were required to 34.2 percent of imported items by 1 September 1979. Also, employment registers are being established where information on skills of workers required for production is being matched with information on job seekers.[3] More important for medium-term solutions has been the establishment of committees to study industry and agriculture at the statewide level and to identify bottlenecks and suggest measures to remedy them. Simultaneously an attempt is being made to improve market structure by increasing credit granted to small- and medium-sized firms and by allowing larger numbers of firms to bid on government and government-agency contracts. A wide variety of additional measures are being taken to increase the ability of the Mexican economy to expand supply more rapidly in response to price increases than it does at present.

*Increased Labor Costs*

The third theory of inflation is that prices rise as a result of increased labor costs. Therefore, the labor movement was asked to limit its wage demands. Minimum wages were adjusted by 10 percent in January 1977 and by a further 13 percent in 1978. In real terms, minimum wages fell 9 percent in 1977 and 3.4 percent in 1978. However, some laborers were able to obtain more than the minimum increase suggested by the guidelines in 1978, and strikes for higher real income increased despite increased government subsidies on-consumption goods. The overall effect of these wage movements was that the share of wages in GDP fell from 41.7 percent in 1976 to 37.7 percent in 1977. The inflaton rate, measured as changes in consumer prices, fell from 27.2 percent in 1976 to 20.7 percent in 1977 and 16.2 percent in 1978. Wage increases granted to public employees were lower than the rate of inflation in 1979.[4]

*Imported Inflation*

The fourth theory of inflation is that prices rise as a result of increased costs of imported goods and services. Although the prices of imports have increased consistently during the last three years, the rate of increase—2.5 percent in 1967, 6 percent in 1977, and 5.5 percent in 1978—was well below the inflation rate. The government is attempting to limit the rise in import costs by eliminating nontariff barriers to trade and replacing them with tariffs. Yet to the extent that the price of Mexican currency is related to that of the dollar, the price of Mexican imports will reflect U.S. rather than Mexican policy, with the result that the Mexican government will have only a limited ability to prevent a so-called imported inflation.

*Impact on Output*

The fifth theory of inflation is that each of the previous four theories is insufficient. To the extent that analysis is directed to the national level, it is misleading since it fails to distinguish between conditions in the different sectors and regions of the economy. Also, to the extent that it does not integrate supply and demand considerations, the analysis does not account for the way that businessmen function. Putting the matter slightly differently, prices of many different products rise during inflation. A price increase for one firm is a cost increase to another. The distribution of price increases among sectors of production determines, for each sector, the level of prices received, costs paid, and therefore profits. Profits, moreover, are strongly influenced by government taxes and subsidies. The distribution of profits across the economy largely determines private-sector investment and output. Once profits by sector are known, estimating the increase in output of a sector and the length of time it will take for output to increase is easy. This theory analyzes the impact of inflation on output.

Such an analysis of inflation probably was carried out by the Mexican government to provide the framework that integrates the many elements of Mexico's strategy to limit inflation and to promote economic growth (see technical note at end of chapter). Similarly, the government likely has examined econometric models of price formation and has used them to examine the impact of various possible revisions of Mexican subsidies on each sector of the economy.

The careful short-run measures taken by the Mexican government reduced inflation from about 33 percent in 1977 to about 18 percent in 1978, and probably just over 20 percent in 1979, rates that are enough greater than U.S. inflation rates to bring continuing implicit pressure for devaluation or for greater oil production and exports yielding sufficient foreign exchange to maintain the value of the peso.

The government's final short-term economic objective was to create detailed plans for the structural modification of the economy. The plans have been made by various groups and cover many aspects of economic development such as industry, urban development, and agriculture. In addition, employment planning is in the process and includes an analysis of the needs for skilled labor. Employment planning has led to the provision of scholarships to study abroad and the expansion of specific kinds of education like research and development at home. The large number of economists in cabinet-level positions has produced a detailed analysis of the workings of the Mexican economy and the ways in which it can be modified.

### Oil, Inflation, and Growth

Oil was central to achieving each of the short-run objectives. The announcement of increased oil reserves heightened investor confidence in general, and direct links between oil and gas expansion and investor outlook were provided by the creation of petrobonds, whose yield was indexed to the price of crude oil, and by the sharp increase in the value of stocks issued by firms that supplied PEMEX. The best-known increase was that of Tubos de Acero, which made pipes for the *gasoducto*. Yet the announcement of oil wealth did not lead to as much growth in nonoil private-sector activity as the government had hoped. It is not clear to what extent the slow private response reflects the ordinary two-year time lag in Mexico between making a decision to expand output and implementing it, and to what extent it represents private businessmen's fears of being crowded out of an economy in which the public-sector share (defined to include the federal government plus the parastatal enterprises) has grown from 26.1 percent of GDP in 1970 to 45.6 percent in 1979.[5]

The limited growth of the private sector doubled government reliance on oil revenues, despite increased tax collection, and may have increased the use of govrnment spending to achieve its objectives in contrast to the use of a variety of incentives to the private sector. As shown in table 6-1, increased spending bears directly on the relationship between oil production and revenues and inflation.

*Regional and Sectorial Considerations*

According to the first theory of inflation, increased spending on oil development would result in rapid price increases regionally, in areas in and around the oil fields, and sectorially, for those goods needed to supply the oil industry. Also, increased government spending made possible by increased receipts from exports of oil would contribute to inflation. These inflationary pressures would continue until the economy could supply sufficient goods and services such that the excess supply of money was eliminated.

Thus a conflict is formed between the desire to limit inflation by restricting government spending and the desire to increase Mexican firms' ability to supply goods by ensuring that they, rather than foreign competitors, obtain government contracts. One way to avoid the conflict is to invest foreign-exchange income abroad in interest-bearing securities. Another way is to repay the foreign debt ahead of time. Both of these measures use oil funds without increasing the competition faced by domestic manufacturers and are useful as long as the absence of skilled labor, rather than that of imported components, is the most-important bottleneck to growth. These measures also aid in fighting inflation according to the second theory—that is, structural bottlenecks.

In fact, the regional impact of oil income has been as expected: Although at first prices rose more rapidly in Mexico City than in other areas, by 1979 the sharpest rises in prices occurred in oil-producing areas. From January through May 1979, prices increased 17.9 percent in Veracruz, Poza Rica, and Tuxpan and 16.9 percent in Yucatan, Merida, and Progreso. Both districts are oil-boom regions par excellence. In contrast, prices in Mexico City rose 15.2 percent, 14.1 percent in Guadalajara, and 12.8 percent in Baja California Norte. The national average increase was 15.7 percent.[6]

The impact on workers in oil regions was worse than these figures imply because of regional variations in the minimum-wage rate. Thus, in 1978 the sharpest fall in real wages was in Yucatan, Guadalajara, Comarca Lagunera, Guerrero, Distrito Federal, and Guanajuato.[7]

The president's representative in oil-rich Villahermosa, in the state of Tabasco, summed up the difficulties of growth: "Everything is happening at once, so we have terrible problems. . . . There are shortages of housing, office space, electricity, water, and all kinds of services. . . . We have developed a plan . . . to meet these problems. . . . But, of course, to do that we have to slow down the boom. We have to control the oil growth."[8]

According to the first theory, demand associated with oil growth would be reflected in different rates of sectorial price increases. As expected, the prices of construction goods are rising more rapidly than others.

PEMEX's imports and debt-service payments required a foreign-exchange outlay greater than its export receipts in 1977 and 1978. During these years, the government used its improved position, which was due to oil, to rearrange its debt structure. As shown in table 6-2, in 1979,

**Table 6-2**
**PEMEX's Net Contribution of Foreign Exchange to the Mexican Economy, 1977-1979**
*(millions of pesos)*

| Item | 1977 | 1978 | 1979 |
|---|---|---|---|
| Income from exports | 1,019.7 | 1,837.9 | 4,469.9 |
| Expenditures | 1,583.3 | 2,417 | 2,370.7 |
| Interest | 193 | 300.2 | 471.6 |
| Imports of capital goods | 560.9 | 852.2 | 708.7 |
| Rental of equipment | 305.6 | 413.1 | 390.6 |
| Other imports | 230.3 | 496.5 | 429.8 |
| Payments for technology and foreign technicians | 294 | 355 | 370 |
| Balance | − 564.1 | − 579.1 | 2,099.2 |

Source: Roberto R. Gutierrez, "La balanza petrolera de Mexico, 1970-1982," *Comercio exterior* 29, no. 8 (August 1979).

projected earnings were greater than expenditures in foreign exchange for the first time. In that year the government repaid a portion of its foreign debt ahead of schedule. Over $550 million of standby credit was repaid to the International Monetary Fund, a transfer of resources abroad that implicitly limited inflation.[9] Yet, on balance the government has signalled that although inflation will be partially contained, protection, growth, and recently, the creation of jobs are its continuing objectives. Regional problems are much more likely to be met by providing services than by slowing oil growth.

*Bottlenecks and Dependence*

According to the second theory of inflation, prices rise due to bottlenecks, and this reflects the fact that producers are not able to increase output rapidly in response to price signals. The government has therefore supplemented price signals by programming its needs for equipment from other sectors so that businessmen can plan to meet PEMEX's requirements. In addition, the Mexican Petroleum Institute designs equipment and makes the plans available to Mexican industrialists so they can manufacture the equipment. Mexican industry currently produces about 60 percent of the tools and equipment used by the oil industry. The measures just described should increase this share.[10]

To some extent, the existence of bottlenecks reflects the limited availability of some categories of technology and skilled labor (an estimate of the cost of importing goods and services not available in Mexico is presented in Table 6-2). PEMEX has therefore attempted to increase the speed of oil development by research and development within Mexico, by arranging for increased training in oil-related professions in various universities, by providing courses for its workers and management, and by using foreign technology and advisers.[11] The latter method has been strongly criticized. For example, a year ago, an economic and financial advisor of PEMEX complained that "the acquisition of foreign services by Mexico to speed its oil development, in the matter of process licenses, patents, transfer of technology and engineering, 'practically is unnecessary' and that PEMEX has 6,000 highly qualified technicians and 3,000 employees of the Mexican Petroleum Institute and an engineering capacity of two million man-hours per year."[12]

Nonetheless, on what is now an increasingly sensitive matter, Dr. Laurence Whitehead stressed that foreign technicians may be necessary for specialized tasks. Writing just over a year before the offshore well Ixtoc 1 blew out in the Bay of Campeche, he stated that "PEMEX's drilling groups are competent enough on land, but have neither the equipment nor the experience necessary for ocean exploration. Thus, U.S. companies have supplied the drilling rigs which PEMEX needs, and even though PEMEX teams manage them, it is known that the number of U.S. 'advisers' (who direct the work) is large.''[13] Similarly, *Excélsior* pointed out in April 1978 that PEMEX was not yet able to act in the case of offshore-drilling disasters and would have to acquire the services of foreign experts. The details of responsibility and performance when foreign and Mexican firms work together are being brought out in the course of lawsuits that involve establishing responsibility for the Ixtoc 1 accident.[14] Yet even before the accident, PEMEX had acted to reduce its dependence on foreign technology by signing joint technology development agreements with some foreign firms and by purchasing technology from others.[15]

The fear of dependence on foreigners has had unfortunate effects. For example, *Excélsior* claims that safety equipment for Ixtoc 1, which could have prevented the ecological effects of the oil spill, was not bought ''for political reasons'': the equipment should have been bought from foreigners.[16] Similarly, the fear of a too-close relationship between government officials and the private sector may create bottlenecks in the future. A case in point is the criticism directed against Jorge Díaz Serano, general director of PEMEX, for granting a contract to Pemargo, which he formerly owned. One can only sympathize with Díaz Serrano's remarks concerning Pemargo: ''I believe that, ethically, a source of work, which has proved to be efficient, and of which there are not many in the country, should not be destroyed because one of its shareholders enters public service and gives up working (for it),'' while wishing for fuller disclosure of the technical details of bidding procedures and prices.[17]

On balance, PEMEX has taken many of the steps required to eliminate bottlenecks in the oil industry, but it is limited in its actions by increasing discussion of the appropriatenesss of relations between business and government officials and by the fear of depending upon foreign technicians and technology.

*Labor and the Cost of Oil Production*

The third theory of inflation is that prices rise as a result of increased costs, most importantly, labor costs. PEMEX suffers from extraordinarily high labor costs and from overstaffing. In 1976, PEMEX's salary and loan bill came to some 119,482 pesos per worker annually—a high figure by Mexican standards. As a result, permanent jobs with PEMEX are said to cost workers about 70,000 to 80,000 pesos in payment to labor leaders. A labor-related problem leading to high costs resulted from the fact that PEMEX signed a contract with the oil-workers' union that requires PEMEX to bring 40 percent of the work to the union and for it to carry out or contract to third parties. The government's attempt to use labor more efficiently in the oil industry included agreements stating that competent workers would be assigned to key jobs. Also, in 1977 the government briefly insisted that PEMEX's employment growth be restricted to 4.8 percent, an order that probably stemmed from the 48.5 percent increase in PEMEX's wages and salaries in that year. However, overtime payments were reduced by an estimated 255 million pesos in 1977 and 250 million pesos in 1978.[18] Moreover, salary increases were limited to 12 percent from 1 August 1978 to 31 July 1979, which implies declining real wages for workers who stayed in the same category of employment during this inflationary period and an increase in employment of almost 17 percent (the increase in PEMEX employment from 1976 to 1 August 1979 was 76.7 percent).[19] The overall increase in salary paid by PEMEX in 1978 was held to 7.5 percent, which is an estimated 30.8 percent for 1979.[20] Attempts to increase labor productivity, and thereby to reduce labor's contribution to inflation, included the establishment of labor-management-productivity committees, regional and national productivity-evaluation programs, increased training of labor, and the provision of benefits that would create a healthy and well-trained work force.[21]

The results of the government's attempts to increase productivity in the oil sector began to be felt in 1978. Physical output per worker increased approximately 4 percent per year between 1976 and 1978, an increase that may also reflect increasing capital per worker and the technical characteristics of the new oil deposits. Labor productivity increases and limited real-wage increases in the oil sector, combined with the rapid increase in export receipts, led to a reduction in labor costs as a share of sales from 22 percent in 1976 to 14 percent in 1979. However, increasing labor costs are not currently the most-important source of inflation either in the oil sector or in Mexico.[22]

*Imports and the Cost of Oil Production*

The fourth theory of inflation is that prices rise as a result of increased costs, most importantly, the increased costs of imported goods and services. PEMEX imports capital goods, whose prices rose about twice as fast as those of crude-oil exports from 1976 to 1978, a fact that helped trigger the latest crude-oil price escalation in 1979.[23] Prices of machines and equipment increased more than 6 percent in the first quarter of 1979; from January to August, PEMEX imported 52 percent of the 26.2 billion pesos of machinery, equipment, and material it acquired.[24] The prices of goods PEMEX imports rise faster than do those of other imported goods, and as a result, the short-run impact of oil development in the economy is more inflationary than that of development on other sectors. Tightness in world supplies of capital goods for the oil industry means that in the short run, until Mexico can economically and technically produce more capital goods for oil development by implementing the decisions indicated here, Mexico will continue to import inflation in the machines and equipment needed for the development of the petroleum sector.

*Profits, Subsidies, and Oil*

The fifth theory of inflation concerns its impact and indicates that the distribution of price increases influences the distribution of profits, which in turn determines the composition and size of output. The distribution of taxes and subsidies, in turn, influences the distribution of prices and profits. The distribution of taxes and subsidies as they affect the oil industry and its customers is therefore of interest both for the development of the oil sector and for that of the economy as a whole.

The oil industry subsidizes the rest of the economy when the prices of its products for domestic sales are set at levels below the prevailing world-market prices. The difference between the price levels times the volume of sales, gives the amount of the subsidy. President López Portillo has often stated that he wishes to use Mexico's oil wealth to serve the nation, and he has used this phrase to justify setting domestic-sales prices below world levels. In theory, the subsidies make possible the limitation of price increases in oil and energy using sectors of the economy. In fact, the subsidies have prevented PEMEX from financing its growth from its revenues and have led to government methods of financing investments in oil that contributed to inflation. This has had the perverse effect of harming the people in the weakest economic position in Mexico through inflation.

Estimates now indicate that the underpricing of oil and petrochemicals will have yielded an implicit subsidy of 1 billion pesos between 1972 and 1982.[25] In 1977, the subsidy was over 70 billion pesos—a sum equal to 4.2 percent of GDP—and in 1978 reached up to 87 billion pesos, equal to about 5 percent of GDP. According to President López Portillo, a barrel of crude oil processed into gasoline and derivatives sells in Mexico for $10.60; at international prices it would bring about $60.00. As shown in table 6-3, the impact of oil subsidies varies among products and users. The largest subsidies in 1968 were for natural gas and fuel oil, followed by diesel, gasoline, and kerosene. Kerosene is largely bought by poor people because cheap gasoline permits cheap transport. Yet the bulk of subsidies go to the Federal District and the northwest and are for industrial use, especially in chemicals, food products, and automotive industries. The subsidies are a factor in cheap energy prices, and make using machines instead of people more profitable, and therefore they contribute to unemployment if wages do not fall. However, this problem will be partly ameliorated by the

**Table 6-3**
**Structures of Components of Mexican-Oil-Product Subsidies, 1976-1978**

|  | Percentage Distribution | | |
| Components | 1976 | 1977 | 1978 |
| --- | --- | --- | --- |
| Product |  |  |  |
| Gasoline | 2.9 | 12.4 | 18.4 |
| Kerosene | 8.1 | 7.6 | 5.1 |
| Diesel fuel | 30.8 | 30.5 | 20.6 |
| Fuel oil | 31.9 | 27.1 | 31.3 |
| Natural gas | 26.3 | 22.3 | 24.5 |
| Total | 100 | 100 | 100 |
| Region |  |  |  |
| Baja California Norte, Baja California Sur, Sonora, Sinaloa, Nayarit |  |  | 7.3 |
| Chihuahua, Durango |  |  | 2.7 |
| Coahuila, Nuevo León, Tamaulipas |  |  | 22.1 |
| Aguascalientes, San Luis Potosí, Zacatecas |  |  | 2.3 |
| Colima, Jalisco, Michoacán |  |  | 6.1 |
| Veracruz |  |  | 15.4 |
| Guanajuato, Queretaro, Hidalgo, México, Morelos, Tlaxcala, Puebla |  |  | 12.1 |
| Distrito Federal, Area Metropolitana |  |  | 26.9 |
| Guerrero, Oaxaca, Chiapas |  |  | 2.1 |
| Campeche, Yucatán, Tabasco, Quintana Roo |  |  | 3 |
| Total |  |  | 100 |
| Sector |  |  |  |
| Industry |  |  | 25.1 |
| Energy |  |  | 33.6 |
| Transport |  |  | 31 |
| Domestic |  |  | 4.2 |
| Service |  |  | 2.7 |
| Agriculture |  |  | 3.4 |
| Total |  |  | 100 |

Sources: PEMEX, *Memoria de Labores*, 1977, 1978, 1979; *Oilweek*, 1976, 1977, 1978; *Petroleum Economist*, 1976, 1977, 1978, 1979; Instituto Mexicano del Petróleo, *Energéticos, demanda regional, análisis y perspectivas* (Mexico, 1977); and Instituto Mexicano del Petróleo, *Energéticos, demanda sectorial, análisis y perspectivas* (Mexico, 1975).

government policy of granting tax credits of up to 20 percent of the cost of investment needed to create additional employment, or 20 percent of the cost of an additional shift of labor valued at the minimum wage for two years, to firms in areas in which economic growth is being encouraged.

Similarly, the nature of subsidies has been broadened. For example, 30 percent reduction in prices of electric energy, fuel oil, natural gas, and petrochemicals below those prevailing in the Mexican market is now given to firms that invest in desired regions under the National Industrial

Development Plan. A 10 percent reduction is given to firms locating in some other zones.[26] These subsidies are also likely to lead to capital-intensive rather than labor-intensive development.

The cheap-oil and cheap-energy policy will not likely be reversed until various labor-training programs have produced workers with the requisite skills. The delay in speeding employment growth may prevent unskilled workers from getting more seniority than workers who will be better able to carry out a job. Skills will be provided in the medium term through government expenditure of about 1 percent of GDP on training in the next several years.[27]

**Subsidies for Petrochemicals.** Hydrocarbon subsidies also effect petrochemical production, which is aided by cheap inputs. The raw materials used by the petrochemical industry are shown in table 6-5. An

**Table 6-4**
**Regional Structure of Oil-Product Subsidies, Gross Domestic Product, Population, and Per Capita Income**
*(percent)*

| Region | Subsidies[a] Percent | Gross Domestic Product Percent | Population Percent | Per Capita Income[b] |
|---|---|---|---|---|
| Baja California Norte, Baja California Sur, Sonora Sinaloa, Nayarit | 7.3 | 9 | 8.4 | $107.7 |
| Chihuahua, Durango | 2.7 | 3.9 | 5.1 | 77.2 |
| Coahuila, Nuevo León, Tamaulipas | 22.1 | 14.4 | 6.9 | 129.7 |
| Aguascalientes, San Luis Potosí, Zacatecas | 2.3 | 2.8 | 5 | 57.1 |
| Colima, Jalisco, Michoacán | 6.1 | 7.7 | 11.8 | 65.2 |
| Veracruz | 15.4 | 5.3 | 7.9 | 66.5 |
| Guanajuato, Queretaro, Hidalgo, México, Morelos, Tlaxcala, Puebla | 12.1 | 7.2 | 18.9 | 38 |
| Distrito Federal, Area Metropolitana | 26.9 | 43.4 | 20 | 216.5 |
| Guerrero, Oaxaca, Chiapas | 2.1 | 4.4 | 10.2 | 43.2 |
| Campeche, Yucatán, Tabasco, Quintana Roo | 3 | 2 | 3.9 | 51.2 |
| Total | 100 | 100 | 100 | 100[c] |

Source: Table 6-2 and Instituto Mexicano del Petróleo, *Energéticos, demanda regional, análisis y perspectivas* (Mexico, 1975).

[a]Subsidies data from 1978.

[b]Per capita income data from 1975.

[c]National average.

**Table 6-5**
**Petrochemical Industry Basic-Sector Consumption of Hydrocarbons as Raw Material, 1976-1979**
*(cubic feet)*

| Hydrocarbon[a] | Consumption | | | |
|---|---|---|---|---|
| | *1976* | *1977* | *1978* | *1979* |
| Dry natural gas[a][b] | 529,136 | 723,542 | 1,153,036 | 1,270,265 |
| Ethane[b][c] | 907,024 | 1,126,390 | 1,580,390 | 1,653,081 |
| Ethylene[c][d] | n.d. | 11,513 | 11,513 | 11,513 |
| Liquid gas | 221,639 | 210,313 | 220,233 | 316,860 |
| Gasoline | 373,513 | 343,460 | 345,598 | 345,598 |

Source: Instituto Mexicano del Petroleo, *Desarrollo y perspectivas de la industrial petro-quimica mexicana*, (Mexico, D.F., 1977).

[a]Equivalent in liquid meters.

[b]6,670.8 cubic feet of gas equal one barrel of liquid.

[c]285.6 cubic meters of ethane gas equal one cubic meter of liquid ethane.

[d]317.7 cubic meters of ethylene gas equal one cubic meter of liquid ethylene.

attempt to indicate the impact of raw-material subsidies is made by estimating the share of raw-material cost to total cost for selected products. In the case of ammonia, the 84 percent subsidy on natural-gas price reduces total cost by about 18.4 percent. As ammonia is used in fertilizer production, much of this subsidy aids agriculture.

The subsidies on other petrochemicals are more difficult to determine because PEMEX purchases all of the ethane it produces, so the subsidy is not known because PEMEX does not publish the accounting price it uses for ethane. The following estimates are based on the assumption that the subsidy for ethane is the same as that on natural gas. Ethane accounts for about 71.4 percent of the ethylene-production costs. Thus, at a subsidy of 84 percent, total costs would be 60 percent below those that would otherwise be paid. Ethylene in turn is used in styrene production. Raw materials account for 68.5 percent of the total production cost for styrene, which is therefore 45 percent below what would prevail in the absence of subsidies. When vinyl chloride is produced by using ethane, the subsidy is about 20.8 percent; using ethylene, it is approximately 21.5 percent. Ethylene is also used in polyethylene production, and the subsidy to polyethylene production is roughly 29 percent. Such subsidies increase petrochemical profits and are likely to lead to overexpansion of this activity—in economists' terms, to a misallocation of Mexican resources.[28]

The net impact on subsidies to the petrochemical industry is complicated by two further considerations. On the one hand, under some circumstances these subsidies may lead to countervailing duties on exports or other retaliatory measures that would limit potential foreign-exchange earnings from this activity and will probably complicate the discussions of Mexico's possible entry into GATT. On the other hand, some petrochemicals imported by PEMEX sell for above world prices in Mexico. Thus the net financial impact of petrochemical subsidies in Mexico, compared to total subsidies in the Mexican economy, is small.[29]

**Effects of Subsidies.** The oil subsidies have had both desired and undesired effects. In the former case, it would be better to pay a cash grant whose value is that of the subsidy, for example, to firms that settle in designated regions. The reason is that the present form of the subsidy (cheap hydrocarbon and electric-power prices) leads to misallocation of resources by making capital-intensive development cheaper than labor-intensive development. The Mexican government has already pointed out that high unemployment leads to weak demand for basic goods, and a consequent low employment rate in these comparatively labor-intensive industries, signalling a possible shift in policy in order to reduce this undesirable consequence of subsidies.[30]

The undesired effects of oil subsidies go beyond those of choosing capital-intensive rather than labor-intensive development. That choice also reflects the fact that, in the absence of a strong private sector, the government has to plan, and it can prepare only a few projects at a time. Planning a small number of large projects is easier than planning many small ones, and large projects tend to be capital intensive. Moreover, the government believes that the number of people skilled to undertake the many investment decisions and perform the varied skilled and semiskilled tasks that labor-intensive development would require is insufficient. Oil subsidies contribute to, but are not the sole cause of, Mexico's emphasis on capital-intensive development.

**PEMEX Subsidy.** The undesired effects of oil subsidies include the fact that low apparent costs lead to an overestimate of oil profits, an increase in their profitability compared to that of alternate investment opportunities, and therefore to greater investments in oil activity than would be warranted if world-market prices were used. For example, in 1979 PEMEX grew three times faster than did the economy, rapidly using up Mexico's nonrenewable oil in the process.[31] The subsidy to PEMEX, in this case, stems from the fact that PEMEX is not charged for the raw materials it uses. Since Mexico owns its crude oil and does not purchase it from a supplier, PEMEX does not subtract the natural-resource cost of its oil from its pretax profit statement to get a net profit statement. If this adjustment were made for 1976, and PEMEX assumed that it had purchased all the crude oil it processed, then its pretax profit of 10 billion pesos would in fact have been a loss of 53.5 billion pesos. For purposes of comparison, a typical U.S. east coast refinery purchased only 30 percent of its crude; for PEMEX the comparable cash outlay (although not resource value) would have resulted in a loss of 9 billion pesos.

An alternate way of looking at the problem is to use the markup between the crude-oil and the refined-product price—crude costs about 75 percent of the price wholesale jobbers pay for refined products. Applying this percentage to PEMEX's sales income implies that PEMEX had a loss of 24.8 billion pesos in 1976. These losses contrast with a GDP of 1.2 trillion pesos in 1976, so that losses accounted for 0.73 to 4.35 percent of GDP.[32]

Since oil prices have been escalating more rapidly than others, and oil is the leading growth sector of the Mexican economy, the implicit loss due to nonreplacable natural resources has increased spectacularly. According to President López Portillo's 1979 state of the union message, subsidies on the domestic sale of oil and oil products reached 380 billion pesos, compared to a GDP of 2.7 trillion pesos. This implies a subsidy of 14.0 percent of GDP.[33]

PEMEX's estimated income in 1979 is 162 million pesos, and its current expenses will be about 126 billion pesos. Thus, the estimated savings are 36 billion pesos. If PEMEX had had to purchase all of its crude, its cost would have been about 245 billion pesos, leading to an implicit loss of 209 billion pesos—equal to 7.7 percent of GDP. If PEMEX had had to purchase only 30 percent of its crude, its savings, instead of being estimated at 36 billion pesos, would have shrunk to a loss of 38 billion pesos, equal to a loss of 1.4 percent of GDP. Note that PEMEX's field operating costs are about double those of the Alaska North Slope and that PEMEX spends more-than-authorized amounts at a rate greater than other public enterprises. Observers are not sure whether the federal government can control PEMEX.[34]

Comparing the size of the subsidies to PEMEX's implicit loss, clearly if the current structure of costs were to be maintained, then the elimination of the subsidies would allow PEMEX to eliminate its losses on current operations. President López Portillo has referred to the oil-sector subsidies as "monstrous subsidies, in order that the Mexican people have cheap energy."[35] A number of commentators since have claimed that this statement is not a defense of subsidies, but instead it is the first step in an educational campaign designed to prepare the public for energy price rises.

**Additional Consequences of Subsidies.** The greatest difficulty with the pervasive subsidies in the Mexican economy is that they make determining costs and profits at world-market prices difficult, with the result that allocating resources efficiently is difficult. Subsidies provided by the oil sector to the rest of the nation have had a number of adverse financial effects, some of which have since been corrected. For example, in 1977 oil financing had an inflationary impact because PEMEX could not finance its own development. Of 35 billion pesos invested, 21 percent came from PEMEX's resources; 86 percent of the remainder came from foreign sources, and it placed 14 percent of its paper with the Bank of Mexico, an operation that undoubtedly contributed to the inflation of 32.7 percent in that year. In 1978 PEMEX's financing was carried out in a less-inflationary manner. PEMEX invested 70 billion pesos, increasing its contribution to 26 percent of the total. It obtained 83 percent of the remainder from foreign sources of finance and placed the rest with Mexican banks. The Bank of Mexico's share was reduced to 1.7 percent of the amount supplied by domestic credit, and the inflation rate in 1978 fell to 18 percent.[36]

In both 1977 and 1978, PEMEX could have financed its own expansion if it had been allowed to charge world prices for its products within Mexico. This would have reduced the inflation that was accompanied by a fall in real wages of 5.5 percent in 1977. In 1978 minimum real wages fell three times more rapidly than in 1977. The government has attempted to mitigate the effects of low real wages by subsidies on popular consumption that cost 40 billion pesos in 1976, 56 billion pesos in 1977, 69 billion pesos in 1978, and 90 billion pesos in 1979, an amount equal to 3.3 percent of government expenditure.[37] Thus, these subsidies did not fully offset the fall in real wages. Further, not all workers have jobs, receive even a minimum wage, or have access to subsidized goods, all of which contribute to continuing labor unrest.

Despite limited wage increases, the hoped-for increase in Mexican private investment, needed to create jobs, did not materialize in the amount needed. Private capital formation increased only 2 percent in 1978 in industry, compared to the 7 percent increase obtained in 1970-1975 and probably reflects the low profitability of manufacturing compared to other sectors before 1977.[38]

In 1979, confidence in nonoil sectors of the economy may be reviving. Affiliates of foreign firms have made several announcements of planned investment. However, the results for the last two years indicate that their direct net investment declined, although short-term loans to the private sector increased.[39] Thus, Mexico's oil-recovery plus stabilization program is financed by inflation and government revenues that increasingly come from exports of oil. The impact of inflationary financing is regressive and is being borne disproportionately by workers.[40]

The financial weakening of PEMEX by subsidies increased its need for foreign financing. Foreign loans to PEMEX facilitate it purchase of imported goods. If PEMEX had had greater peso revenues, it could have possibly furnished supplier credits (directly or through greater contributions to the federal government, which would then spend the funds appropriately) that would have enabled it to purchase a larger share of goods from Mexican suppliers.

PEMEX's need for foreign financing has a number of implications for Mexico's external position. The fact that Mexico has oil has eased the terms on which it obtains loans. The fact that Mexico needs to borrow abroad in order to bring in the oil implicitly creates pressure on the forward-exchange rate, while domestic inflation more rapid than that of the United States also creates pressure for a devaluation. Thus, heavy foreign borrowing obligates Mexico to find ways of earning foreign exchange for repayment, promoting traditional and new exports, increasing sale of services abroad, or borrowing still more. One result of heavy foreign indebtedness has been the increase in the amount of oil Mexico is willing to produce and export as other sources of foreign exchange are insufficient. Also, to make matters worse, Governor William Clements of Texas claims that the too-rapid development of Ixtoc 1 contributed to the blowout.

Another effect of the need for rapid development of the export of oil is the need to carve out a share of the market. For the first year or two of its exports, Mexico granted more than normally favorable credit terms to purchasers of its oil, so that the price it charged was slightly below that prevailing on world markets. Having secured customers, it now charges the world price, or slightly above it, for crude oil. This pricing policy is made possible by the technical characteristics of Mexican oil, Mexico's location, the nation's willingness to provide secure long-term contracts with escalator clauses, and the tightness of the spot market.

Finally, in addition to the effect of subsidies on PEMEX's financial strategies, oil subsidies in some cases directly benefit foreigners. Long lines of American cars in Mexican border areas testify that buying the relatively inexpensive Mexican gasoline is worth a considerable wait. Also a large incentive exists to buy Mexican-hydrocarbon products in border areas and bring them to the United States, rather than pay the world prices that Mexico charges for delivery by the shipload. Similarly, foreigners benefit from Mexican subsidies to the extent that they own part of the Mexican industry. For these reasons, as well as Mexico's desire to use gas internally in place of oil, it has been suggested that Mexican-oil price for domestic sales will rise and approach world levels sooner than will the Mexican price of natural gas for domestic sales.

## Oil Development and Ecology

So far, it has been suggested that oil is the motor of Mexico's recent increase in growth and the key to its development plan but that the domestic-pricing policy and subsidies associated with oil development have had a number of unfortunate effects. Yet within Mexico, until recently, far less attention has been focused on pricing policy and subsidies than on the ecological effects of oil development, regarding both pollution from the use of gasoline and other oil products and from oil development.

The official position on the relation between ecological considerations and the need for economic development is that "Mexico endeavors to bring about a complete social and economic development and simultaneously sustains a pitched battle against contamination and deterioration of the environment."[41] The problem is intensified because more than 50 percent of Mexican industrial production has been located in Mexico City, the geographical setting of which aggravates the effects of pollution. The government has attempted to move industry away from Mexico City and has set pollution standards. Many people argue that it is difficult to take ecological and pollution considerations into account due to the dispersal of authority among many government agencies. Specific action to reduce energy-related pollution has not yet been recommended by the National Energy Commission.[42] Nonetheless, the government has taken a number of actions to limit specific contributions to pollution. For example, automotive vehicles contribute 70 percent of the air pollution in Mexico City. The government chose diesel-powered busses to reduce pollution but did not maintain them properly, so that they in turn contributed to pollution. Ecological considerations are taken into account in reaching siting decisions for oil and petrochemical plants. PEMEX, for example, is adopting the use of directional wells in order to limit the damage to the environment. Similarly, PEMEX states that it repairs environmental damage that results from building pipelines and other activities. At first glance, direct government action seems to be easier to control than private action. In part, this stems from the low level of fines attached to private violation of pollution standards and the preference of many local officials for growth instead of environmental improvement. Yet most of the evidence suggests that despite intermittent concern with the environment, the most-important environment-related decisions are made for other reasons. For example, although the switch from oil to gas for electricity generation will reduce pollution, the decision was made both to limit the burning of natural gas and to free oil for export. Similarly, although PEMEX announced its concern with environment, its budget contains funds to pay fines for environmental damage that it expects to incur in the course of its development.[43]

Finally, PEMEX's many offshore developments have brought numerous complaints from fishermen and nature lovers, increasingly so since the blowout of Ixtoc 1. Domestically, the problem is how much of existing agriculture, stock raising, and fishing should be allowed to be damaged for the benefit of PEMEX's land and offshore development. Internationally, the problem is how to handle damage from oil spills that affect other nations' shores and fishing. This problem will only be settled in the context of broader negotiations on environmental issues, especially those regarding the United States, since the United States had contaminated more of the Mexican water supply and air than vice versa. Yet because PEMEX expects to concentrate its efforts on offshore development, environmental damage is likely to increase and to have an international impact because offshore-oil development is intrinsically more difficult than land-based drilling. PEMEX has less experience with offshore than with land operations, so that the chances of accidents are higher. It will have an international effect both because spilled offshore oil reaches other nations' shores and fishing grounds and because Mexican ocean products are sold in international markets. For example, Mexico's fishermen have already asked the president to downplay stories of pollution from Ixtoc 1 so that Mexico's fishing and shrimping catch may be sold in foreign markets, either at all, or at a price that will not be reduced as a result of stories of possible oil-pollution damage to the catch.[44]

Environmental concerns will probably increase somewhat in U.S. foreign policy due to the strongly organized environmental pressure groups in that country. One unfortunate effect of this is that environmental concerns may come to be identified mainly with the United States and with offshore-oil growth in Mexico. If this happens, then environmental considerations probably will be taken even less into account than they are now, and the resources available to Mexico's future generations will be fewer and more damaged than they would have been in the absence of international conflict.


## Final Considerations on the Political Economy of Oil Development

### Private-Sector Participation

Evaluation of the political economy of Mexican oil must be placed in the context of Mexico's economic policy of the 1970s, which is to reduce welfare spending and replace it with spending on directly productive activities. This policy is subject to the constraint that the public sector must not increase its expenditure so fast that private investors will prefer to invest in foreign assets and thus bring pressure on the exchange rate. Similarly, the government would have to be careful not to crowd out private enterprise in Mexican-credit markets.[45]

The collapse of private confidence in the Mexican economy in 1976 was so great that the government had little choice but to spend. Credit to the government increased 30.4 percent in 1976, compared to a 21.0 percent increase to private industry. The government spending was in part used to develop oil, which in turn attracted some private investment. By 1978, credit extended to the government increased 14 percent, while that used by private industry grew 31 percent.[46] These figures suggest that once the worst of the 1976 crisis was past, although some segments of the private sector may have had trouble obtaining credit, the private sector as a whole was not crowded out of Mexican-credit markets. Similarly, the return of the capital that had left Mexico in 1976 suggests that the Mexican government's spending in 1978 was not at levels that would cause the private sector to stagnate.

*Employment*

The more-complex question in evaluating the political economy of Mexican oil is whether Mexico's oil development and recovery program increased unemployment compared to what would have occurred if funds had been spent on other sectors of the economy. The government admits to urban unemployment of about 7 percent in 1976, 8 percent in 1977, and 7 percent in 1978. During these years, the labor force increased 13.9 percent and employment increased 14.9 percent. By 1978 the share of people in the 12-years-and-older population with jobs fell one or two percentage points to about 49 percent of the age group. In comparison, 61.2 percent of people aged sixteen and over in the United States had jobs in 1975, which implies that Mexico has substantial hidden unemployment in its potentially economically active population.[47] The government has dealt with this problem in part by the measures to create employment discussed previously, but far more by passively accepting a large export of unskilled workers to the United States as illegal and legal migrants and an import of skilled labor.[48] Moreover, the share of public investment in agriculture and in rural areas has increased from 15 percent of government investment during the Echeverría years to about 23.2 percent in 1979.[49] Even greater increases in such investment would help job creation, but very possibly they would need to be accompanied by reform measures that would not frighten away private investment. Similarly, the question of how fast the government can increase rural employment and wages when Mexico cannot yet feed itself is one of the most politically difficult problems to face. Building up new areas is apparently more acceptable than greatly changing economic and power balances to favor workers in existing areas. Within the political constraints set out at the beginning of this chapter, the government may not be able to do much more in the short run to increase employment by direct spending. However, measures already mentioned, such as granting larger shares of bank credit to labor-intensive industries, providing them with technical assistance, and allowing them to bid on government contracts, should be of increasing importance and perhaps should have been more-strongly emphasized earlier in the López Portillo administration.

## Remaining Questions

The key question then is not whether the medium- and long-run strategies for Mexican-oil development and economic development are well conceived, but whether the government can avoid adopting a series of short-run measures that are continuously so conservative that they prevent the medium-run measures designed to increase popular participation in Mexico's economic growth and improve the income and power distribution from taking effect. If it is possible to continuously implement the medium-run measures that have been announced, oil-led development, despite the short-run costs, will lead to an economically advanced and complex economy with improved living conditions for much of the population. If the medium-run measures are not continuously implemented, then the high-technology strategy, currently accompanied by decreasing income shares for workers, will lead to a potentially explosive political and economic situation.

## Technical Note

The time lags were estimated by using a dynamic-adjustment model of the Mexican economy. The details of constructing such a model are given in Randall, *An Economic History of Argentina in the Twentieth Century* (New York: Columbia University Press, 1978). In the Mexican case, the economy was divided into the following sectors: agriculture (including hunting and fishing), cattle, mining, oil, petrochemicals, manufacture, commerce, construction, and services. Output for each sector in any year was estimated as a function of profits in each of the sectors of the economy and past output of the sector whose output is estimated. In the series of estimates for Mexico, profits were lagged, successively, one to four years. The results of the estimating equations were compared, and the equation having both the highest corrected multiple-correlation coefficient and the largest number of significant independent variables within the equation were chosen as indicating the correct estimate of the time lag of response-to-profit signals. The results were: agriculture, three years; mining, three years; oil, four years; petrochemicals, two years; manufacture, two years; commerce, two years; construction, one year; services, one to two years; and cattle, less than one year. The difference in the length of lag among the sectors results in the fact that the model works well for individual sectors, but it does not predict GDP well if GDP is predicted directly based upon average lagged profits and output. The correct estimating method is to estimate sectorial output, based on the lags appropriate to each sector, and then to sum the results to obtain the gross product. The values used for change in profits in the equations are shown in the following table.

**Change in Unit Profits from 1960 Levels for Eight Sectors of the Mexican Economy, 1960-1977**

| Year | Agriculture[a] | Oil and Petrochemicals | Commerce and Services[b] | Government and Services[c] | Cattle | Manufacture | Construction | Mining |
|---|---|---|---|---|---|---|---|---|
| 1960 | 0 | 0 | 0 | 0 | 0 | 0 | 0 | 0 |
| 1961 | 56 | 5 | -18 | 22 | -23 | 7 | -103 | -54 |
| 1962 | 76 | -3 | -45 | 57 | -19 | 8 | -199 | -75 |
| 1963 | 97 | 2 | -53 | 59 | -64 | -16 | 24 | -10 |
| 1964 | 80 | -31 | -21 | +51 | -44 | -28 | -74 | 37 |
| 1965 | 80 | -47 | -43 | 74 | -79 | -73 | 0 | 152 |
| 1966 | 11 | -98 | -36 | 97 | -95 | -30 | 59 | 203 |
| 1967 | 15 | -137 | -63 | 122 | -74 | -13 | 89 | 227 |
| 1968 | 4 | -170 | -67 | 144 | -121 | -5 | 46 | 412 |
| 1969 | -5 | -207 | -79 | 166 | -75 | -4 | 87 | 349 |
| 1970 | 10 | -258 | -83 | 182 | -99 | -9 | 116 | 395 |
| 1971 | -19 | -311 | -86 | 206 | -16 | 13 | 102 | 233 |
| 1972 | 18 | -331 | -102 | 221 | -144 | 8 | 127 | 254 |
| 1973 | 194 | -390 | -104 | 199 | -142 | -21 | 150 | 265 |
| 1974 | 216 | -306 | -89 | 136 | -263 | -1 | 197 | 310 |
| 1975 | 254 | -320 | -105 | 167 | -296 | -4 | 237 | 241 |
| 1976 | 262 | 399 | -124 | 191 | -271 | 13 | 273 | 284 |
| 1977 | 263 | -323 | -109 | 140 | -222 | 20 | 247 | 498 |

Rank Order of Profit Opportunities[d]

| Year | Agriculture[a] | Oil and Petrochemicals | Commerce and Services[b] | Government and Services[c] | Cattle | Manufacture | Construction | Mining |
|---|---|---|---|---|---|---|---|---|
| 1961 | 1 | 4 | 5 | 2 | 6 | 3 | 8 | 7 |
| 1962 | 1 | 4 | 6 | 2 | 5 | 3 | 8 | 7 |
| 1963 | 1 | 4 | 7 | 2 | 8 | 6 | 3 | 5 |
| 1964 | 1 | 6 | 4 | 2 | 7 | 5 | 8 | 3 |

**Change in Unit Profits from 1960 Levels for Eight Sectors of the Mexican Economy, 1960-1977** *(continued)*

| Year | Agriculture[a] | Oil and Petrochemicals | Commerce and Services[b] | Government and Services[c] | Cattle | Manufacture | Construction | Mining |
|------|------|------|------|------|------|------|------|------|
| 1965 | 3 | 7 | 6 | 2 | 8 | 5 | 4 | 1 |
| 1966 | 4 | 8 | 6 | 2 | 7 | 5 | 3 | 1 |
| 1967 | 4 | 8 | 6 | 2 | 7 | 5 | 3 | 1 |
| 1968 | 4 | 8 | 6 | 2 | 7 | 5 | 3 | 1 |
| 1969 | 5 | 8 | 7 | 2 | 6 | 4 | 3 | 1 |
| 1970 | 4 | 8 | 6 | 2 | 7 | 5 | 3 | 1 |
| 1971 | 6 | 8 | 7 | 2 | 5 | 4 | 3 | 1 |
| 1972 | 4 | 8 | 6 | 2 | 7 | 5 | 4 | 1 |
| 1973 | 3 | 8 | 6 | 2 | 7 | 5 | 3 | 1 |
| 1974 | 2 | 8 | 6 | 4 | 7 | 5 | 3 | 2 |
| 1975 | 1 | 8 | 6 | 4 | 7 | 5 | 2 | 1 |
| 1976 | 3 | 8 | 6 | 4 | 7 | 5 | 3 | 1 |
| 1977 | 2 | 8 | 6 | 4 | 7 | 5 | 3 | 1 |

[a]Includes agriculture, fishing, and forestry.

[b]Includes commerce, electricity, communication, and transportation.

[c]Includes government and other services.

[d]Assuming that profits actuated for risk were the same among sectors in 1960. Otherwise to be interpreted as index of change in profit opportunities after 1960.

## Notes

1. *Excélsior,* 2 September 1979; and Ted Wett and Shannon L. Matheny, Jr., "México," *Oil and Gas Journal* 77, no. 34 (20 August 1979).

2. Comisión Económica Para América Latina, *México: notas para el estudio económico de América Latina, 1978* (Cepal/Mex/1009/Rev. 2, May 1979); International Monetary Fund, *International Financial Statistics,* October 1979.

3. *Excélsior,* 2 September 1979.

4. Comisión Económica, "México: notas"; *Excélsior,* 2 September 1979; and José López Portillo, *Tercer informe presidencial, Anexos*

5. Lópex Portillo, *Tercer informe presidencial,* Anexos, 1979.

6. Data from Comisión Nacional de los Salários Minimos and Banco de México.

7. Ibid.

8. Joseph Kraft, "A Reporter at Large: The Mexican Oil Puzzle," *New Yorker,* 15 October 1979 (citing Pedro Rodríguez), p. 162.

9. *Excélsior,* 8 October 1979.

10. *Excélsior,* 26 April 1978.

11. *Excélsior,* 8 October 1979; 20 March 1979.

12. *Excélsior,* 4 August 1978.

13. *Uno Más Uno,* 3 May 1978.

14. *Excélsior,* 28 April 1978.

15. *El Sol de México,* 17 March 1978; and *Excélsior,* 5 August 1978.

16. *Excélsior,* 11 July 1979.

17. *Excélsior,* 27 July 1979; and Excélsior, 31 July 1979.

18. PEMEX, *Informe, 1977* (March 1978).

19. PEMEX, *Memoria, 1978* (March 1979); and López Portillo, *Tercer informe presidencial, Anexas.*

20. PEMEX, *Memoria, 1978* (March 1979); and López Portillo, *Tercer informe Presidencial, Anexos* II B, p. 614.

21. PEMEX, *Memoria,* 1976, 1977, 1978, 1979.

22. *Excélsior,* 19 March 1979.

23. Roberto R. Gutierrez, "La Balanza Pertolera de México, 1970-1982," *Comercio Exterior* 29, no. 8 (August 1979); and United Nations, *Monthly Bulletin of Statistics,* August 1979.

24. Ibid.; López Portillo, *Tercer informe presidencial, Anexos II B, p. 614;* and *Petroleum Economist,* 1976-1979.

25. *Excélsior,* 8 October 1979.

26. *Plan Nacional de Desarrollo* (Mexico, 1979).

27. *Excélsior,* 8 October 1979.

28. Arthur M. Brownstein, *Trends in Petrochemical Technology: The Impact of the Energy Crisis* (Tulsa, Okla.: Petroleum Publishing Co., 1976); and Brownstein, *U.S. Petrochemicals: Technologies, Markets, Economics* (Tulsa, Okla.: Petroleum Publishing Co., 1972).

29. PEMEX, *Memoria,* 1977, 1978.

30. López Portillo, *Tercer informe presidencial,* IV, p. 288.

31. Ibid., II, p. 614.

32. Adrian Lajous Vargas and Victor Villa, "El sector petrolero Mexicano 1970-1977, estadísiticas basicas," *Foro Internacional* 72, table 2; John M. Blair, *The Control of Oil* (New York: Random House, 1976), pp. 300-01; Federal Energy Administration, Office of Regulatory Programs, *Preliminary Report: Preliminary Findings and Views Concerning the Exemption of Motor Gasoline from the Mandatory Petroleum and Price Regulations* (Washington, D.C., August 1977), p. 44; and *Petroleum Intelligence Weekly,* 31 June 1978. For earlier estimates, see G. Fernandez de la Garza and A.S. Manne, "Energeticos," in *Multilevel Planning: Case Studies in Mexico,* ed. Louis M. Goreaux and Alan S. Manne (New York: America and Elsevier Publishing Co., 1973), p. 255.

33. López Portillo, *Tercer informe presidencial, Anexos;* and *Excélsior,* 2 September 1979.

34. López Portillo, *Tercer informe presidencial, Anexos,* p. 115; and Excélsior, 2 September 1979.

35. *Excélsior,* 2 September 1979.

36. PEMEX, *Memoria,* 1977, 1978; López Portillo, *Tercer informe presidencial*; and Comisión Económica "México: Notas."

37. Comisión Económica, "México: Notas," pp. 52, 53.

38. López Portillo, *Tercer informe presidencial, Anexos,* p. 288.

39. Ibid., p. 274.

40. Comisión Económica, "México: Notas," p. 43; and López Portillo, *Tercer informe presidencial, Anexos.*

41. Maria Alberto Chavez Gonzales, "Legal Protection of the Environment in Mexico," in *Legal Protection of the Environment in Developing Countries,* ed. Ignacio Carrillo Prieto and Raul Nocedal (Mexico, D.F.: Universidad Nacional Autónoma, 1976), p. 297.

42. Julian Jergensmeyer and Earle Blizzard, "Legal Aspects of Environmental Control in Mexico: An Analysis of Mexico's New Environmental Law," in *Pollution and International Boundaries,* ed. Albert E. Utton (Albuquerque: University of New Mexico Press, 1973); Mario Alberto Chavez Gonzales, "Legislación Mexicana sobre el medio ambiente: su aplicación en el golfo de California," *Natural Resources Journal* 16, no. 3 (July 1976); *Excélsior,* 26 November 1978 and 11 December 1978; and Lucio Cabrera Acevedo, "Legal Protection of The Environment in

the Environment in Mexico," *California Western International Law Journal* 8, no. 1, (Winter 1978).

43. PEMEX, *Memoria,* 1977, 1978.

44. *Excélsior,* 25 July 1979.

45. Leopoldo Solís and Sergio Ghigliazza, "Estabilidad económica y política monetaria," *El Trimestre Económico* 30 (April-June 1963).

46. Comisión Económica, "México: Notas," table 16.

47. Ibid., table 13; and *World Almanac and Book of Facts* (New York: Newspaper Enterprises Association, 1976).

48. Gustavo Cabrera, "Política demografica de México, 1978-1982: objectivos y metas," *Ciencia y Dessarrollo* (May-June 1979).

49. López Portillo, *Tercer informe presidencial, Anexos,* II and III.

# Comments

*Sidney M. Leveson*

These comments critique chapter 3 by Dr. Bernardo Grossling and chapter 4 by Dr. Isidro Sepúlveda. They are followed by remarks on some broader issues that perhaps will provide a setting for further reflection.

## Commentary on Chapter 3

Dr. Grossling presented material that implied the possibility of a more-favorable worldwide environment for resources that is important for controlling inflation and achieving high growth rates for the entire world.

His outlook for the Mexican situation is very similar to my sympathies—that is, viewing the situation as an economist. Oil prices have increased dramatically. Reserve estimates around the world have not been increased to reflect the economically recoverable reserves at 1979 prices. More than that, no effort has been made to systematically estimate how much more oil could be found and recovered as a result of exploration that is economic at 1979 prices. Dr. Grossling has made a valuable attempt to do that for Mexico. Whether we agree with his estimates or not, we must recognize that a fundamental difference exists between what is economically recoverable at 1979 prices (assumed to increase from this level at the inflation rate) and the estimates usually being used. Dr. Grossling used an assumed 40 percent recovery rate for oil in place in his estimates, which is the percentage that probably is used for the long term based upon the economics. In fact, we could say that even this figure does not take into account the extent to which the economics will induce research and technological development that may ultimately raise recovery rates. The important point is that there has to be a large element of truth to this estimated recovery rate, not only for Mexico but also for other places around the world.

Dr. Grossling's paper suggests that the long-run solution to economic problems is not to put money in Switzerland. An investment solution instead would suggest putting money in oil stocks because oil-producing countries have more reserves than they show and because the governments of the world probably will not do what is necessary to solve economic problems. However, if they are solved, given the possibilities for petroleum reserves in place, then Dr. Grossling's view that the price increases, which took place in January 1980, may be the last hurrah for OPEC is probably accurate. Of course, this view assumes no disruption to production for political reasons in the Middle East.

117

**Commentary on Chapter 4**

Dr. Sepúlveda's chapter offers an accurate characterization of PEMEX as having dual roles in export and import substitution. The subsidies to encourage development, which have been given largely in the form of cheap energy and particularly natural-gas prices, usually can be justified. Situations involving import substitution must consider whether this course is inconsistent with the country's own comparative advantage and whether it is being taken simply as the easiest way, in the short run, to deal with balance-of-payments problems. In the case of Mexico, clearly the kinds of activities that are being subsidized are ones in which tremendous economies of scale must be achieved in order to compete on the world markets. This is one effect of these subsidies. A second effect is that comparing Mexican industrial requirements when a plant is built with the situation in the United States and elsewhere shows that a large amount of infrastructure must be built by the company itself, and a good part of the subsidies can be justified on that basis.

PEMEX is a bureaucracy. Sometimes it is too slow. The building of some petrochemical plants has been delayed one-and-a-half years, during which time production is still not being realized. Many stories demonstrate this situation. For example, the mayor of a town sat in the middle of the road with the whole town's population, and refused to move until PEMEX built a schoolhouse. When the schoolhouse was built, PEMEX was able to proceed. Obviously many political negotiations, at various levels of government, must take place when an organization of the size and responsibility of PEMEX is involved. In fact, a high government official made the following comment about PEMEX, "If we push any harder, it will break." However, PEMEX is basically doing the job that it is supposed to be doing. Therefore, instead of focusing on the responsibility of PEMEX, where PEMEX might be going in the future may be a more-beneficial consideration.

The government has established an official limit for petroleum production of 2.25 million barrels per day, which is supposed to be reached in 1980. Yet conversations with officials in manufacturing companies, engineering companies, and so forth, who have various reasons to know what is really going on in the oil industry, indicate that the production peak may rise to 3.75 million barrels per day. Businessmen have to be aware of these trends in order to estimate the growth rate for the economy and the impact on their business. They also have to know in order to determine what effect oil production is going to have on the balance of payments because of the ever-present possibility of devaluation in Mexico, especially in light of recent high rates of inflation. In fact, long-term investment is already taking place at a rate consistent with a petroleum-production rate of

3.75 million barrels per day. This investment, however, cannot be announced because it is not customary in Mexico for one president to make public statements about what the succeeding president will do in the following term. (However, the first ten-year plan, which was made public in 1979, may be viewed as a major policy change in that direction.) The 3.75-million-barrel number could be achieved somewhere in late 1983 or certainly 1984 at the latest, and a production level of 4.5 million barrels per day is possible for 1985 if further decisions to do so are made.

PEMEX is constrained by its own available capital despite the large oil revenues. It was a net borrower in 1979. Also, considerable competition for funds exists in Mexico, which for many years had a policy of concentrating on growth in the private sector and then went through a period of concentrating on growth in the government sector. In 1979 Mexico was trying to grow in both the private and government sectors simultaneously. The pressure will always be on PEMEX to transfer its funds into private projects that are less capital intensive and that will create more jobs. However, that pressure has been resisted to a large extent so far. Also, within PEMEX's own capital budget clearly some shift toward a greater concentration of available funds on upstream investments has occurred.

A constant growth rate of 8 percent or better would indicate that Mexico will have to increase its production annually. This is clear, first of all, because petroleum is a significant sector of the economy, and if it grows less than 8 percent per year, it will drag down the growth rate. Second, it is true because this is the area in which a large portion of the savings is generated in the economy. Third, it is true because, with the level of Mexican inflation, if oil exports are not increased, periodic devaluations will become necessary, not of the magnitude of 1976, but of several percent per year. When these repeated devaluations first start to occur, the market will not be prepared for this regular event, as are some other countries, and a real risk exists that in the first year or two it could lead to some disruptions in relationships in international financial markets. In addition to that, devaluation itself tends to perpetuate inflation. Therefore, inflation will not be decreased if oil exports fail to increase.

## U.S.-Mexican Relations

The comments in this section focus on some of the implications for relationships between the United States and Mexico. A clear consensus seems to be appearing in this book that it is about time that Mexico and the United States treated each other as equals. Equally true is the fact that any negotiations must be based on the premise that the oil is Mexican oil. Further premises for negotiations must reflect an understanding of what the impact of oil development is going to be on Mexico itself. The United States might like to see as much production as possible, but Mexico must face the difficulties to which greater investment in oil could lead—for example, the creation of fewer jobs because of the capital intensity of the petroleum industry.

The type of agreements sought between the two countries should help overcome these difficulties through international financing, imports from Mexico, and similar measures. More importantly, Mexico, through major increases in oil production from the present level, would impact its own price. It would get a lower price on every barrel now produced as a consequence of producing additional barrels. Mexico already represents a significant portion of the world trade in oil, and as that portion increases the net benefit to Mexico from increased production will decrease considerably. The reverse is true for the United States. When another barrel of oil is produced, the United States benefits from it not only in terms of a secure barrel of oil but also in terms of a lower world oil price. A U.S. Department of Energy study estimated that the true cost of an additional barrel of imports to the United States is approximately $100 per barrel. Mexico has a right to negotiate based on that recognition and the recognition that the true increment they will get on an additional barrel is much less, taking into account the decline in the price of their existing barrel. How then does one deal with the negotiation problem? After these factors have been considered, terms must be found that are mutually beneficial to the United States and Mexico.

Other factors also complicate the negotiations. It has been pointed out that when the United States pays more for Mexican natural gas, it must also pay more for Canadian natural gas. The real price, therefore, is much higher than the nominal price. In terms of natural gas, the problem is probably more complicated than this. Considerble debate occurred regarding whether natural gas prices should be based on number 2 oil or number 6 oil. Natural gas certainly has a higher value than number 6 oil, and thus its price might be based on number 2 oil. However, since the United States has more gas than it needs in Texas and less gas than it needs in Ohio, the logical price based on strictly economic grounds would be the price of number 2 in Ohio minus the transportation costs from the Mexican border. This calculation would result in a figure considerably lower than what was actually negotiated. Thus, we pay the premium for both security and for developing a relationship that hopefully will lead to more gas. Incidentally, much more than the minimum amount of natural gas likely will be available to the United States because the associated gas related to the oil production will assure increased natural-gas supplies. Furthermore, Mexican energy policy is not always consistent, just as U.S.-energy policy is not always consistent. For example, the United States could buy natural gas from Mexico for much less if it bought in the form of ammonia.

The specifics of negotiations must provide for an arrangement that will take into account the interests of both parties. This perspective, on the one hand, could lead the United States to insist that the Mexican government increase oil production by substantial quantities over an extended period of time as a condition of the signing of the natural-gas contract. On the other hand, the United States has a responsibility to negotiate as equals and to recognize the disadvantages to Mexico from too much production. Therefore, an equitable agreement should consider U.S. imports from Mexico, perhaps on a preferential basis in some cases, such as agricultural commodities. The agreement should also include provisions for the trade of petrochemicals as well as other products Mexico considers important for its own development. Financial agreements with Mexico must be included in order to make sure that the capital necessary for this oil development does not take capital away from job-producing activities in Mexico. Finally, efforts should be made through negotiation to contain long-range security problems that could threaten the oil supply, which would include recognizing the possible Cuban threat to Mexico.

**Conclusions**

In short, the United States must start with a complete understanding of what is important to Mexico and reach an agreement as equals from which both countries benefit. Such an agreement might not result in production of the magnitude that Dr. Grossling's estimates imply, but the United States can certainly negotiate an agreement in which Mexican production would exceed 5 million barrels a day, possibly by a substantial amount, and that is consistent with the benefits to both parties and their people.

# Comments

*John H. Christman*

## Recent Statistics of Mexican Economy

Before addressing specific remarks to chapter 5 by Dr. Villarreal and chapter 6 by Dr. Randall, it is useful to touch very briefly on some recent statistics concerning Mexico's economy, not covered in the two chapters, since they are definitely linked to the topics at hand.

### Economic Growth

Current indications suggest that Mexico's growth, in terms of real GDP for 1979, will reach 8 percent, and this figure will likely be repeated in the following year, albeit with somewhat more-intense inflationary pressures. Very strong growth in the petroleum, petrochemical, manufacturing, and construction sectors is expected in 1980. This progress is anticipated notwithstanding the continuous, serious problem presently of shortfalls in raw-materials production and severe strains on the country's outmoded transport system.

### Investment

In 1980, despite some limiting factors, considerable new expansion of private investment, both domestic and foreign, should be occurring. The latest forecasts indicate that new, private fixed investment in 1980 should reach the equivalent of $18.4 billion in current prices, which is $3.7 billion more than the projected 1979 total. Even discounting the very real impact of domestic and imported inflation, that is a healthy and much-needed increase. Within that total, U.S. direct investment in Mexico in 1980 should reach a record high of $770 million, including $661 million in manufacturing-sector investment. The projected U.S. investment compares with just $347 million in 1978 and an estimated $569 million in 1979, although the figure for 1979 still represents only about 6 percent of total private investment in Mexico.

Without shunting to one side Mexico's traditional and shorter-term socioeconomic problems, these figures help to underscore the current confidence in the country's economic-development potential. Mexico's oil, while obviously an important factor, is not the only factor in this confidence.

*Petroleum Exports*

As shown in table 6-6, crude-oil production by PEMEX as of 7 December 1979, had reached just over 1.3 million barrels per day and should get to the planned 1.9-million-barrels plateau by year's end. Meanwhile, as shown in table 6-7 PEMEX's crude-oil exports accounted for 47.8 percent of Mexico's total merchandise exports in the first ten months of 1979. In the same period in 1978, the figure was just under 30 percent. The most-reliable recent projections indicate that by 1985, PEMEX exports of crude, gas, and petrochemicals will represent $24.7 billion in foreign-exchange revenues. This is a very sizable increase over the projected revenues of $4.3 billion in 1979 and $8.7 billion in 1980.

**Commentary on Chapter 5**

Dr. Villarreal has presented a clear view of the government's possibilities for development with petroleum. However, in this reviewer's judgment he may be too optimistic about the possibilities of export substitution. While hopefully realizable, chances are that many years will pass before Mexico's manufacturing sector is geared up for an ongoing exports program in both real and psychological terms.

Mexican entrepreneurs have for too many years been accustomed to a guaranteed domestic market regardless of price and quality, thanks to high protective barriers. Knowing from firsthand experience the mentality of many companies toward exporting on a programmed basis, forecasting a definite new thrust in the export of manufactures is difficult regardless of Mexican-government trade incentives or direct pressures. The implementation of an export-substitution program as described by Dr. Villarreal would require a dramatic change in the export mentality before the companies would produce exports in an ongoing, competitive fashion. This change would be desirable if it would happen in the near term. However, if Mexico

**Table 6-6**
**Production Programs of PEMEX, 1979-1982**

| Year | Refinery Capacity (barrels) | Refinery Capacity (barrels per day) | Petrochemicals (metric tons per year) |
|------|------|------|------|
| 1979 | 481 million | 1.31 million | 7.26 million |
| 1980 | 564 million | 1.51 million | 10.64 million |
| 1981 | 582 million | 1.59 million | 12.33 million |
| 1982 | 655 million | 1.79 million | 15.39 million |

Source: *Petróleos Mexicanos.*

**Table 6-7**
**Forecasted Export Revenues of PEMEX, 1978-1985**

| Year | PEMEX Export Revenues (millions of dollars) | PEMEX Exports as Percentage of Mexico's Total Merchandise Exports |
|------|------|------|
| 1978 | $1,805 | 31 |
| 1979 | 4,270 | 47.8 |
| 1980 | 8,738 | 63.4 |
| 1981 | 13,000 | 70 |
| 1982 | 14,894 | 70.9 |
| 1983 | 17,419 | 72.4 |
| 1984 | 20,478 | 73.7 |
| 1985 | 24,737 | 75.5 |

Source: Wharton Econometric Forecasting Associates, Inc., and Department of Economic Studies, American Chamber of Commerce of Mexico, A.C. Projections made in October 1979.

does adhere to GATT, as is now more probable than not, it could force many companies in the manufacturing sector to reevaluate their long-standing approach to competitive production. This reevaluation would be extremely positive since the production of competitive-manufactures exports, including processed agricultural commodities, on a systematic and wide-ranging basis would contribute much more in the long run to Mexico's economic development, stability, employment, and balanced regional income distribution than would increased oil exports as such.

## Commentary on Chapter 6

Dr. Randall's well-presented and thought-provoking paper is useful in placing the political economy of Mexican petroleum in perspective. These comments are confined to four points, that further elaborate some of the ideas in chapter 6 and point up areas of disagreement from this reviewer's perspective.

First, Dr. Randall pointed out quite correctly that Mexico has many ongoing problems that are not likely to be solved, or even noticeably alleviated, in the short run, the country's rapid return to oil-power status notwithstanding. However, to the problems she mentioned such as population growth, the stagnation of farm production, unemployment levels, and so forth should also be added the prospects for a continuing high rate of inflation; uncertainty concerning the peso and the government's "float" management policy; current lack of an exportable surplus aside from oil and, to a lesser degree, gas; and the fact that 1980 will be a year of intensified positioning for the 1982 presidential succession, with the multiple potential implications of this positioning on government economic policy and decision making.

Second, her discussion of the different reasons for inflation was interesting since Mexico likely will have annual rates of retail inflation of between 18 and 25 percent well into the next decade. The pressures on Mexico's government to develop rapidly and to create as many new jobs as possible will not permit determined and pronounced antiinflation measures for the forseeable future.

Mexico, during the first three years of the López Portillo administration, was directly and concurrently affected by all of the inflationary factors mentioned by Dr. Randall, except that created by excessive wage contract agreements. Inflation will continue to be affected by all the factors for the forseeable future, and this includes the probability that the government's wage policy will be of necessity much more liberal. The data in table 6-8 reinforce this view, and other data also indicate the following:

Real-wage increases for workers have been negative over the past three years.

Worker productivity has been increasing.

Real unit labor costs have been dropping.

The purchasing power of workers has been declining.

Income distribution has been shifting away from wage earners in favor of public and private owners of capital assets.

These events have led to an increase in pressure from organized labor on the government. Meanwhile, upward pressures on wages have resulted from competitions between unions affiliated with the Labor Congress and the so-called independent unions, which are headed by seemingly more-aggressive labor leaders. This competition has been provoked by the pending departure from the labor scene of the long-established union leader, Fidel Velázquez. As a result, unions have been more successful in raising wages by means of collective bargaining. For example, in the three months of

**Table 6-8**
**Mexican Wage Statistics, 1977-1980**

| Item | 1977 | 1978 | 1979 | 1980[a] |
|------|------|------|------|---------|
| Nominal wage increase | 10 | 12.5 | 16 | 22 |
| Real (deflated) wage increase | −2.5 | −2.4 | −0.1 | 1.9 |
| Increase in worker productivity | 2.9 | 3.1 | 3.5 | 2.7 |
| Wage bill as percent of GDP | 30.9 | 29.3 | 28.4 | — |

Source: Department of Economic Studies, American Chamber of Commerce of Mexico, A.C.
[a]Projected.

September, October, and November 1979, the average wage increases agreed upon were 15.23, 16.71, and 17 percent respectively. Quite possibly the secretary of labor will loosen its hold on organized-labor demands, which suggests that salary demands will be even higher next year.

Third, Dr. Randall strongly indicated that private investment in Mexico has not been keeping pace in recent times. This was true in 1977 primarily because of the urgency of decapitalization and debt renegotiation resulting from the peso devaluation of late 1976. Since then, however, private investment, as shown in table 6-9 with strong support from the López Portillo administration, has registered a constant and dynamic ascent to the point that it once again accounts for more than 50 percent of the country's gross fixed investment—that is, 55.4 percent in 1978 and projections of 55.7 percent in 1979 and 1980.

New private investment in manufacturing always involves an eighteen- to twenty-four-month time period between the investment decision and the installation of the new production capacity. This has been true in Mexico, and furthermore, lead times recently have been adversely affected by a lack of available expansion financing in pesos and serious delays in deliveries of equipment and material. These delays have resulted from bottlenecks in Mexico's transport system, which first became evident in the spring of 1978 and since have become increasingly serious during the country's economic recovery.

Interest in new investment is very high and should continue indefinitely. For example, all private companies in the manufacturing of oil-industry equipment, ranging from line pipe to drill bits, now are actively involved in expansion, which in most cases will mean at least a doubling of installed capacity as well as an introduction of product lines that hitherto have

**Table 6-9**
**Projected Gross Fixed Investment in Mexico in the Private and Public Sectors, 1978-1985**
*(percent)*

| Year | Private | Public | PEMEX[a] |
|------|---------|--------|----------|
| | | *Gross Investment* | |
| 1978 | 55.4 | 44.6 | 31.9 |
| 1979 | 55.7 | 44.3 | 28 |
| 1980 | 55.7 | 44.3 | 23.1 |
| 1981 | 55.1 | 44.9 | 14.5 |
| 1982 | 54 | 46 | 13.2 |
| 1983 | 53.4 | 46.6 | 10.6 |
| 1984 | 51.9 | 48.1 | 14.8 |
| 1985 | 50.6 | 49.4 | 13.5 |

Source: Wharton Economic Forecasting Associates, Inc., and Department of Economic Studies, American Chamber of Commerce of Mexico, A.C.

[a]Percentage participation of PEMEX in total public-sector gross fixed investment.

not been manufactured in Mexico. Most of these companies already sense that within three to five years, they will have to double capacity again because of PEMEX's equipment requirements. Traditionally, up until the current oil boom began, imports accounted for about 33 percent of PEMEX machinery, equipment, and material needs. This figure jumped to 57 percent in 1978 and probably will be around 75 percent in 1979. Thus, the imperative need is for a much-greater domestic-production level of oil-sector equipment, a need to which private companies are responding via accelerated expansion investments. Recall that the PEMEX capital-expenditures projections for the 1979-1982 period total $8.2 billion.

Fourth, exception should be taken with Dr. Randall's remark that transnational corporations are restricting Mexico's access to technology. Technology transfer did slow down in the 1974-1976 period because of concerns as to the political, economic, and philosophical leanings of the Echeverría government and an initial reaction of uncertainty to the new transfer-of-tecnology law. However, although both reactions were understandable, this slowdown has now been reversed. At present, interest in selling technology to Mexico appears to be at an all-time high, an interest that is combined with more sophistication and flexibility from the government's transfer-of-technology registry.

# Discussion Summary

Elihu Bergman opened the discussion session with the generally prevailing observation that oil revenues are expanding options for economic remedies and developmental processes for Mexico. No one has claimed, however, that enough revenue will be available to do everything that all sectors might desire. Therefore, he proposed that the participants speculate as to the political dimensions of the choices, given these limitations. The remarks that followed touched upon the roles of three primary groups in this regard: PEMEX, the United States and the international community, and public and private investors.

Sepúlveda was the first to respond. "Any change that will occur in Mexico will not come about without political consequences." Furthermore, the political consequences will be either civil or military authoritarianism or democratic pluralism, depending on the political choices selected. PEMEX, Sepúlveda believes, will have an important role in determining the direction of this decision making. If it chooses an exclusive business orientation, it may cause a breakdown in the political system. He cited examples of other Latin American countries, like Brazil, in which the continued business orientation has promoted difficulties between the government and society: "They have been successful, but they have often fostered totalitarian regimes." Alternatively, if PEMEX opts for a mixed orientation that considers productivity and social concerns, it may cause the formation of a more-open society.

Rapp questioned the actual PEMEX role in the decision-making process. Sepúlveda responded that PEMEX will not ultimately make the decision on how the oil revenues are to be used nor will it have exclusive influence on the decision. He elaborated, however, that at least PEMEX will have a role, along with other members of the political establishment, and at most it will have a crucial role in the usage of revenue to be reinvested.

Puente Leyva supported the importance of PEMEX in the political decisions Mexico will make concerning the overall development of the country. "PEMEX is a political and social entity more so than the international-market-oriented oil companies." He expressed the opinion that a historical and social rationality exists in the current oil boom—it is not a miracle. This rationality, he said, is based on the fact that PEMEX is a national company and persisted as such in the lean years when nonnational companies might have retreated from Mexico. The Mexican oil boom exists, according to Puente Leyva, for two reasons: (1) PEMEX has done good technical work, and (2) prices increased fourfold between October 1973 and early 1974, at a time when PEMEX was prepared to take advantage of the market.

Williams speculated that, with or without the PEMEX role in political decision making, the outlook for the benefits of oil production appears pessimistic if this is defined as equitable distribution of income. His conclusion was based on two perspectives. First, the historical trend since 1940 has been an increasing maldistribution of income in Mexico. Second, the experience of other Latin American oil-distributing countries like Venezuela has been an increasing maldistribution of wealth.

Ayres interjected that the discussion was lapsing into a discussion of Mexican issues, as opposed to U.S.-Mexican issues. He emphasized the need to maintain an awareness that the consequences of Mexican-oil production may depend on the evolution of U.S. policies toward Mexico and U.S. willingness to search for mutually accommodating arrangements. As examples he cited the U.S.-tariff policies that would effect efforts toward expanding Mexican exports, the nature of U.S. accommodation to Mexican comparative advantage, potential U.S. investment in Mexico, and U.S. policies that are now inadequate for dealing with changes in the international division of labor. Wionczek agreed that a broader perspective of the discussion would be beneficial, but that this broadening should move beyond U.S.-Mexican relations. He suggested that an understanding of the Mexican-oil situation would become clearer if the United States would recognize interests beyond its own—that is, "The world for Mexico is not made up only of the United States and Mexico." Mexico should be viewed as having other interests such as Cuba, OPEC, and the United Nations. He concluded that because Mexico and the United States operate from different conceptual views of the world, their relationship would benefit from the relaxation of the framework of that relationship.

Puente Leyva turned the focus of the discussion to the role of private and public sectors in the political consequences of the oil boom. He disagreed with the concept that increased public investment will probably need to be accompanied by reform measures that would not discourage private investment. He suggested that this situation was probably the case in the early 1960s, but in the context of today's fast-growing Mexican economy and the international recession, Mexico is most attractive to private investors. In addition to these circumstances, Mexico offers a variety of subsidies to private investors, particularly the investors conducting business in the oil regions. He concluded his comments by suggesting that a primary concern for both private and public investment will be to increase the rate of savings. "The hope of Mexico," according to Puente Leyva, "is that together they will fill the gap in domestic savings in order to take advantage of foreign income from oil exports."

**Part III
The U.S. Perspective**

# 7

# Mexican Energy Resources and U.S. Energy Requirements

*Bruce C. Netschert*

## Implications of the Juxtaposition

The juxtaposition of "Mexican energy resources" and "U.S. energy requirements" in the title of this chapter should not be interpreted to mean that the purpose of the former is to satisfy the latter.[1] Rather, the issues should be taken in the context of international trade.

Resource endowment versus need is, in fact, the fundamental basis of all international trade. Each country sells to another what it has and the other needs. Classical economics, moreover, demonstrated with the elegant logic of comparative advantage the basis for mutually beneficial trade, even in circumstances in which both of two countries have the same two resource endowments. On another level, the mutual interdependence of all the nations of the world was well summed up by President López Portillo in his address to the United Nations General Assembly in September 1979: "No country on earth is entirely self-sufficient. We all have need of the others." Therefore, there need be no invidious element in the suggestions that the existence of Mexican energy resources and U.S. energy requirements can logically and justifiably be paired. Before going further, however, a brief review of the nature and size of those resources is presented.

## Mexican Energy Resources

### Petroleum

The latest official figures announced by President López Portillo in September 1979 indicated that the combined proved reserves of crude oil and natural gas were equivalent to 45.8 billion barrels, with another 45 billion barrels of probable reserves. Although no official figures are available for oil and gas separately, the commonly accepted assumption, which has been neither denied nor corroborated by the Mexican government, is that approximately 60 percent of the total is oil, and 40 percent is gas. On this basis, the proved and probable reserves of oil are each some 27 billion barrels. Potential reserves are estimated at a combined 200 billion barrels, which translate into 120 billion barrels of oil.

The figures for natural gas alone that can be derived from the official totals are subject to greater uncertainty because of the need to assume not only the gas-oil ratio in the totals but also the calorific equivalent of gas versus oil. Using the conservative assumption that one barrel of oil is the equivalent of 5,000 cubic feet of gas, the indicated proved and probable reserves of gas are each approximately 90 trillion cubic feet.

## Coal

The most-recent authoritative estimate of Mexico's coal resources is given in an international summary of world energy resources prepared for the Tenth World Energy Conference in 1977. According to this source, Mexico's "technically and economically recoverable reserves" are 875 million tons.[2]

## Geothermal

Like other countries that border on the Pacific Ocean in the low and middle latitudes of the Western Hemisphere, Mexico has resources of geothermal energy. Estimation of these resources is speculative because of the difficulty of defining such resources, which in turn is related to the determination of the technology that can be applied. "It has been estimated by the Mexican Federal Electric Commission that there can be 400-1,400 megawatts of geothermal capacity on line by 1985 and 1,500-20,000 megawatts by the year 2000. The ultimate geothermal potential of Mexico is variously estimated at 4,000-20,000 megawatts (e)."[3]

## Uranium

Mexico also has significant uranium resources. According to one report, probable reserves of the uranium compound $U_3O_8$ are 600,000 tons, but exploration for uranium resources throughout the country is still in its early stage.[4] A processing plant under construction will produce 400 tons of $U_3O_8$ a year beginning in 1982, and the country's first nuclear-power plant will go into operation with 675 megawatts of capacity in that year.[5]

In summary, Mexico's endowment of energy resources gives it, beyond any doubt, the capability of expanding energy production well above its domestic needs, regardless of any plausible rate of growth in those needs, well into the next century. Mexico is already exporting crude oil and will soon be exporting natural gas and electric power as well.[6] Expanding those exports severalfold would be physically possible if the policy of the Mexican government were to do so. As an illustration of the scale of such expansion, Mexico could export to the United States quantities such as 3 million barrels a day of oil and 5 billion cubic feet a day of gas in 1985 and provide several thousand megawatts of firm power based on geothermal and hydro plants as well as plants fueled with oil or gas. Coal and uranium can be dismissed from consideration in the present context because U.S.-Mexican issues do not concern them. That such expansion of petroleum exports could be very much in the interest of both United States and Mexico should become apparent from a review of existing circumstances and policies in the two countries.

### Circumstances and Policies in the United States

The existing energy circumstances in the United States have received so much attention, not only within the United States but also throughout the world, that they scarcely need elaboration. Domestic production of oil has been unable to keep pace with even the reduced-demand growth of the past several years. Imports, as a consequence, have increased, and this in turn has led to an increasingly adverse trade deficit. Under other circumstances this deficit would not necessarily cause concern, but because of the importance of the dollar in international financial and monetary affairs, it creates severe problems of the U.S. Treasury and causes instability in international money markets. By contributing, moreover, to the growth in the world demand for OPEC exports, the U.S. import demand has contributed to OPEC's ability to continue to raise prices by the classic cartel tactic of restricting production.

Therefore, for a congeries of reasons, the United States has arrived at a policy goal of reducing oil imports. Agreement on the appropriate policies to accomplish this goal unfortunately cannot be said to have been reached as yet. Most people agree that over the long term (ten years or more) that goal should be achievable through a combination of developing previously submarginal and alternative resources on the supply side, including the production of synthetic fuels from coal and the large-scale use of renewable resources and conservation on the demand side.

Although enthusiasts of each of these avenues contend that with appropriate actions and policies, quick results would follow—even within five years—it is fair to say that objective opinion is not optimistic. Increased production from heavy oil and enhanced recovery of conventional crude oil could conceivably lead to some increase in total domestic-oil production in the next five years, and continued conservation efforts should reduce demand growth, if not the absolute level of demand. Such results, however, although unquestionably helpful, will not achieve a massive reduction in the level of oil imports. As for the contribution that can come from synthetic fuels and renewable resources, technical and institutional obstacles preclude any significant results throughout most of the 1980s and certainly in the next five years.

Thus, although U.S. policy is aimed in the right direction, it will not solve the import problem in the near term. Given the apparent inability of OPEC to restrain its more-aggressive members in the frequency and size of successive price increases, this delay in effecting a substantial decrease in U.S. oil-import demand can aggravate the problems not only of this country but of the world as well. To view the need of the United States to solve the oil-import problem as second only to the need to avoid a nuclear-arms race and holocaust is no exaggeration. The results of anarchy in Iran only underscore this conclusion.

**Circumstances and Policies in Mexico**

As a modern nation, Mexico can take pride in an impressive record of political stability and the achievement of an economic position well above that of most Latin American nations. Economic progress has been hampered, however, by high rates of population growth, unemployment, inflation, and insufficient capital to modernize agriculture. In these circumstances the discovery that Mexico is blessed with one of the richest concentrations of petroleum resources on earth is of epochal importance. Few nations in its position have been fortunate enough to be given the clear and untrammeled opportunity, in one single revelation, to make the transformation from the ranks of the less-developed countries to those with high living standards and a powerful voice in world affairs.

The full extent of that opportunity is dazzling. Mexico has not merely followed in the path of Taiwan and South Korea, whose achievements in three decades or less have astounded the world, but it has become the first nation in history to emulate the earlier transformation of Japan into a fully industrialized world power. In this respect Mexico starts with many advantages. Japan, on the one hand, with almost no indigenous mineral resources, accomplished the feat solely through two social transformations—the first in the nineteenth century and the second after World War II. Mexico, on the other hand, has substantial mineral resources in addition to its energy resources. Mexico could conceivably, in the early twenty-first century, surpass Japan's achievement and attain a standard of living above that currently enjoyed by some of the countries of Western Europe. Little wonder that a sense of excitement emanates from Mexico City.

The stated goal of President López Portillo and his administration is to make sure that this opportunity is not lost through default. The goal of his policy is to see that the revenues from oil will contribute to economic growth and not be wasted in nonproductive use. Meanwhile, by the pace of its development of the newfound resources, PEMEX is confounding the opinion of some members of the international-oil fraternity who doubted that Mexican capabilities were equal to the task. At the same time, the government is mindful of the dangers attendant on rapid expansion and ballooning revenues. It is fully aware of the dismal examples provided by countries such as Iran, in which the income was squandered, and by other countries such as Norway, in which even severe restraint on the pace of oil development has been unable to prevent inflation.

Given these circumstances, Mexico would be expected to seek to tread the exceedingly narrow and difficult path between, on the one hand, a rate of development that is too cautious and that results in thwarted public expectations, and on the other hand, a rate that is too ambitious and that results in inflation that cancels the benefits of expansion. The government has repeatedly emphasized its intention of avoiding the latter, which it appears to regard as far more dangerous than the former.

Mexican production will be increased to a level of 2.25 million barrels a day by the end of 1980, and under present plans it will remain at that level indefinitely, even though it would be physically feasible to attain a production level of twice that amount, if not more. Production thereafter will depend on the circumstances at the time. The government has also announced that it will diversify the countries to which it sells and that it will sell to the United States only some 60 percent of its exportable surplus rather than the 90 percent it sells currently.

Therefore, a conflict of interests exists. From the U.S. viewpoint large oil imports from Mexico during the 1980s would greatly reduce the dimensions of the oil-import problem in general.[7] From the Mexican viewpoint such large imports would require production levels in excess of the level deemed compatible with established inflation targets. Thus, what would satisfy U.S. interests would be harmful to Mexican interests.

On the face of it, this aspect would seem to end the matter. What point is there in talking of greater Mexican-oil exports for the benefit of the United States if, in Mexican eyes, the benefits—that is, the increased revenues—are outweighed by the risk of unwanted and harmful inflation? Let us be not so naïve as to suggest that Mexico should defer to U.S. wishes—that would indeed be outrageous Yanqui-ism. I suggest, rather, that the existence of common interests provides the basis for an approach to greater production and exports to the United States that would take care of Mexican fears or, even better, would provide such great benefits to Mexico that it would be in the Mexican self-interest to agree to appropriate U.S. proposals.

**Conservation and U.S. Import Needs**

It should be emphasized that this proposal does not imply that the United States should attempt to convince Mexico to export its oil in order to allow continued unrestrained growth in the U.S. import demand. An import ceiling has already been established by President Carter. Nevertheless, a widespread feeling exists in the international community that the United States is remiss in not having reduced its demand for petroleum before this time so that it would be importing less than it is at present.

However, people do not usually recognize, even within the United States, that simple demand elasticity, especially in the industrial sector, has already produced significant results. As shown by table 7-1, energy consumption by U.S. industry grew by only 7 percent between 1971 and 1976, and at the same time the industrial output (as measured by the Federal Reserve Board Index of Industrial Production) grew by almost 50 percent.

Petroleum conservation *is* occurring, and continuing price increases will stimulate it still further. The industrial use of energy in the United States in 1990, if not sooner, probably will be less than it was before the oil embargo, even with continued growth in output.

Amid all the backing and filling on domestic-energy policy, moreover, most people also do not recognize that progress in gasoline conservation due to measures already adopted is beginning to be apparent and will be highly significant in the 1980s. As automobile manufacturers meet the mileage-per-gallon guidelines established by the government, and as the new, more-efficient cars constitute an increasing percentage of the total car population, not only will average mileage per gallon of that population increase but also, despite the continued increase in the total number of cars, total gasoline consumption will actually decrease. Consumption in 1985 has been projected to be almost 10 percent less than 1980 consumption.

**Table 7-1**
**Industrial Energy Consumption versus Industrial Production, Selected Years**
*(index for 1967 = 100)*

| Year | Federal Reserve Board Index | Industrial Energy Consumption |
|------|-----------------------------|-------------------------------|
| 1967 | 100 | 100 |
| 1971 | 108.2 | 110.2 |
| 1974 | 129.4 | 114.4 |
| 1975 | 116.3 | 101.7 |
| 1976 | 146.8 | 106.8 |

Source: Federal Reserve Board Index of Industrial Production, 1967-1976.

Much as one may deplore the inability of the United States to settle on a coherent, rational energy policy that will solve the oil-import problem, nevertheless on one score, at least, policy clearly has been settled. The United States is determined to have a substantially lower oil-import requirement in the 1990s (President Carter's goal is a 50 percent reduction by 1990). Whether this goal is achievable remains a matter of dispute, but there are good grounds for expecting significant progress by that time. Every OPEC price increase and supply perturbation can be expected to increase the progress that will be made.

Could the United States reduce its import requirements more rapidly? Of course it could, but to achieve truly large results within five years would require drastic measures such as gasoline rationing. Some people argue that this is indeed what should be done, but political realities must be considered. One of these realities is that the U.S. public does not view the present circumstances as constituting an emergency that would justify rationing, with all its enormous problems of equity. Another reality is that, barring the public perception of an emergency, a democracy cannot reasonably be expected to act other than as a democracy—that is, if no emergency is perceived, society may deplore the government's misperception, but it cannot be condemned for failure to take the supposedly correct action.

In summary, it is not presumptuous to take the existence of a sizable U.S. demand for imported oil during the 1980s as a given in discussing Mexican energy resources and U.S. energy requirements. The problem of undue dependence on imports is recognized and is being grappled with in the clumsy, muddled fashion that so frequently characterizes the actions of a democratic society. Impatience with this process is understandable, but it must be accompanied by tolerance. U.S. import needs for oil during the 1980s are therefore justified in the sense that the country is moving in the right direction, that conservation is taking place, and that those needs will progressively decrease. Furthermore, OPEC actions will reduce U.S. demand for imported oil and thus silence the argument that increased Mexican exports of oil to the United States would lessen the pressure to reduce the reliance on imports.

Such an increase is also justified in a wholly different context. The United States is the world's largest oil importer. Thus, to the extent Mexican exports come to this country, the pressure on OPEC supply is reduced to the benefit of all other importing countries, which is not to imply that Mexico would do this to break the market power of the OPEC cartel. As an exporter, Mexico has no interest in such a move. However, the Mexican government would recognize the distinction between lowering the world price of oil through increased exports and preventing or ameliorating further price increases. As is universally acknowledged, and recognized by

President López Portillo in his public statements, troublesome as the OPEC price actions are to the United States and the other industrialized countries, the Third World ultimately bears an intolerable burden. Indeed, this thought would be chilling to anyone contemplating the prospect of the indefinite escalation of OPEC prices. At some point the fragile Third-World economies could collapse under the increasing strain, with a resulting danger to the maintenance of the global economy.

## U.S. Attitude in Dealing with Mexico

In approaching the Mexican government with the idea of increased oil exports to the United States, the U.S. government must create an atmosphere of mutual trust. The past record on this score, unfortunately, is not good—for instance, the well-known example of the aborted negotiations on natural gas should suffice.

### Recognition of Mexican Attitudes

The Mexican government brings suspicion along with it to any dealings with the United States. On the basis of past experience this suspicion is fairly justified. The United States in the past has often abused its position, frequently through sheer inadvertence but sometimes deliberately. The first requisite for successful negotiations to induce greater Mexican-oil imports, therefore, is for the United States to demonstrate that it is sincere in its desire to pursue mutual interests, which will not be easy. In part this can be accomplished by the nature of the proposals themselves, which are presented in the following sections. However, in the last analysis this demonstration of sincerity will depend on the *tone* of the negotiations. Whether an agreeable tone can be achieved is a matter of conjecture, but it is essential to success.

### Recognition of Mexico's New Position

Having been so long on the fringes of world affairs and the object of diplomatic neglect by the United States, Mexico understandably is fiercely proud of its new position as an emerging world power and vocal in its demands that this be recognized. The U.S. response to date can be characterized as a grudging acceptance of the changed circumstances. However, common sense would seem to call for full and unqualified recognition of Mexico's new status in official U.S. policy and diplomatic dealings with Mexico. Beyond this, the creation of a mutual trust would be immensely aided by the declaration that the United States not only welcomes Mexico's new status but also wishes to do what it can to help Mexico attain the full world-power status of which it is capable.

If Mexico becomes fully industrialized in the face of continued U.S. indifference and only reluctant acceptance, the United States will find itself with a world power on its border, with relations between the two, at best, strained. Even in the absence of the question of oil imports from Mexico, such a strained relationship should be avoided. Remember, moreover, that the best trading partners for any industrialized nation are other industrialized nations.

### Recognition of Mexican Political Realities

Another requisite for successful negotiations is U.S. recognition of the realities of Mexican politics. As in most countries, the Mexican political spectrum covers the full range from left to right, and although Mexico is a one-party state, the party itself includes a wide part of that spectrum. Traditionally, the Mexican Left has enjoyed baiting the United States as a tool to achieve its own ends. Thus, any Mexican president must proceed with caution in any dealings with the United States. Any action or proposal that conceivably could be interpreted as having made concessions to the United States will be seized on by the Left to embarrass the president and to gain advantage in Mexican internal politics. The president must therefore avoid putting himself in a position in which the Left can label him a yanqui dupe or claim that he has given away Mexican interests under U.S. pressure.

In negotiating for increased Mexican-oil exports, the United States can avoid putting the Mexican president in this position by making the quid pro quo it offers so attractive from the Mexican viewpoint that attempts by the Left to exploit acceptance would only make the group look foolish and clearly against the best interests of the Mexican people.

### The Quid Pro Quo

The task of fashioning the proposal or proposals that would be irresistibly attractive to the Mexican government is one for diplomats and expert negotiators. Some examples of what could serve as the basis for an irresistible proposal are offered in the following sections.

### Immigration

The most-obvious example is the matter of illegal immigration. The pressures within Mexico that cause this immigration are themselves irresistible. One of the goals of the Mexican-development plans is to reduce the unemployment and underemployment from which the immigration stems and thus to begin to reduce its magnitude and eventually eliminate it. The present situation is an acute embarrassment for both countries. Thus far they both have looked the other way, not seeing any solution and preferring not to bring the issue to a head for fear of damaging already shaky relations.

Clearly in the interest of the United States is to bring the matter under some kind of control. The new oil wealth makes possible the new development plan. The scope of this chapter is not to suggest specific solutions, except to say that the U.S. government could explore the concessions it could make in officially recognizing and permitting the immigration that would be both politically and economically tolerable. The politics are especially sticky. However, it seems to be one thing to offend a political constituency such as organized labor, which contends that the immigration displaces U.S. workers, with an action that would seem to be permanently adverse to its interest, and another thing altogether if it can be demonstrated that the adverse effect will be only temporary and will be ultimately to its benefit, such as the resultant expansion of U.S.-Mexican trade. Thus, the United States could present Mexico with the proposition of increased oil exports in return for concessions on immigration. Such action would assuage Mexican pride and at the same time aid in the solution of one of its thorniest domestic problems.

*Trade Policy*

A second example of quid pro quo is in the area of trade policy. The domestic market for manufactured products in Mexico is too small to support many of the industries for which Mexico has the resources, and therefore, if these resources are to be utilized, domestic industry must be able to produce for the export market as well. The neighboring U.S. market is the first natural export market for Mexican products. At present the entry of Mexican products into the United States is considerably more restricted than it is for products from countries such as Japan and Taiwan. Mexico would benefit greatly from the increased ability to export products such as fertilizers, petrochemicals, steel, and machinery to the United States.

Again, the domestic political implications in the United States are nettlesome. Any liberalization in trade policy must always contend with strong protectionist sentiment in the industries concerned. This sentiment has not, however, prevented relaxation of import restrictions in the past through the argument that the greater good of more free trade outweighs limited interests of trade barriers.

*Electricity*

A third example of quid pro quo is an extension of across-the-border deals already in progress. Utilities in San Deigo and San Antonio are proceeding with arrangements to import electric power from Mexican generating stations, with the San Antonio plant using generating capacity based on geothermal energy. The quid pro quo would be to propose to Mexico that it build generating capacity in its northern states specifically to supply U.S. systems and that this capacity be based on oil- and gas-fired, as well as geothermal, units. This use of oil and gas generation for exports of electricity would bypass the Mexican political problems inherent in increased direct exports of petroleum. In addition, the establishment of large generating capacity in areas in which the demand is now too low to justify such investment would provide the initial step in adding to the economic development of those regions. As domestic Mexican demand developed, the generating capacity would be available. Identical arrangements have been made previously with Canada, and indeed, similar arrangements are made between neighboring electric utilities in the United States. Therefore, it seems plausible that the U.S. government would enter into negotiations with the Mexican government for arrangements that would clear the way for new electric utilities with the Mexican Federal Electric Commission.

**Conclusion**

Have no delusions about the difficulty of carrying out what has been suggested in this chapter. The odds for success are less than even. It may not be possible to change attitudes within the U.S. government, and given such a change, the Mexican government possibly would see it as hypocrisy rather than a true change of heart. Even with Mexican acceptance, the influence of the political Left could prevent the reaching of agreement. Finally, domestic political pressures in the United States could preclude the offering of the necessary quid pro quo.

None of these reasons is sufficient for not making the attempt, however. For Mexico, the resolution of outstanding major issues with the United States would be immensely helpful in its use of the oil wealth as a basis for the economic transformation of the country. For the United States, the potential benefits of the approach suggested in this chapter are so great that it deserves the highest priority and emphasis in the government. Not only would the great dangers of dependence on Eastern-Hemisphere oil be lessened but also there would be more room for maneuver in the U.S. transformation of its own energy economy. Failure to even try to induce Mexico to increase its oil exports would truly be folly. If the attempt fails, so be it, but at least the opportunity would not have gone by default.

**Notes**

1. I do not mean to imply that the organizers of this conference had this in mind. I am confident that the implication was wholly inadvertent.

2. World Energy Conference, *World Energy Resources: 1985-2000* (New York: IPC Science and Technology Press, 1975), p. 66.

3. *Geothermal Energy Prospects for the Next 50 Years*, Electric Power Research Institute, EPRI Document, ER-611-SR, February 1978, pp. 2-5.

4. *Journal of Commerce*, 14 December 1977, p. 32.

5. *Journal of Commerce*, 26 September 1979, p. 7-A.

6. Agreement has finally been reached in the matter of gas exports and projects involving the export of electricity to California and Texas.

7. It may be argued that the maintenance of a high level of U.S. oil imports by importing from Mexico rather than from other countries does nothing whatever to alleviate the problem. To be sure, a reduction in oil imports reduces the trade deficit, pressure on the dollar, and so forth, and because of this it is obviously to be desired. But this desire overlooks the fact that the paramount danger to the United States in the present import situation is the threat to national security. Serious as the economic problems of inflation, limited maneuverability in monetary policy, and the like may be, they cannot compare with the consequences of a major supply interruption. The OPEC embargo and the Iranian Revolution have demonstrated the reality of this danger. Mexico is not Arab and its oil-export policy is therefore not automatically involved in Israeli-Arab relations, nor does it have a despotic government totally out of touch with the people that would make Mexico susceptible to the political and social disintegration that occurred in Iran. Beyond this, from the purely military viewpoint, the problem exists of the vulnerability of long supply routes from the Persian Gulf and Africa. Every barrel of oil from Mexico that substitutes for a barrel imported from the Eastern Hemisphere must therefore be preferable in the interest of the United States.

# 8

# Impact of Alternatives to Petroleum on U.S.-Mexican Relations

*Lawrence Goldmuntz*

At what price should the United States export oil after 1990? Should the United States then become a member of OPEC? Perhaps it should follow Mexico's lead, charge the same price as OPEC, but leave the joining to others. While these questions are not high on the agenda of U.S.-policy experts, and while oil-exporting countries should not be overly concerned immediately, neither is this possibility pure fantasy.

Four major elements underlie this possible reversal of current U.S. policy. First, oil prices have increased by more than a factor of ten in current dollars in the last decade. Second, the huge U.S. economy was built on cheap fuel, but by 1990 two decades will have passed since oil prices increased sharply, and substantial adjustments to expensive fuel will have been achieved. Third, U.S. reserves of coal and shale exceed the fossil-fuel resources of any other country. Fourth, many conservation efforts and clean coal-burning technologies are economic even when oil sells for less than $20 per barrel, and synthetic fuels based on shale, additional conservation efforts, and some coal-conversion technologies become economic when oil prices are in the range of $20 to $30 per barrel.

## Growth of U.S. Energy Demand

Macroeconomic statistics concerning energy consumption, and the relationship of incremental energy demand to growth in the GNP, indicate that the U.S. economy has already reacted meaningfully to the increase in real energy prices that began in 1973. The overall annual U.S.-energy-consumption growth rate in the 1950-1973 period was 3.5 percent, and in the 1973-1978 period it was 0.9 percent for a decline in energy growth rate of 75 percent between the two periods. The annual average GNP growth rate declined approximately 45 percent over the same two periods. This implies that changes in the U.S. economy are occurring that have broken the 1940-1970 historical trend of the relationship between energy growth and GNP growth. Estimates are that the decline has been about one-third.

The decline in overall energy growth rate is particularly evident in the oil and gas sectors. Over these same two time periods, the rate of increase in the consumption of oil has declined from 4.2 to 1.6 percent, and the rate of increase in the consumption of gas has declined from 5.8 to −2.5 percent. In the case of oil, the decrease was due primarily to an average increase in real crude prices by a factor of four and in the case of gas (for which the price was fixed for much of this period) the decline was due primarily to supply shortages, which in turn increased the demand for oil.

Many estimates have been published on the energy future of the United States with some consensus now emerging that energy consumption will grow from 76 quads (37 million barrels per day of oil equivalent) in 1977 to approximately 100 quads by 1990 and to approximately 115 quads by 2000, assuming growth in the GNP of 3.2 percent during this period. These estimates of overall energy growth are supported by sectorial studies of energy demand for residential, commercial, industrial, transportation, and electrical requirements.

## Prospects for Supplying U.S. Energy

Less consensus exists as to how this energy demand will be supplied as between oil, coal, nuclear, gas, and solar sources or how this demand might be abated by additional conservation efforts. Imported oil is the balancing fuel for any supply shortfalls in coal, nuclear, gas, and solar or any failure in conservation.

Environmentalists have a predilection for renewable resources such as solar energy, and they include hydro and wood fuels in the definition of renewable resources. Nuclear advocates defend that source's low cost and good comparative historical safety record, even taking into account the accident at Three Mile Island. Senators from Appalachian coal states want their coal used, despite its high sulphur content, and senators from western coal regions want their states to be compensated for the economic and environmental impact of coal development on their constituents. All these special interests complicate the task of U.S.-energy planners.

A baseline scenario of U.S.-energy balances in 1990 has been developed by the Energy Information Administration of the U.S. Department of Energy (see table 8-1). Without any federal intervention oil imports would increase from 8.3 million barrels per day to 11.2 million barrels per day. However, the federal government has mandated some programs and is planning additional steps to reduce this projected import level. There are two generic types of programs, one dealing with the conservation of oil and gas and the other with the substitution of domestic resources such as coal and shale for oil and gas. Oil and gas are treated as equivalents because domestic demand for both are partially supplied by imports and because these two fuels can be used interchangeably in many sectors—home and commerical heating, industrial-process heat and steam, and the generation of electricity.

**Table 8-1**
**Base Case U.S. Energy Balances in 1990**

| Balances by Sector | 1977 | | 1990 | |
|---|---|---|---|---|
| | Quads | Million Barrels of Oil Equivalent | Quads | Million Barrels of Oil Equivalent |
| Demand | 76.3 | 36.9 | 101.2 | 48.5 |
| **Residential** | | | | |
| Oil | 3 | 1.5 | 2.6 | 1.3 |
| Natural gas | 5 | 2.4 | 5.4 | 2.6 |
| Electricity | 7.6 | 3.6 | 11.2 | 5.3 |
| Coal | a | a | a | a |
| Total | 15.7 | 7.5 | 19.2 | 9.2 |
| **Commercial** | | | | |
| Oil | 3.4 | 1.7 | 2.4 | 1.2 |
| Natural gas | 2.6 | 1.2 | 2.4 | 1.1 |
| Electricity | 6.3 | 3 | 10.4 | 4.9 |
| Coal | a | a | a | a |
| Total | 12.3 | 5.9 | 15.2 | 7.2 |
| **Industrial** | | | | |
| Oil | 6.9 | 3.4 | 10.2 | 5 |
| Natural gas | 8.5 | 4 | 10.7 | 5 |
| Electricity | 8.8 | 4.2 | 16.9 | 8 |
| Coal | 3.8 | 1.8 | 7.1 | 3.4 |
| Total | 28.1 | 23.4 | 44.9 | 21.4 |
| **Transportation** | | | | |
| Oil | 19.6 | 9.6 | 21.4 | 10.5 |
| Natural gas | 0.6 | 0.3 | 0.5 | 0.2 |
| Total | 20.2 | 9.9 | 21.9 | 10.7 |
| **Electricity[b]** | | | | |
| Oil | 4 | 2 | 5 | 2.5 |
| Natural gas | 3.3 | 1.6 | 0.5 | 0.2 |
| Coal | 10.3 | 4.9 | 20.2 | 9.5 |
| Nuclear | 2.7 | 1.3 | 9.4 | 4.4 |
| Other | 2.6 | 1.2 | 3.5 | 1.6 |
| Total | 22.8 | 11 | 38.6 | 18.2 |
| Supply | 76.3 | 36.9 | 101.2 | 48.5 |
| **Domestic** | | | | |
| Petroleum liquids | 19.8 | 9.7 | 17.9 | 8.6 |
| Natural gas | 19.5 | 9.2 | 17.4 | 8.2 |
| Coal | 15.9 | 7.5 | 29.4 | 13.9 |
| Nuclear | 2.7 | 1.3 | 9.4 | 4.4 |
| Other | 2.6 | 1.2 | 3.5 | 1.6 |
| Refinery gain | −0.4 | 0.3 | −0.3 | 0.5 |
| Stock change | −1.8 | −0.9 | − | — |
| Total | 58.3 | 28.3 | 77.3 | 37.2 |

**Table 8-1** *(continued)*

| | 1977 | | 1990 | |
|---|---|---|---|---|
| *Balances by Sector* | *Quads* | *Million Barrels of Oil Equivalent* | *Quads* | *Million Barrels of Oil Equivalent* |
| Imports/(Exports) | | | | |
| Oil | 18.2 | 8.8 | 24 | 11.3 |
| Natural gas | 1 | 0.5 | 2 | 0.9 |
| Coal | −1.4 | −0.7 | −2.1 | −1 |
| Other | 0.2 | 0.1 | — | — |
| Total | 18 | 8.7 | 23.9 | 11.2 |

Source: U.S., Senate, Committee on the Budget, *Synthetic Fuels*, 27 September 1979. 96th Congress.

[a]Less than 0.5 quads.

[b]Includes previous sector totals—that is, electric-generation losses are allocated to final consuming sectors.

Table 8-2 is a comparison of typical conservation options with coal- and shale-substitution programs. Two of many possible conservation opportunities are the conventional weatherizing of homes involving a $600 investment per home and resulting in a 20 percent saving in fuel, and the substitution of a gas-heat pump involving an incremental capital cost of $1,350 per home for present gas heaters and resulting in an additional 45 percent saving in fuel. Two of the many domestic fuel-substitution programs are (1) the use of advanced fluidized-bed-combustion techniques to burn coal cleanly for commercial and industrial-process steam and heat and (2) the extraction of synthetic fuel from shale in Colorado and Utah.

Modern fluidized-bed coal-combustion systems have a five-year payback period when utilized 50 percent of the time and when oil costs $1.75 per billion BTU more than coal. Of course the pay back is quicker if the capital plant is used more than 50 percent of the time, as it is in many process heat and steam applications. The price differential today in the United States between oil and coal is more than $2 per million BTU. If only 15 percent of the current demand for oil and gas in the commercial and industrial sector was replaced by modern coal-combustion systems, there would be a saving of 1.5 million barrels per day of oil equivalents. President Carter's program, announced 16 July 1979, contemplates a minimum 0.4 million barrels per day of synthetic fuel from shale, but federal leases that are already let could support production of 1.5 million barrels per day. This fuel can be produced to sell for $24 per barrel. A $24,000 investment is necessary to obtain a production capability of one barrel per day.

A comparison of the investment costs, the cost-per-barrel equivalent of oil or gas displaced, and the ratio of the investment cost to the annual reduction in the balance-of-trade deficit is displayed in table 8-2. The table shows that the investment-costs-per-barrel equivalent displaced is higher for

**Table 8-2**
**Comparison of U.S. Conservation and Production Options to Replace Imported Oil**

| Option | Million Barrels of Oil Equivalent | Investment costs | | | Decrease in Annual Balance-of-Trade Deficit ($23 per barrel; billion $) | Investment Cost / Annual Reduction in Balance-of-Trade Deficit |
| --- | --- | --- | --- | --- | --- | --- |
| | | Total (billion dollars) | Dollars per Barrel per Year Displaced | Dollar Costs per Barrel Displaced (20-year lifetime) | | |
| Conventional weatherizing | 0.7 | 44.7 | 174 | 9 | 5.87 | 7.6 |
| Gas-heat pump | 0.34 | 39 | 314 | 15.7 | 2.8 | 14 |
| Coal conversion (15 percent of present commercial and industrial stock) | 1.5 | 27 | 50 | 10.5 | 12.6 | 2.1 |
| Shale extraction | 0.4-1.5 | 9.6-36 | 65.7 | 24 | 3.36-12.6 | 2.8 |

Sources: Dennis L. O'Neal, *Energy and Cost Analysis of Residential Heating Systems*, Oak Ridge National Laboratory, July 1978; Cameron Engineers, *Overview of Synthetic Fuels Potential to 1990*, report prepared for Senate Budget Committee, 27 September 1979; and personal communication from Wormser Engineering, Middletown, Massachusetts during 1979.

the conservation of options than for the fuel-substitution options, and therefore, the ratio of investment cost to annual reduction in balance-of-trade deficit is also higher for the conservation possibilities than are the fuel-substitution options. However, the costs per barrel of fuel equivalents displaced tends to be lower for the conservation options as compared to the fuel-substitution possibilities. If U.S. policy is designed to reduce trade deficits at minimum investment costs, then fuel substitution would be emphasized. If U.S. policy is designed to displace oil and gas equivalents at the lowest cost over the lifetime (assumed to be twenty years) of the conservation or conversion program, then weatherizing and coal conversion would be preferable to gas-heat pumps and shale extraction. The major conclusion, however, that can be drawn from table 8-2 is that all described options are economically attractive at current world prices for oil and gas.

Various presidential and congressional conservation and oil- and gas-substitution suggestions are identified in table 8-3 along with new, clean coal-burning technologies applicable to the commercial and industrial sector. These programs are summarized in table 8-4 in order to avoid double counting and to compare the summary of oil- and gas-substitution programs with projected imports in 1990.

As can be seen from table 8-3, the president recommended a substantial initiative to produce synthetic fuels and decontrols to stimulate production of domestic crude. The Senate Budget Committee recommended stronger conservation programs than did the president. While neither the president nor the Senate Budget Committee recommended substantial coal conversion in the industrial and commercial sector, both recognized this potential in their supporting documentation. A coal-fired fluidized-bed combustor was recently dedicated for space heating at Georgetown University, and a 30-million-BTU-per-hour advanced fluidized-bed system is now scheduled for Lowell University in Massachusetts. The Power Plant and Industrial Fuel Use Act of 1978 permits the secretary of the Department of Energy to prohibit the construction of large industrial boilers that use oil or gas. Therefore, to assume that 60 percent of new industrial boilers will be coal fired is reasonable. This would eliminate 1.5 million barrels per day of oil equivalents. Also, because of the favorable economics associated with the current difference between oil and coal prices, to assume that 15 percent of current industrial and commercial boilers will be switched from oil and gas to coal is reasonable. This would also eliminate 1.5 million barrels per day of oil equivalents. Furthermore, the federal government is now considering tax credits for industrial and commercial coal installations, a phaseout of fuel pass-through charges, and a phasein of individual metering to stimulate commercial coal conversions.

When these programs are summed, as shown in table 8-4, and compared to projected oil imports, the indications are that oil and gas substitution

**Table 8-3**
**Oil- and Gas-Substitution Programs**
*(million barrels of energy per day)*

| Program | Present Consumption | President's Program, 16 July 1979 | Senate Budget Committee Report 27 September 1979 | | Other Possibilities |
|---|---|---|---|---|---|
| | | | *$20 per Barrel* | *$30 per Barrel* | |
| Conserve residential and commercial building energy | 6.8 (6.2 projected in 1990) | 0.5 | 2.9[a] | 4.1 | |
| Reconvert coal-capable utility boilers | | | | | |
| Accelerate replacement of oil- and gas-fired utility boilers | 3.6 | 0.7[a] | 0.19 | 0.43 | |
| Synthetic fuels | | 2.5[a] | | 1 | |
| Decontrol of domestic crude | | 1.5[a] | | | |
| Decontrol of heavy oil | | 0.5[a] | | | |
| Mass-transit and automobile efficiency | 5.2 | 0.25 | 0.61[a] | 0.71 | |
| Asphalt substitutes | | | 0.25[a] | 0.43 | |
| Prohibit oil and gas use in new industrial boilers | 2.6 (projected growth until 1990) | | | 0.8 | 1.5[a] |
| New coal-burning technology retrofit for commercial building and industrial heat and steam | 10.3 | | | | 1.5[a] |

Source: The White House, *Fact Sheet on the President's Import Reduction Program*, (Washington, D.C., 16 July 1979); U.S., Senate, Budget Committee, *Synthetic Fuels*, 27 September 1979. 96th Congress.
[a]Summed on table 8-4.

**Table 8-4**
**Summary of Oil- and Gas-Substitution Possibilities**

| Starred Summation | Projected Oil Imports, 1990 |
|---|---|
| 2.9 | |
| 0.75 | |
| 2.5 | |
| 1.5 | |
| 0.5 | |
| 0.61 | |
| 0.25 | |
| 1.5 | |
| 1.5 | |
| Total 12.0 | 11.2 |

exceeds projected oil imports in 1990. How realistic is this possibility? All the programs listed are economic at present oil and gas prices—with the probable exception of the production of some synthetic liquids derived from coal. The total incremental demand for coal for the coal-conversion and synthetic-fuel options is 300-400 million tons annually, depending on the proportion of synthetic fuel provided by coal as compared to shale and unconventional gas. Currently an excess coal-mining capacity of 100 million tons exists on top of a base production of 600 million tons. The additional 200-300 million tons annually required by 1990, the equivalent of 20-30 million tons a year of incremental production, seems achievable. The Colorado Department of National Resources has concluded that enough water is available in the Upper Colorado River Basin for production of 1.5 million barrels per day of synthetic fuels with no displacement of agriculture and no preferences in court decisions on water allocation for synthetic fuels. With some preferences on water allocation, oil-shale production could reach 2-3 million barrels per day.

Not all oil- and gas-displacement possibilities have been considered, however. For example, General Motors intends to produce an electrically powered car by 1985. Their new nickel-zinc battery provides a car with a range of 100 miles. This range, in combination with the 300-deep discharge cycles, permits the battery to go a total of 30,000 miles before being replaced. Additional improvements also are expected. Operating costs are lower than conventionally powered cars, but overall costs reflecting the capital cost of the battery are 20 percent higher. However, electrically powered service vans that operate a greater percentage of time seem to be economic today. The U.S. Postal Service is now testing 1,000 electric vehicles. They have found the total amortized cost of 352 electrified jeeps to be slightly less than the amortized cost of gasoline-powered jeeps. They expect to be able to replace one-third of the postal-service-owned fleet of

100,000 vehicles with battery-operated vehicles. The Bell System and General Telephone Electronics are planning comparable programs. Congress is reviewing legislation that would provide substantial incentives to the automobile industry to produce electric vehicles. As another example, the National Aeronautical and Space Administration is developing the testing of new multiblade propellers driven by turbine engines. They are expected to improve aircraft-fuel economy by up to 45 percent as compared to the ducted fans used today.

**Conclusions**

This chapter has hypothesized what may have appeared at the beginning as fantasy. Yet the data that have been presented suggest that this scenario is at least plausible and perhaps realistic. We tend in energy policy, as well as in other policies, to be overly impressed with the experience of the moment at the risk of overlooking the longer-term evolution of structural developments. The fact is that the various components of U.S. society—industry, consumer, commerce, and government—have, each in its own fashion, adjusted and are continuing to adjust to high energy prices. This continued path of adjustment can reasonably lead by 1990 to the condition I have suggested in this chapter, in which the U.S. becomes an energy exporter.

The investment necessary to conserve or substitute domestic resources for imported energy is very large, in the hundreds of billions of dollars. Once made, however, a reasonable expectation is that these investments will be protected against lower energy and gas prices. For example, price guarantees are now being considered by Congress to stimulate synthetic-fuel production. Restriction of imports is unavoidable if traditional suppliers of oil and gas cut prices to regain markets, a realistic prospect because of the substantial spread between the price and the production cost of the world's oil and gas resources. Clearly, such a development would have considerable impact on U.S. relationships with other countries from which it imports energy and consequently on the very structure of international-energy trade. It would have an important influence on U.S.-Mexican commercial relationships and in the way these relationships are perceived and expected to evolve. While this chapter has not developed fully the implications of such events, clearly not only is the described evolution technically and economically feasible but also, and perhaps more important, it is politically attractive in the United States.

# Mexican Economic Development and the United States

*Clark W. Reynolds*

The discovery of large petroleum reserves in Mexico has awakened interest on the part of most countries in prospective relations with Mexico, and the United States is no exception as this book illustrates. However, unlike most other countries, the United States and Mexico are joined by a common history and a common border—neither of which is fully perceived in terms of implications for the future, large oil reserves notwithstanding. Indeed, the actual and prospective influx of large petroleum revenues into Mexico gives it a sense of increased freedom and power, vis-à-vis the United States, especially with regard to capital requirements.

Foreign investment, trade, and migration are the three key links that have increasingly bound the two countries together. With these links has come the vulnerability of each country to the political and economic stability of the other, but whereas in the past the main direction of vulnerability has been from north to south, in the future the direction of casuality is likely to shift. The very magnitude of petroleum rents, which already amount to a sizable fraction of a $10-billion value of gross international sales, has made rapid growth an even more-viable option for Mexico, but perhaps paradoxically that very growth process may substantially increase the interdependence of the two economies, even if oil rents reduce Mexico's dependence on foreign borrowing.

In order to put in perspective the magnitude of Mexico's intended growth between now and 2000, this chapter begins with a thumbnail sketch of the economic development of the U.S. Southwest since the beginning of World War II. The reason is that Mexico plans to grow from a GNP of approximately $80 billion in 1980 to a GNP four times that large, or $320 billion, by the year 2000. Today, the GNP of California, with a population of 23 million, is around $300 billion. What Mexico proposes to accomplish in only twenty years took California, today the world's seventh-largest "economy," thirty years to achieve.

Mexico's advantage is oil and a burgeoning labor force. However, both advantages contain serious pitfalls since the rents from oil can swamp diversified growth if not channeled into productive investments perceived by the population at large to be socially as well as economically efficient. Also, soaring labor-force growth can place demands for job creation and distribution of income well ahead of growth of output.

**Implications of the U.S.-Southwest Experience
for Mexico**

Before 1940 little manufacturing was being done in the Southwest. Tourism.
was a principal industry, along with mining and agriculture. These resource-
based industries depended heavily upon government expenditure on roads,
dams and irrigation systems, and government land grants to the railroads.
Large public-sector investments in infrastructure permitted the private accumulation of economic rent from land and natural resources, much of
which was deposited in regional financial institutions. California's banking
system, including the Bank of America, was built on the basis of income
from California's mining, fisheries, and irrigated agriculture. However,
before World War II few of these resource rents were recycled into regional
manufacturing. The Great Depression, which temporarily slowed southwestern development, is a partial explanation for the failure of the regional
economy to diversify. Perhaps more important, however, was the fact that
before the war the western market was not large enough to generate scale
economies sufficient to attract capital into regional manufacturing, while
eastern markets were too remote and external trade was limited.

With the advent of a world war in two theaters, a need was created to
establish continentwide supply lines for the U.S. military as well as to
enhance security by diversifying production away from the East and the
Midwest. This caused the federal government to provide massive support
for southwestern industrialization. Federal loans, guarantees, and procure-
ment were provided for the establishment of an integrated structure of
heavy, medium, and light industry. Between 1940 and 1944 approximately
$18 billion of government investment was poured into California alone.
Steel, cement, aluminum, and other heavy industries were established in the
region with the help of government programs.

In addition, the regional-university system received substantial state and
federal support for teaching and research, which helped to generate the
technology on which the subsequent aerospace, electronics, and light-
manufacturing booms were based. Before the war-induced period of intense
development of the Southwest, few barriers to trade, migration, or investment had existed between the western states and the rest of the United States
other than transport and location costs. Finance, technology, and population were permitted to flow freely in both directions. Yet interregional exchange was not enough to permit California to develop a diversified
economy. Not until the impetus of war did government and the private sector join forces in a common cause that created an industrial structure in a
matter of years that, under normal circumstances, might have taken generations. Yet without this relatively free trade on a continentwide basis, the initial system of government support would have been inadequate.

From a social and political perspective, the experience of the Southwest in the past forty years has little in common with the Mexican situation today. However, many similarities are evident from an economic viewpoint. The transformation of the Mexican economy, which is planned to quadruple in size in the next twenty years, will require an even more-massive investment of resources and skilled labor than took place in the U.S. Southwest from the 1940s to 1980. California's population was relatively well educated, but the economy's labor supply in 1940 was inadequate to meet the challenge of wartime development. Large numbers of workers were recruited from beyond its borders so that from 1940 to 1945 its labor force grew from 3.1 million to 3.9 million, a 26 percent gain in five years. Mexico today has over six times the labor force that California did in 1940. By the year 2000 it will have doubled again. Out-migration is therefore likely to continue for decades, even if Mexico's ambitious economic goals are achieved, while the country must increasingly draw upon external resources of skilled labor and management to balance the skill requirements of rapid growth, even given the rapid expansion of Mexico's educational and training programs.

What are some of the implications of the development experience of the U.S. Southwest for Mexico? In both cases resource rents were the basis of historical development. After a long history of mining for export, Mexico began its first petroleum boom at the turn of the century. By the end of World War I, it led the world in oil production. Scarcely affected by the Revolution that devasted agriculture and slowed production in much of the rest of the economy, the oil sector continued to produce at rising rates, but these rents accrued for the most part to foreign owners. Today new oil discoveries place Mexico again among the world's top nations in hydrocarbon reserves, and since the ownership of the reserves and the drilling and exploration rights shifted to the Mexican government in 1938, command over oil rents and the responsibility for their use has fallen squarely on the shoulders of the federal government.

Much speculation has occurred in this book about the level of Mexican reserves. Within any reasonable range, though, the potential for resource rents available to be channeled through the Mexican economy is almost unprecedented. At a 50 percent rental share of gross value of production, and at $30 per barrel, reserves of 60 billion barrels represent $900 billion in rents that could become available over the next few decades. Also, since Mexico's reserves are likely to be at least double that amount, even if recovery costs of the second $50 billion are much higher, the total amount of rents available to the Mexican government could well surpass $1 trillion or twelve-and-one-half times the current GNP.

The portion of this immense purchasing power spent on goods and services will have an initial multiplier effect on aggregate demand and the price level, at least until it leaks out into imports. To the extent that mineral-induced price increases provide incentives for investment in agriculture, manufacturing, and services, capacity will eventually expand but not without first causing severe inflationary pressures. Induced growth in capacity will eventually ease pressures on the price level. Because of a lag between the phases of oil-induced demand growth and expanded supply, the economy is likely to face continuing inflation that will grow with the expansion of oil production unless imports are allowed to flow freely to supplement domestic capacity. Even today, gross oil revenues amount to over $10 billion per year, much of which is injected into the spending stream.

In the U.S. Southwest the inflation that might have resulted from demand pressures of the World-War-II economy was repressed through wage and price controls. Free trade with the rest of the country (except for some rationing of basic commodities) also helped to diminish the regional inflationary impact of wartime growth, and expansion of the Southwest provided a stimulus for growth in the rest of the United States. In the case of Mexico's current situation, neither wage nor price controls are being employed, except in a limited way, nor is free trade being contemplated by policymakers who see continentwide free exchange as a threat to national industry, employment, and political autonomy. Yet rapid expansion of the Mexican economy could do more to expand continentwide trade, employment, and productivity than did the remarkable growth of the U.S. Southwest. Mexico could be North America's new frontier.

In addition to the problem of providing resources, skilled labor, intermediate goods, and technology during the time lag between increased oil exports and expanded growth capacity, another important aspect of the Mexican recycling problem exists. Beyond *economic* recycling of mineral rents into diversified manufacturing and agricultural production, there is growing recognition of the need for *social* recycling to shorten the lag between output growth and social welfare. Pressures are being applied on the government to use an increasing share of the oil surplus to improve the living conditions of the impoverished mass of the Mexican population, 40 percent of which receives less than 10 percent of national income. If economic recycling is difficult owing to the need for a high degree of cooperation between the private and public sectors, social recycling is even more problematic. Since the Cardenas administration (1934-1940), the government has become increasingly centralized, self-perpetuating, and out of touch with the rural poor or with urban workers whom its decisions crucially effect. Many spokesmen for the working class have become strongly antagonistic, not only to private-sector "capitalists" but also to the government itself, as the gap between revolutionary goals and social reality widens. However, much as this antagonism may be justified, it poses a severe problem for the joint achievement of economic and social recycling. Instead, a danger of conflict exists between the two uses of the oil surplus, and that danger grows daily.

Mexico's growth plans from 1980 to 2000 will require the kind of sustained big push, with strong government impetus and massive response from private investors, that it took a war to induce in the U.S. Southwest. In effect, Mexico must mobilize its economy as though for war. Today the economy has little excess capacity, and much of it is obsolete. Instead of being labor scarce, with freedom to import workers as needed as was California in the 1940s, Mexico is a labor-surplus economy in which at least 20 percent of its workers have at one time depended upon emigration for their livelihood. Instead of beginning with high levels of education, investment, social integration, and political participation, Mexico begins with a minimally educated work force, a majority of which is impoverished and effectively outside of the political process. This means that the component of petroleum rents used for social recycling must be increased, leaving a smaller share of the surplus for investment. It also means that much of the skilled labor, technology, and management needed to achieve a quadrupling of the economy will have to come from outside of Mexico, and much of Mexico's unskilled labor will have to find employment in the United States.

## Mexican Supply and U.S. Demand for Labor

Labor projections for the United States and Mexico have important implications for the future of both countries—implications that should be reflected in the migration policy of each.[1] Mexican-labor demand and supply projections were derived from output and productivity forecasts based on the government's economic growth and investment plans extended to the year 2000 and on historical trends in labor participation and demographic change. Similar labor demand and supply projections were made for the United States, reflecting modest rates of output and productivity growth and the lagged effect of decelerating population on the supply of labor.

The Mexican population is expected to grow from around 63 million in 1977 to 109 million in 2000, or at a decelerating rate averaging 2.4 percent per annum over the next twenty years, owing to expected continued declines in fertility rates. However, the demographic transition between now and the end of the century will not affect people already born who will be seeking employment over the next twenty years. Indeed, if fertility rates continue to decline, the already rising female-participation rate may be expected to increase still further, raising the rate of growth of job seekers even higher than the 3.5 percent annual rate of growth in these projections. Even at that rate Mexico's labor force is expected to grow from 19 million people in 1980 to over 40 million people by the end of the century. For a country to absorb a doubling of its labor force in only twenty years is unprecedented. For instance, many European countries in the period between 1850 and 1920 were only able to cope with a much-slower rate of population growth by "exporting" up to one-third of their additional workers. Even with all its advances in technology and remarkable growth, Sweden was unable to affect a transformation of agriculture or a rate of industrialization capable of employing more than two-thirds of its increase in population during that period. Mexico now faces a much-greater challenge, attempting to do within its own boundaries and with temporary migration what other countries have only been able to accomplish with a significant amount of permanent emigration.

According to the World Bank's *1979 World Development Report*, Mexican agriculture employed about 7 million workers in 1977. The number of job seekers coming out of agriculture will amount to at least another 7 million workers by the year 2000. By way of comparison this increase will be more than twice the total agricultural employment of the United States in 1977 (about 3 million). At a current capital cost of $20,000 per additional job created in Mexico, $140 billion of new investment will be required to absorb 7 million additional workers. This amounts to the total surplus from the export of 9 billion barrels of oil over the next twenty years. At a profit of $15 per barrel of oil, exports of 1.23 million barrels per day would be required just to cover the capital costs of job creation for new workers from the rural sector. This figure does not include the additional investment needed to absorb 13 million more workers from nonagricultural households. Demands will be placed upon oil rents for the purpose of education, training, and other forms of social recycling.

In short, the government's present petroleum plan, the limitations of which seem realistic in terms of Mexico's need to achieve financial stability and diversified economic growth, will not be able to provide the resources needed for effective absorption of Mexico's rural job seekers unless the capital intensity of nonagricultural production is drastically reduced, which would tend to slow productivity growth, and unless new labor-using technologies are introduced into agriculture. Whether Mexico's increasingly educated rural youth will be content to remain on the farm or in labor-intensive local industry, even with rising wages, remains to be seen. Even in China, force had to be used to slow the rate of urban migration. Emigration to the United States, at least on a temporary basis, will probably have to increase significantly if the government's goals of full employment and improved living levels for all are to be achieved. Oil alone cannot solve these problems.

The problem of labor absorption in Mexico also has implications for its functional distribution of income over the next twenty years. The share of net national income representing wages and salaries is currently about 43 percent in Mexico compared to 80 percent in the United States. Given the ten-to-one wage disparity between the two countries, this enormous gap will have to be narrowed if political stability is to continue between Mexico and the United States. Will it be possible to raise the labor share of Mexican income from 43 percent to even 60 or 70 percent in twenty years? The United States took a century to reach its present wage-profit distribution, even after starting from a much-higher wage share and only after passing through crises, including two world wars, that fundamentally changed the social and institutional fabric of the country and increased the bargaining power of labor.

Mexico has given itself twenty years to carry out a more-difficult redistribution task than the one that took the United States one hundred years to do, and it is relying presumably on changes in the wage bill to accomplish this task. Increased employment, it is argued, is the key to effecting a massive redistribution of income. While I would agree that increased employment is crucial to any major social-distribution scheme in Mexico, wage increases alone will not be sufficient to accomplish a major rise in the labor share of national income if the labor supply doubles and even if output quadruples. What will be required is a much-greater participation of workers in the income from capital and resources. But how might a rising share of profits and rents be channeled to the working class without upsetting the present system of asset ownership?

We have seen that from the rural sector alone Mexico will have to absorb an additional 7 million workers between 1980 and 2000, while 13 million more job seekers will come from Mexico's cities and towns. Our demand projections are based upon the labor requirements for compound real rates of growth of GNP of between 4 and 7 percent. These projections indicate that the demand for labor in the year 2000 will range from 30 million (at a 4 percent rate of GNP growth) to 41.5 million (at an annually compounded 7 percent growth). If output were to grow at a 6.6 percent rate over the next twenty years, demand for labor would just equal projected supply. In other words, only under extremely optimistic projections will Mexico be able even to keep pace with the growth of its labor force, much less absorb those employed all or part of the year in the United States and an estimated 8 million underemployed in Mexico. Given these facts, a rate of growth of output as high as 7 to 8 percent betwen now and the end of the century will still leave over 12 million Mexican workers underemployed or forced to migrate even under the best of circumstances. Also, even though relative wage gaps begin to narrow between the two countries, absolute wage differentials will widen for many years so that incentives for migration based on absolute-income differentials will remain.

Reverse migration may be expected for those people with higher skills, as Mexican wages (after taxes) surpass U.S. levels, just as they already have for managers and professionals in Brazil. Our research indicates some degree of symmetry between the projections of Mexico's labor surplus and future U.S. shortages. The demand for labor in the United States is likely to surpass supply since:

There is compelling evidence that the aging demographic structure of the United States will lead to an increasing shortfall of labor to fill low-skilled jobs.'' The demand for migrants to fill the gap will rise from 3 to 9 million workers between 1980 and 1985 and may be as high as 15 to 30 million workers by the year 2000, if the U.S. GNP is to continue to grow at past rates of 3 percent or better, unless one of two circumstances occurs: (1) Either a massive increase in participation rates will have to occur or (2) much-accelerated investment and productivity growth coupled with a much-higher rate of savings than has obtained in recent decades.

In short, an almost certain need exists for migrant labor in the United States, if it is simply to maintain its position in the international economy. That migration may not have to come from its neighbor to the south, but given the likelihood of a sustained surplus of unskilled labor in Mexico, even by its highest likely growth projections, taking the fullest possible advantage of its petroleum resources, and owing to the geopolitical and security interrelationships of the two nations, migration from Mexico would seem in the greatest mutual interest.[2]

Since the United States is currently in a recession, our 3 percent GNP growth projection between 1980 and 2000 may seem high. In addition to the current economic downswing, many Americans advocate policies of slower growth in the United States leading to a corresponding reduction in its share of world resources. Clearly, no growth in output would mean no increased demand for labor. However, that such a strategy is socially or politically acceptable either at home or abroad is unlikely since U.S. trading partners depend on their own growth on exports to the United States.

## Proposal for Increasing the Participation of Mexican Workers in the Distribution of Income

We have seen that the impact on the United States of Mexican economic development is as likely to arise from social as from economic factors. Population and labor-force growth accentuate the need to pursue policies that will narrow the income gap between rich and poor within Mexico and between workers with the same qualifications north and south of the border. We have also seen that continued growth of the U.S. economy will require an even-closer connection with Mexico than has existed in the past. The oil boom provides a means for Mexico to pursue greater economic interdependence yet with increased national autonomy, but it will not be an easy process. Within Mexico, the large and growing inequalities in distribution of income, wealth, and power threaten the stability of government, the security of enterprise, and the incentives to invest on which growth depends. Hence, even though this is a matter for Mexicans and for those foreigners whose businesses fall under Mexican law, a list of a number of conditions on which successful interdependence between Mexico and the United States may well depend seems appropriate:

1.   Employment of a large and growing share of the population in occupations that are productive, remunerative, stable, and that offer opportunities for advancement;
2.   Provision of workers with a sense of participation not only in the wage bill but also in the returns to capital and natural resources (including land and mineral-resource rents);
3.   Greater access to decision making in both political and economic matters across regions and social classes so that workers in Mexico have a growing sense that they are helping to shape the destiny of their nation;
4.   Adaptation of the pattern of production and consumption to the tastes of the Mexican population at large, with an attempt to maximize the Mexican character of economic and social life and not to simply reproduce the patterns of demand and values of other developed countries (particularly the United States);
5.   Achievement of a vigorous competitive system of production leading to every-greater levels of efficiency so that Mexico will become a competitive participant in the international market (and particularly in the growing market of the Third World).

The first positive steps in the direction of the Alliance for Production might be set in this larger framework of basic requirements for economic democracy that must accompany economic growth, if the latter is to take place in an atmosphere of continued social and political stability and increased political democracy.[3]

Some people would argue that the five objectives listed here could only take place after a radical transformation of the entire system of business and politics in Mexico. The government and business communities are challenged to demonstrate, at least in the Mexican case in which output is planned to quadruple in two decades and large surpluses from petroleum and natural gas will be available, that evolution toward economic democracy can in fact occur, facilitating greater political democracy as well. While the possibility always exists that such an evolution would meet overwhelming obstacles, and while an increasing number of Mexico's educated elite might feel that the internal contradictions of capitalism make such a road impossible, the very fact that cooperating enterprises are now moving forward with a program for the production of low-cost basic products for the working class, reflecting some aspects of points 4 and 5, is a sign that these critics might well be wrong. The rest of the chapter makes suggestions for what might be done in addition to the present program, as part of a medium- and long-range strategy of cooperation between the private and public sector, in the interests of full economic democracy, with the primary focus on point 2.

One of the most-important aspects of broader participation of workers, and especially the poorest workers (including the unemployed and underemployed), in the future growth of Mexico is to receive a share of the returns to capital. If the economy is to quadruple in twenty years, then the capital stock will increase several times over. This means that the wealth of the country, expressed in terms of productive assets (leaving aside that portion of wealth expressed as "human capital" or worker productivity), must increase proportionately in real terms. A tremendous opportunity exists for a dynamic redirection of wealth in favor of the working class, and especially the lowest-income households. However, such a redirection is not going to occur unaided through the normal flow of market forces. Instead, with such a large supply of underemployed and impoverished labor as Mexico possesses, and with a certain doubling of the labor force over the next twenty years, normal market forces may bring about a modest improvement in real wages of higher-skilled workers, but the unskilled are likely to face a holding action at best in terms of wage levels (expressed in real purchasing power) in the absence of subsidies. Also, Mexico's wage share of national income, which remains among the world's lowest, is unlikely to significantly increase without a major new approach to the distribution of profits and rents. The benefits that do occur through the labor market will favor middle- and upper-income groups that already constitute a "labor elite." Political pressures from the poorest workers in urban slums and subsistence agriculture will grow, calling for a larger piece of the action. Vociferous critics of the system, many of them from the middle class and the intellectual elite, will demand drastic change in ownership of the means of production "on behalf of the impoverished and disenfranchised poor." The growing number of university-educated youth will be looking for jobs as managers in the economic system and as political operatives.

The proposal here is that this problem be anticipated and that a program be considered to provide *all* workers with growing participation in the capital stock of Mexico. This could be done in the following manner, subject to elaboration by people more familiar with the institutions and political-economic realities of Mexico. A "workers'-bond" program could be devised in which a capital fund would be established in the name of the working class. All workers would receive bonds as participants in the fund, in proportion to a combination of factors that would be determined to give "labor points." The points would be based on labor time and intensity of work effort rather than on earnings per se.[4]

One of the main criticisms of capitalism made by proponents of the labor theory of value is that under capitalism, workers are rewarded not in terms of effort but in terms of arbitrary patterns of demand and natural-skill endowments, so that great artists yet unaccepted by the public die in poverty, and manual laborers in labor-surplus economies live wretched lives, while those born to privilege or who are capable of meeting the public's arbitrary tastes earn millions. The workers'-bond program would begin to address this criticism by providing workers with capital assets in terms of their labor efforts rather than in terms of the market value of their skills. These bonds would be redeemable by the recipient primarily for other forms of accumulation such as housing, education, purchases of durable consumer goods, tools, small-business investment, and the like. The bonds also could be redeemed for cash in case of emergencies such as sudden loss of job, health problems, and for other purposes to be determined, but not for current consumption unless absolutely necessary. Hence, the bonds would represent a growing labor participation in the capital stock of Mexico.

How would the program be financed? At the outset the fund could receive a share of returns from petroleum as the primary source of funds. All workers would participate as asset holders. The fund would grow as the financial assets were invested by trustees including labor, management, and regional representatives in new, economically productive activities. The fund would be available as a source of financial capital to private, public, and mixed enterprise and could be used to leverage equity capital. Since the fund would provide financial resources for investments in Mexico's future development, it would be appropriate to have representatives of the workers of Mexico sit on boards of directors of those enterprises drawing on the fund. In addition, as enterprises developed they would be encouraged to allow the fund to participate in the expansion of their capital. This could be favored by fiscal incentives such as tax advantages for those enterprises that set aside retained earnings for the workers' fund and by financial incentives such as lower reserve requirements for financial institutions that allocate reserves for increased participation in the workers' fund as part of loan packages.

One of the most-fundamental needs is for the decentralization of decision making in the development process, and especially for greater fiscal and financial leverage for local communities (*municipios*) that are currently severely constrained by their miniscule tax base. (The base is often not miniscule, but the majority of revenues collected are channeled to the federal and state governments.) The workers'-bond program could help to alleviate this problem in the following manner.

A share of the assets represented by the workers'-bond fund could be allocated to local communities on the basis of labor points from that locality, rather than on the value of past production of the region. Committees could be established comprised of representatives of all sectors of the community to determine the use of those funds for local development. While certainly some of the funds would be used for infrastructure and public works that might not be immediately productive in economic terms, it would give greater dignity and self-determination to local areas of Mexico and a greater sense of participation in the nation's progress, even if some of the funds were used for public plazas, libraries, baseball stadiums, parks, or other such facilities. Of course, the majority of the funds would go into productive investments, and at any rate, only a share would be decentralized.

The same local communities could determine the basis for local-labor participation in the program, and they could administer the allocation of bonds accordingly, following general guidelines established in cooperation with the federal government. In the past, national governments such as that of Cárdenas established wide popular base and immense credibility by offering assets to the rural workers in the form of land. Cárdenas also nationalized the oil industry by indirectly promising all Mexicans a share in that part of the "national patrimony." Mexico's patrimony of the future will be the growing capital stock, technology, and skills. The government could establish a new era of credibility even greater than that of Cárdenas by offering to the workers a share in the capital stock. The advantage of this approach is that broadened participation by workers in the national patrimony can occur without transferring assets to the state and without the inequities that arise when the assets of given enterprises with different profitabilities and productivity are shared only with the workers of the same enterprises. Such an approach tends to perpetuate and even exacerbate conditions favoring the labor elite and does little or nothing for the poorest households.

Since accumulation of labor points would depend upon some form of gainful employment, to be fully equitable the program requires attention to point 1 in the previous list. Full-employment policies are essential and represent a major challenge to the Mexican community. In the case of the U.S. Great Depression of the 1930s President Roosevelt had to provide massive employment programs in which all people willing to work could find a job for a few dollars a day. While many of those jobs were of dubious productivity in a strict economic sense, they helped to restore the dignity of U.S. workers. The underemployed and unemployed in Mexico must be given such an option. To keep this policy from being unduly inflationary will be a major challenge. But the gradual "trickle down" approach to job creation that is presently being pursued will be far more costly in terms of inflation and inefficiency than one in which specific activities are focused upon, clearing houses are formed for the underemployed, and workers are being helped to find and keep jobs by joint efforts of business and government.

A tight labor market is the only way that a turning point in real wages of unskilled labor can be achieved. It is the only way that the wage share of national income can increase, insuring a broadened market for the basic products to be produced under the Alliance for Production. Over time, as real wages rise, and as workers become holders of assets through the workers'-bond program, business must be prepared to adopt labor-saving technology. This will help to achieve the goals of point 5—that is, increased efficiency and competitiveness of production. Basic products should eventually cost less than similar goods in the international market, as firms involved in their production benefit from economies of scale and learning by doing. To convince workers that these goods are in fact beneficial will be difficult until their price is competitive with similar goods produced in other countries such as Korea, Taiwan, and Japan, where wages are rising above Mexican levels for unskilled labor but where higher labor productivity continues to offset wage increases.

Businesses cooperating in the Alliance for Production might invite students, faculty, and graduates from Mexico's major universities to participate in the program through:

Market research;

Establishment of distribution channels in working-class areas;

Investigation of new products and technologies appropriate to the production of basic products;

Monitoring of the program of basic-goods production to determine the realistic costs of production, distribution, and returns to labor and capital under the program;

Establishment of credit programs for working-class areas;

Task forces to work on the regional decentralization of marketing of basic products;

Task forces for the establishment of cottage industries and cooperatives to produce basic products or their components;

Studies of working-class households, communities, and their behavior patterns as they relate to the practical needs of the program;

Studies of the feasibility of decentralization of political and economic decision making to the community level.

Implementation of the basic-products program and adoption of a medium-run strategy to establish a workers'-bond program would provide

multiple opportunities for socially oriented university students and graduates of secondary and professional schools to be involved in practical measures to achieve greater economic democracy. Business, government, labor,
and educational institutions could work together for this common goal.

## Conclusions

The United States stands to gain from successful development in Mexico
just as it has from the growth of its own Southwest, and it would lose as
much from a Mexican failure as it would have through a failure of the
sunbelt economy to prosper during and after World War II. It is no longer
possible to live behind a political-economic curtain, whether it be iron,
bamboo, or tortilla, however stressful may be the international relations of
global interdependence.

Given the huge surplus unlocked from Mexico's hydrocarbon reserves
and the profits accruing to Mexican investment, its problem is seen to be
that of recycling part of that surplus for both economic growth and social
participation. Even the immense petroleum rents likely to accrue over the
next twenty years will not begin to resolve Mexico's social problem without
major changes in the distribution of wealth plus sustained migration of unskilled labor to the United States. These factors must be accompanied by
greatly increased trade and large-scale inflows of skilled labor, management, entrepreneurship, and technology.

A proposal is made for the establishment of a workers'-bond program
as a joint effort of business, labor, and government that could provide all
Mexican workers with a growing share in the increments to national wealth.
While the specifics of such a program must be worked out by those involved, I am convinced that only a program of this magnitude can provide
the framework within which social demands will be consistent with political
stability and sustained economic progress. Since those goals are essential for
continued U.S. prosperity and national security, its role is to provide the external dimensions of policy space within which Mexico may forge its own
destiny.

## Notes

1. The material for this section is taken primarily from Clark
Reynolds, "Labor Market Projections for the United States and Mexico
and Current Migration Controversies," *Food Research Institute Studies* 17,
no. 2 (1979-1980).

2. Reynolds, "Labor Market Projections," p. 31. Reprinted with permission.

3. The Alliance for Production program was begun by President López Portillo as an effort to bring business and government together after their relationship was stressed during the previous administration of Luís Escheverría (1970-1976).

4. This "workers'-bond" idea is still in its preliminary stage and should not be advanced as a cure-all before its equilibrium implications for savings and investment are worked out more fully in a future paper.

# Comments

## Thomas Blau

Several of the previous chapters have assumed that oil in the ground is worth more than extracted oil. They have also assumed that the world price for oil will exceed the rate of inflation, and therefore, the prudent strategy for oil producers is to minimize production in the near future in favor of the far-off future. Oil reserves already discovered are assumed, in this view, to be almost the last of a dwindling and irreplaceable substance. As for the oil consumers such as the United States, many participants have assumed that little can be done to increase oil imports, except to importune producer countries more. This view sees consumers as having little to offer producers in exchange.

## Commentary on Chapters 7 and 8

### Conservation versus Production

These assumptions were undisturbed until the presentation of the chapters in this section. Dr. Netschert has indicated to both Americans and Mexicans the range of opportunities in the creative development of the bilateral relationship. Dr. Goldmuntz has shown the range of opportunities for what could become antioil-import self-defense by the industrialized countries.

Indeed, conservation by oil producers may well not be revenue maximizing. To the extent that oil producers withhold supplies and thereby succeed in boosting price, they force the industrial nations to speed the development of renewable and very long-term sources such as synthetic fuels. The result is that industrial countries make political and institutional, as well as economic, commitments to avoid oil purchases. Therefore, it is conceivable that oil-exporting countries may seriously damage the market for oil in a decade or so by withholding supplies, such that they may be left with considerable conserved oil at sharply reduced prices. At that point conservation may be easy. This potential scenario suggests that if the producers want to maximize revenues in the long run, they should increase current production and not conserve as much oil as at present.

### Benefits of Oil Revenues

Mexicans and Americans both tend to be unclear about the relationship between revenue maximization and benefits to the Mexican people. The

171

example of Iran may suggest, at first glance, that revenue maximization contributes to unrest and topples regimes. But Mexico is Catholic, not Islamic; Western, not Eastern; technically and socially sophisticated, not primitive; traditionally revolutionary in its ideals, not atavistic; secular in governance, not theocratic; with multiple centers of power and initiative, not just one, and with orderly succession of government, not cataclysmic. Finally, while the measured use of massive new revenues is a significant administrative problem for anybody, little reason exists to assume that Mexico would adopt the Iranian "policy" of squandering money on dreams of unneeded nuclear plants and advanced military equipment while the poor continue to hunger.

Perhaps the most-destabilizing choice of all would be for Mexico to choose the theoretical possibility of not absorbing revenues. People's expectations move fast. Governments may believe themselves immortal and may be largely indifferent to the choice of benefits soon or in the next century. Governments tend to plan using excessively low discount rates. People, however, do not.

It would not be easy to foresee that the Mexican government would follow this route and limit economic growth for the following major reasons:

Mexico has a historical growth ethic.

President López Portillo has been open and frank in public about the extent of the reserves.

The hopes of the Mexican poor have been raised, and the government would not choose to dash them openly.

Mexico has an extraordinary opportunity to create social justice effectively without forcing redistribution.

Mexico has considerable and extensive needs for infrastructure—for example, dams, harbors, and transportation—that can foster economic development and be financed by oil revenues.

**Conclusions**

It is not unreasonable, therefore, to see the U.S.-Mexican energy relationship as inherently complementary to the mutual benefit of both nations. Fundamentally, the United States needs oil and Mexico needs money and technology. Moreover, the extent of the underlying U.S.-Mexican common interest is broad in politics, economics, culture, and society. In fact, the large number of common interests makes possible the repeated attentions to our mutual sensitivities that take place in so many U.S.-Mexican discussions. Most relations are sensitive, especially between friends, neighbors, relatives, and economic partners, all of which characterize the United States and Mexico, especially but not only, in northern Mexico and the southwestern United States. Obviously we have a profound interest in each other's success. Given the extent of our interrelationship, neither the United States nor Mexico is likely to prosper if the other does not.

# Comments

*Robert E. Ebel*

## Observations on World Oil Supplies

From the previous chapters, two issues evidently warrant elaboration: the oil-reserve estimates and the scope of world energy relationships.

### Oil-Reserve Estimates

Dr. Grossling's Mexican-oil-reserve estimates were quoted on the front page of the *Phoenix Republic* on 14 December 1979. He said that Mexican-oil reserves are equal to reserves in the rest of the world combined. The newspaper reader has to come away with the impression that no oil shortage exists in the world, that plenty of oil is available, but that the valve is deliberately kept partially closed in order to keep prices high. However, the public must be educated to understand that one cannot operate automobiles, run factories, or make current operational policies on potential oil. Rather, one must refer to those amounts of oil reserves that are proved—that is, oil that can be produced under today's economic and technical constraints.

Proved petroleum reserves in Mexico in 1979 are placed at 40 billion barrels. In order to calculate an accurate figure for policy development, natural-gas reserves, which are thought to represent about one-third of the total, must be subtracted from this amount. This defines proved Mexican-crude-oil reserves at about 27 billion barrels. Next, divide by 20, which is the rule of thumb many experts use in trying to determine the life of an oil field. Divide further by 365 to ascertain what the daily production rates would be under these circumstances. If this statistical exercise is followed, the results equal the estimates of Sidney Leveson—3.75 million barrels per day. If Leveson's figure is accepted as a reasonable level of production, and if the amounts of oil Mexico might be consuming by 1984 or 1985 are deducted, the remainder then becomes an exportable surplus. Of this exportable surplus, 60 percent apparently will be available by Mexican policy for purchase by the United States. This available oil, in volume, would represent what the United States imported from Mexico in 1979 plus what it lost from Iran.

### Energy Relationships

The second issue arising from this section was the belated recognition that other countries in the world besides Mexico and the United States are interested in oil. Also belatedly apparent is that U.S. better interests would be served if it examined Mexican oil and its oil-supply problems outside of the very narrow context of U.S.-Mexican energy relationships. A more-realistic context would consider the background of current and anticipated events in the Middle East, North Africa, and China.

**China.** Not long ago a number of experts saw an alternative to dependence on Middle East oil in Chinese oil resources. These experts estimated that 8 million barrels per day would be produced in China by the year 1990. After examining the indigenous oil industry in China and applying some measurements to that industry and to the economy in general, the results indicate that China's oil-export capability would be of short duration. The maximum export capability that could be expected is approximately 1 million barrels per day. This level could possibly be sustained until the latter part of the 1980s. Thereafter, China could revert to being a net importer of oil.

The international oil companies involved in offshore-oil development in China in 1979 are only in the very first phase of oil-resource development— that is, the seismic-survey stage. These companies have gone to China because off China's shores lies one of the last large, but unknown, potential areas for oil in the world. This area is equal in size to that extending from Maine to the Florida Keys. Under the seismic-survey program, data will be gathered, evaluated, and handed over to the Chinese authorities at no cost. The next step toward oil development will be the offering by the Chinese of offshore blocks for competitive bidding. However, China likely will protect its own interest and keep those blocks in which oil is known to be present. Perhaps one-third of the remaining blocks will be offered for bidding. Once the blocks have been secured, the companies will initiate exploratory drilling, followed by developmental drilling, presuming oil is found. Given the time constraints prevalent in exploratory and developmental drilling, offshore oil in reasonable volumes might be expected to be flowing by 1985. Some of that oil will find its way into the onshore market, but most will be directed to the export market until demand for oil onshore catches up with supply.

China likely will find itself in the same vicious circle that most exporting countries eventually find themselves. Exports of oil are used to generate hard currency, and hard currency is used to pay for imported goods and services. Demand for these imports, however, is not easily satisfied, and historically it generates a still-greater demand for similar imports and, in turn, a greater demand for oil exports. A polarization develops in the country between those people who want to move the country ahead on the basis of oil-derived revenues, and those people who believe that Western influence is becoming too strong and that traditional values are being lost. The solution to these concerns is to be found in a cut in exports.

**Saudi Arabia.** An interesting scenario developed in 1979 in Saudi Arabia, the world's largest oil exporter. The polarization within the country was being led by the so-called "California Mafia," a term applied to people in policymaking positions in the Saudi Arabian government who completed their education at various California institutions of higher learning. These officials stand against further increases in oil exports and instead advocate a reduction in export levels. Estimates, in fact, indicate that the economy could function using the revenues generated by the production of 3.5 million barrels per day, which is some 6 million barrels per day less than the 9.5 million barrels per day that Saudi Arabia was producing in 1979. This latter figure is Saudi Arabia's limit, and at this rate the country no longer has unused producing capacity to fall back on when other countries in the Middle East seek higher prices for their oil. This point is important because Saudi Arabia has been a moderating influence in the past by suggesting that it would increase production if necessary in order to bring prices back to more-desirable levels. At this 1979 figure the economic and political tool is no longer available.

Future concerns for world oil developments must consider how much oil Mexico might be producing by the year 1984 or 1985. The possibility of political instability in Saudi Arabia necessitates this concern. The implications of a withdrawal, over a period of time, of 6 million barrels per day of oil from the world market is earthshattering.

**USSR.** The U.S. CIA reports that oil production in the USSR will peak in 1979 or 1980. In 1980 it should produce about 12 million barrels per day, but production should then decrease. No more large oil fields are available for production, and thus no more opportunities exist for immediate growth. What happens when demand continues to grow in the USSR, but production begins to decline? The CIA speculates that oil sales to the West will be withdrawn, but this alone would not provide sufficient oil supplies for the USSR. The next action for the USSR to take, speculates the CIA, would be a move into the Middle East and North Africa in search of oil that would increase its supply some 2 to 3 million barrels per day. This move would mean a withdrawal in oil supplies for the rest of the world of 4 to 5 million barrels per day, considering the needs of Eastern Europe in addition to the USSR. Can the marketplace adjust to a swing of 4 to 5 million barrels a day without serious disruption?

The CIA speculation may be incorrect. The USSR could reach a peak in oil production in 1980, but a plateau of production could result in the years that follow. Any sharp decline would be a very pessimistic forecast.

**Middle East.** Some countries in the Middle East do not need to continue to produce at current levels simply because the earnings are not needed.

Among those is the United Arab Emirates. In 1979, for example, the per capita income in Abu Dhabi from oil-derived revenues, using population calculations based on only the native-born people, is $180,000. The problem with this calculation for Abu Dhabi is that the native-born inhabitants are outnumbered by imported workers by a ratio of about 5 to 1. In Abu Dhabi and elsewhere in the Middle East, the overwhelming role that expatriate workers play signals a real danger. This issue is likely a great concern for the governments of Abu Dhabi, Dubai, Kuwait, Qatar, and Saudi Arabia.

Across the water in Iran, oil-consuming nations find that they have lost 2.5 to 3 million barrels per day of oil supplies. As long as Western technicians are denied access to the oil fields, those oil fields are going to suffer. Restoration to the 6-million-barrel-per-day level, even if the government wanted to do so, seems doubtful. For planning purposes, the 2.5 to 3 million barrels per day must be forgotten.

**Political-Risk Analysis**

The very recent emergence of Mexico as an oil exporter of international rank, and one whose ultimate potential is still being measured, will play prominently in the plans of the importing countries as they try to assemble oil-supply contracts for the coming years. Pressure will come from Japan, Brazil, Canada, France, Italy, and numerous other oil importers who will volunteer to buy Mexican oil. Mexico will probably attempt to diversify its customers, which would be in Mexico's political and economic interest. However, too many commitments for oil could place an unwanted burden on the oil industry that might exceed the normal economic and technical capacity to respond.

Political-risk analysis is something relatively new for many corporations. However, some corporations have begun to rely on the interaction of political-risk analysis and economic-risk analysis simultaneously. Indeed at times, political-risk analysis may override economic-risk analysis. The acceptance of this interactive analysis has been slow in coming. Management has not been quick to think in these terms because political risks cannot be quantified as can economic risks; it can be only subjective analysis. Yet a good track record and appropriately placed confidence has increased managements' acceptance of evaluation based on these techniques. In order to enhance this type of research, many international corporations will have to develop their own intelligence-gathering systems. There is no reason why any moderately sized transnational corporation cannot, on its own, develop commercial, economic, and political intelligence of reasonable scope and depth, which would allow management to make their decisions in confidence.

What would a political-risk analysis of Mexico reveal? Should corporations expand their efforts in Mexico, or should they think about other areas around the world? One issue that clouds this and other political-risk analysis is the Iranian syndrome that, if care is not taken, could easily obscure analysis. Whether "other" Irans are lurking out there is a lingering question. What was overlooked in Iran that might have alerted it to the coming overthrow? Why was it caught short, and what could it do to make sure overthrow does not happen again? Failures in the past have dervied from an inability in part to develop a sensitivity to the desires of the host country—the kind of sensitivity that cannot develop from Washington or Dallas or Houston but only from within the country itself.

A political-risk analysis of Mexico would discuss the issues of unemployment, underemployment, inflation, high birth rate, extremely young population, growing expectations, and concomitant frustrations. All of these issues together should be examined, not within the context of the Mexico in 1979 but rather in the context of what Mexico, under President López Portillo's successor, look like. By that time researchers will have a better understanding of what the future holds for Mexico's petroleum industry. Among other aspects, the ability of Mexico to use its oil revenues to create new jobs will be clearer.

## Conclusions

In sum, the real test of the viability of U.S.-Mexican relations will not come until after the 1982 Mexican presidential election. In the meantime, the insurance that the political risk of corporations and individuals is minimal depends on the character of the partnership that Mexico and the United States develops. This must be a partnership in which the interests of both parties can be satisfied. Mexico should be viewed as a supplier of oil, not wherein the United States demands a production level and a price but as a partner with whom to bargain in good faith.

At the same time both the U.S. government and business corporations must consider a wide range of issues in their planning. Possible instability in Saudi Arabia, the possible impact of Pan-Islam on the Middle East and North Africa, the role of Mexico, and the activities of the USSR all must be contemplated. The course of oil developments in China remains unclear. Perhaps more oil might be made available than now appears probable. These issues must be coped and dealt with interactively, not in isolation. Thus, Mexican petroleum and U.S.-Mexican energy relations must be considered within the context of probable events throughout the world.

# Discussion Summary

The chapters designed to elicit the U.S. perspective on U.S.-Mexican energy relations evidenced several themes that focused the discussion session. The first theme involved the U.S. search for alternative-energy sources to oil. The second theme referred to energy planning, and the third pertained to issues of immigration.

Wionczek opened the discussion by welcoming the presentation by Goldmuntz. His chapter indicated that the United States had the capacity to reduce its imports of oil and improve the domestic supplies through the use of coal and shale, among other sources. The compatibility of this view of U.S. supplies with the Mexican position is apparent if it is assumed that Mexico wishes to export oil only to the extent of its absorption capacity. "In fact," Wionczek continued, "there appears to be no conflict of interest between the industrial oil-importing countries and nonindustrial oil-exporting nations in this regard."

Goldmuntz responded that he was not convinced that his presentation was as optimistic as interpreted by Wionczek. The success of the United States in developing oil substitutes would depend on both government energy policy and the response by the public to adopting energy-saving measures. He expressed skepticism that the U.S. energy policy would reflect the tenacity necessary to make his calculations realistic. Although he admitted the unpredictable nature of the U.S. government and its citizenry made any speculation difficult.

Energy-planning issues emerged when Dr. Netschert objected to the suggestion that planning be based on proved reserves to the exclusion of potential reserves. "If that were done," he speculated, "the world oil industry would have been written off sixty years ago." In addition, he expressed confidence in the estimates of Dr. Grossling, which would indicate that the Mexican fields are probably the largest in the world. This geological research would imply, he concluded, that ". . . oil is not a resource problem, but [it is] a political problem."

Whether the problem is one of resources or politics, it was suggested that if energy planning does not become effective, a trade war might result, especially involving those countries that cannot substitute for oil supplies easily, like Japan. The question arose as to the possibility of countries attempting to isolate cheap oil supplies in the future. In this regard, Goldmuntz offered his projection that an international market may develop for alternative-energy resources such as coal that would serve to mitigate the possibilities of a trade war.

The final subject discussed in this session involved immigration issues. Rapp commented that "if mutual interests are the important basis for an agreement . . . immigration has been ignored.'' He speculated, on the one hand, that the avoidance of the topic in formal negotiations has probably occurred because the issue's direct linkage to oil is not politically feasible in either country. Reynolds, on the other hand, felt that although it has not been explicitly part of the negotiations, the relation of migration to employment is implicitly a vital issue for Mexico. Also, Mexican employment problems suggest that a massive transformation will likely occur that will involve the energy industry, and future studies may make apparent the advantage of the linkage of oil and migration issues in an explicit form. Dr. Netschert emphasized that this linkage cannot be avoided and that the simultaneous consideration of the issues may not be difficult if the initial reluctance of both countries to discuss the issues could be hurdled. In contrast, Puente Leyva commented that immigration was not an issue of negotiations. It is not a problem to be discussed, but rather it is a solution to both countries' problems. According to this perspective, he explained, Mexico has a surplus of laborers, and the United States has a demand for workers to undertake undesirable work. Given this mutually advantageous situation, he said, ''it is useless to have an agreement over a labor-force issue when it is not an issue.''

# Part IV
# The Changing Conditions of Mexico's External Relations: United States, Hemispheric, and Global

# 10 Oil and U.S. Policy toward Mexico

*Olga Pellicer de Brody*

A notable effect of the reappearance of Mexico in the block of oil-exporting countries is the amount of attention given to its relations with the United States. This effect is understandable. The accelerated growth of U.S. imports of crude oil, the difficulties in modifying the so-called American way of life based on the senseless waste of energy, the price rises of oil set by the OPEC countries, and the uncertainty of the world supply of oil created by the policies of the new Iranian government all contribute to the fact that energy is currently the major preoccupation of U.S. leaders. In such circumstances, indifference to the oil wealth south of the border is unthinkable. The search for a relationship with Mexico that will allow significant agreements on energy has become a priority objective of U.S. foreign policy. The modalities and characteristics of the overall outline of U.S.-Mexican relations and the factors, both international and domestic (in the United States and Mexico), that would act in favor of or against its implementation and maintenance are yet to be defined.

Thus, it is not surprising that so many journalistic efforts and major essays are dedicated to the analysis of the actual state and possible evolution of relations between Mexico and the United States. A few of these studies have emphasized the influence that oil has on assigning a new place to Mexico in the security plans of the United States.[1] American strategists also are concerned with Mexico's long-term economic and political stability and the delineation of more-intense and subtle intervention in future events south of the border. However, the majority of the studies transmits an optimistic vision of the effect petroleum will have on Mexico's economic development and its bargaining position with the United States. This last point has been the object of hasty commentaries. Keeping in mind the dimensions of the energy crisis and the inevitable desire of the United States to establish good relations with Mexico, some observers arrive at the conclusion that the United States will assume a more-flexible position in dealing with the most-urgent problems existing between the two countries—problems such as undocumented workers and commerce. Furthermore, these observers assume that the United States will seek a framework for U.S.-Mexican relations that will contribute to the resolution of Mexico's social problems. In other words, petroleum will give rise to a new situation in which it will be possible to overcome the opposition to Mexican interests that comes from certain well-defined sectors of U.S. society (producers that come into conflict with Mexican exports or strong opposition to the presence of foreign workers in the United States being the most conspicuous examples). Mexico will have, in oil, the instrument it needs to establish a "genuine interdependence" with the United States that would discredit the concept of the inevitability of conflict between a great capitalist power and an underdeveloped country that seeks to overcome its economic and social problems within a framework of late-developing capitalism.

If this were the case, U.S.-Mexican relations would be on the path to a better world. However, a brief review of the U.S. policy toward Mexico in the last few years gives the opposite impression. The negotiations that have taken place in the area of energy or in the treatment of commercial and migration problems reveals that structural motives exist in the United States that prevent a positive response to the demands and needs of Mexico. The U.S. policy toward Mexico is, and will continue to be, that of a superpower. Mexican petroleum will not likely change this situation.

**Agreements on Energy Matters
and Bargaining Power**

The subject of crude-oil exportations and its long-term volume and price has not yet been the object of official negotiations between Mexico and the United States. U.S. companies have bought increasing volumes of crude oil reaching approximately 400 million barrels a day in 1979, 80 percent of the total exports of PEMEX. In the coming years these purchases are expected to increase in absolute terms but decrease in relative terms as a result of the Mexican government's decision to diversify its market. The oil price follows the tendencies of OPEC—that is, it is slightly higher than the price of the same type of crude oil coming from the Middle East, but the low cost of transporting the oil makes the overall price very attractive to the United States.

U.S. leaders have been extremely cautious in formulating policy with respect to Mexican oil. We know that they consider it to be technically possible and highly desirable for Mexico to increase its production to 4.5 million barrels a day in 1985 and to double this amount in the 1990s in order to satisfy U.S. needs. Nevertheless, they are also aware of the enormous political obstacles to such an increase. On the one hand is the strength of sectors inside Mexico that are in favor of a conservationist policy, and on the other hand is the fear of the negative effects that a rapid increase in oil production would have on Mexico's economic stability and policies.[2]

The knowledge and assessment of these obstacles has permitted opposition to the people who press for a policy toward Mexico that would convert it into a producer the size of Saudi Arabia. Such a situation could be easily altered. A change in U.S. political leadership, the worsening of political conditions in the Middle East, or the failure of the attempt to lower consumption of energy in the United States could open the door to new tendencies. As was suggested in the introduction, in the next decade the U.S. government most probably will try to induce Mexico to increase its exports of crude oil and to assure its delivery to the United States. It is difficult to predict Mexico's reaction to this type of situation and the degree to which it could maintain its bargaining power so as to be able to decide autonomously the rhythm of growth of the country's oil industry. Be that as it may, this situation has not yet come to pass, and for now the most-interesting negotiations have occurred in the area of the sale of natural gas.

It would be beyond the scope of this chapter to go into detail about the negotiations for sale of gas that lasted more than two years, from August 1977, when the Mexican government announced its intentions of selling 2,000 million cubic feet of gas a day to the United States, to September 1979, when the governments of both countries agreed on the conditions for the sale of a moderate amount of gas—300 million cubic feet a day.[3] However, it is important to recall the various stages of the negotiations in order to detect just what, in this case, the conciliatory position of the United States was in relation to Mexican interests.

When Mexico announced the construction of the pipeline, which would transport large volumes of gas to the United States, many people thought that the price of gas would be based on the price of other types of energy that were similar in quality and caloric value to natural gas. Thus, the price of gas was to be fixed at a price equal to that of the so-called fuel oil number 2, or diesel, at its original price in New York harbor. Changes in the price of fuel oil number 2 would determine changes in the price of Mexican gas. If this arrangement had been approved, Mexico today (December 1979) would receive more than $5 per million cubic feet (mcf) of gas.

At the end of 1977, pressured by some members of the U.S. Congress and taking into account the impact Mexico's asking price would have on the price of domestic gas, and on the agreements for the purchase of gas with Canada, the U.S. Department of Energy firmly rejected the formula. Mexico then lost interest in exporting massive quantities of gas to the United States and initiated a program of internal utilization that would permit the domestic use of almost all of the gas associated with the production of crude oil predicted for 1982. Nevertheless, some excess still remained, and at the request of the United States, negotiations to export this excess began after President Carter's visit to Mexico in February 1979.

Among the various motives behind U.S. interest in reopening negotiations for the sale of gas were the pressure of public opinion, expressed in the country's most-important newspapers, against the Department of Energy's decision on the negotiations; the desire of the Carter administration to reach an agreement with Mexico that could be presented in the next election as a triumph of his foreign policy; and finally, the belief that an agreement on gas was an indispensible antecedent to a more-extensive energy relationship. The approval of the U.S. Energy Plan in late 1978 that provided for the lifting of internal price controls on natural gas was added to all these factors. This plan allowed for a considerable increase in the price of gas over the following fifteen years and thus weakened one of the arguments used in 1977 to oppose the price solicited by Mexico.

These conditions created an atmosphere favorable to the United States' taking a flexible position in relation to Mexico's demands. Nevertheless, U.S. negotiators firmly opposed Mexico's attempts to link the price of natural gas to that of other similar combustibles on the international market. At the end of August 1979, the U.S. press announced that Mexican representatives had proposed that the price of fuel oil number 6 (a low-quality residual combustible that the United States proposed as a point of reference) and of fuel oil number 2 be averaged. The resulting figure oscillated between $3.60 and $4.18 per mcf.[4] Fearful of the effect that such a price would have on the gas agreements with Canada that were to be renegotiated in October, the United States did not accept the proposal. However, they urged that a search be made to find a "reasonable" price that would allow them to reach an agreement before the Carter-López Portillo meeting that was to take place in Washington in September. Finally, a few days before the meeting, an agreement on the sale of gas was announced.

From the Mexican perspective, that agreement included the following favorable provisions: a reduction in the sale of gas to 300 mcf per day, the linking of the base price of gas to the changes in the price of crude oil on the world market, and the inclusion of a clause that would permit Mexico to eventually renegotiate the agreement under more-satisfactory conditions. These achievements, however, do not hide the fact that, in arriving at a base price, Mexico gave in significantly. The price was fixed at $2.65 per mcf, a negotiated price that was not explicitly linked to other energy prices on the international maket. Nevertheless, it corresponded in general terms to fuel oil number 6, a combustible that most experts do not consider equal in quality or ease of transport to natural gas.[5]

Multiple explanations exist for the Mexican concessions. They range from the current conditions of international-energy commerce, in which natural gas still plays a secondary role, to the necessity of maintaining a good climate for U.S.-Mexican relations that will allow the Mexican government a margin in which to maneuver in other problem areas such as undocumented aliens and hemispheric politics. Whatever the reason, the fact is that the first important petroleum agreement in the new era of Mexican oil was far from being a confirmation of an increase in Mexico's bargaining power of a sign of a more-tolerant attitude on the part of the United States when it comes to attempts to revalue natural resources. What has happened in other areas of U.S.-Mexican relations? Has oil altered the hostility toward undocumented workers that reached unsuspected large dimensions at the beginning of the Carter administration?

## The Undocumented Worker and Energy

The fact that the problem of undocumented Mexican workers in the United States will play a central role in the negotiations between Mexico and the United States in coming years has frequently been pointed out. Although the explicit interrelationship of undocumented workers and energy has been avoided at the official level, observers believe that a situation acceptable to Mexico in the area of migration is a sine qua non condition for the initiation of an era of understanding in energy matters.[6] The hypothesis is simple: advances in energy agreements will probably take place without notable changes in the situation of the undocumented worker, or the conflicts in this area may diminish without a broader energy relationship. Whatever the case may be, it is interesting to reflect upon some of the changes in the migration policies of the United States that, in one way or another, are attributable to its interest in Mexico's petroleum potential.

During the period from 1976-1977, the influence of energy concerns on President Carter's view of Mexican immigration was not evident. The immigration policy presented by Carter for consideration by Congress in 1977 was based on strictly domestic considerations. Essentially, he responded to the demands of workers that had supported him during the election.[7] As is well known, the economic policy of the new administration, publicly announced at the beginning of 1977, did not respond to the demands of the workers in terms of employment. Its major proposal was a tax rebate, leaving investment for the immediate creation of new jobs in the background. Under these circumstances it seemed advantageous to offer a project to deal with illegal workers that was to free up millions of jobs for the American people. This is why one of the supposed principles of the proposal was that illegal workers would displace the U.S. worker and therefore contribute greatly to the high U.S. rate of unemployment.

This last type of consideration seems to have determined the contents of the proposal on matters of immigration. Its impact on Mexico's economic problems (particularly on unemployment, which reached one of its highest levels at that time) or on the good-neighbor atmosphere between the two countries did not upset the president. A similar attitude was apparent in Congress. In the interventions made in favor of, or against, the proposal, no one referred to the need to consider the negative effects the plan would have south of the border or the advantages of having a good relationship with Mexico.[8]

This situation began to change around mid-1978 when Mexico's oil riches conquered the imagination of the U.S. public. At the end of that year, Mexico's principal newspapers evidently had mounted a campaign destined, in part, to convince the U.S. government and the public of the importance of Mexico's oil potential and to pressure the Carter administration into elaborating a policy toward Mexico designed to smooth out the rough spots that had originated with problems such as undocumented workers.

Attempts to modify the public's attitude toward migrant workers were made. For example, an editorial in the *Wall Street Journal* pointed out that the Mexican migrants are ". . . not an economic problem. . . ." It went on to say that they ". . . are productive workers that . . . contribute to making the economic process more viable." Further, that their economic contribution in the United States is a factor in creating ". . . respectable jobs for workers born in America."[9]

The way in which the leaders in Washington began to link the subject of undocumented workers and energy problems in the United States was excellently depicted in the famous cartoon in the *Washington Post* in which, upon being asked about the best policy toward Mexico, an official finds the solution and exclaims: "Why don't we ask each illegal worker to bring a barrel of oil with him?"[10]

New attitudes toward migratory matters, influenced by interest in oil, exceeded the scope of political cartoons. Since 1978, new ways of approaching the subject have been seen in both the executive branch and Congress. For now, short-term plans, similar to those contemplated in the 1977 proposal, that oppose immigration to the United States probably will not be approved. This is due to the creation of the Select Commission on Immigration and Refugee Policy whose findings will be ready in March 1981. Except in the event of a major crisis, neither the president nor members of Congress are likely to propose legislation on matters concerning undocumented workers before hearing the results of these studies.

In addition to this, new conciliatory-sounding proposals have recently emerged in Congress. For example, in June 1979 Senators Hayakawa and Goldwater introduced a proposal called "The Mexico-United States Good Neighbor Act" that called for a program of temporary visas to be given to Mexican workers similar to the bracero programs that existed until 1964. Even though the number of visas to be granted was not specified, the spirit of the proposal indicated it would be higher than what had been previously considered.[11]

Another conciliatory proposal was presented by Senator Kennedy in October 1979 that increased the number of visas granted annually to neighboring countries from 20,000 to 35,000. In Mexico's case, the proposal stated that Mexican nationals could use visas not used by Canada. Keeping in mind that the average number of visas solicited annually by Canada is 10,000, the visas given to Mexico would number around 50,000—more than double the number currently allowed.[12]

Such are some of the innovations in policy matters dealing with migration that, together with the declarations about the contributions of the undocumented worker to the U.S. economy, show a desire to maintain a friendly attitude toward Mexico. Nevertheless, these innovations are not very far reaching. As some observers have pointed out, proposals such as the one made by Senator Kennedy benefit skilled labor, which is the type of worker that usually solicits a visa, but is not representative of the great mass of unskilled labor that makes up the stream of undocumented workers.[13] In addition, note that while no legislation explicitly dealing with immigration has been approved, other legislation, which indirectly worsens the already difficult conditions in which the Mexican worker functions in the United States, have been passed.[14] Examples include the measures that were approved by Congress in May 1979 prohibiting organizations that receive federal funds from granting free legal assistance to anyone who is in the United States in violation of the immigration laws.

The attitudes that have supported this type of measure and the frequent detention and mistreatment of the undocumented workers in work centers suggest that there is not, and possibly cannot be, a profound modification in the U.S. public's opinion of the presence of foreign workers. The majority of the experts on the subject point out that U.S. society is going through a time in which fears are growing about high inflation, the incapacity of political leadership to confront the country's problems, rising unemployment, and the integration of new migratory currents in the traditional "melting pot."[15] Changes in public opinion will depend on the political and economic situation in the next few years. If the recession and energy crisis become more acute, the search for a scapegoat will continue, and the undocumented workers will be an easy target. The effect of Mexican petroleum on the situation is relative. It probably will not exceed the stylistic changes that have already been pointed out.

**Petroleum and Commercial Relations**

In the last few years two types of problems in the area of commercial relations between Mexico and the United States have been evident. First are the problems that stem from the U.S. producers' traditional opposition to imports from Mexico, and second are the problems related to Mexican commercial practices, especially the protectionist measures, that the United States wants to see substituted by a greater opening up of the Mexican economy to international business.

Much attention has been given to the so-called tomato war waged by farmers in Florida. These farmers asked the U.S. Treasury Department to carry out an investigation on the conditions under which Mexican tomatoes are sold in the United States and to decide if antidumping laws could be applied to the case. Their demands provoked a strong and immediate wave of uneasiness in Mexico. A decrease in the export of tomatoes would affect a considerable volume of sales calculated at $200 million dollars a year and would reduce the possibilities of employment in agriculture in northern Mexico at a moment when unemployment in the Mexican countryside was already severe.

This uneasiness was also felt in the U.S. press that had been advocating a climate of harmony in U.S.-Mexican relations. Thus the *Wall Street Journal* pointed out that a decision against Mexico by the Department of Treasury would impinge negatively on U.S. relations with Mexico. ". . . For those who are worried about energy problems it is obvious that this is not the way to induce Mexico to share its petroleum and gas with us; for those who are worried about Mexican immigration to the United States, it is an obvious error to take measures that would increase unemployment in that country.[16]

Criticism of this protectionist petition also came from those people who perceived its inflationary impact on the price of food. Alfred Kahn, White House advisor on antiinflationary measures, pointed out that a decrease in Mexican agricultural exports could raise vegetable prices in the United States in the winter of 1979 by 0.5 percent. Therefore, those in favor of Mexico hoped both to preserve a favorable atmosphere for an energy relationship with Mexico and to avoid inflation in the United States. It is fitting to mention the opinion of one of the members of Congress who added, "Mexican tomatoes taste better."[17]

This matter was particularly irritating because of the moment in which it arose. The Treasury Department was to give its reply to Florida farmers in mid-July when preparations for López Portillo's visit to Washington were being made and when the talks on the sale of gas were at a standstill. The application of the antidumping law and the persistence of maintaining a conflictive positive with respect to the price of gas forewarned of an even less-friendly and probably stormier meeting than the one held in February.

Because of these conditions and a request made by the Department of State, Florida farmers opted for a truce. They temporarily retracted their demands and decided to enter into private talks with Mexican producers to explore the possibility of arranging "voluntary restrictions" on exports.[18] The talks were not successful, and in October demands were once again made to the Treasury Department. In a decision that "could both favor Mexican-North American relations and maintain low food prices this winter," the Treasury Department decided against the U.S. farmers.[19]

It is difficult to tell just how much the desire to maintain a cordial relationship with Mexico affected the Treasury Department's decision. The press clearly desired to promote a just and friendly treatment of Mexico, but it would be wrong to conclude that Mexico's bargaining position in commercial matters is improving. The most-interesting aspect of commercial relations between the two countries in the coming years will not be the retreats or advances of Mexico's traditional exports, but rather what agreements on fuels may be reached and the modification of Mexico's commercial practices and its effect on the overall relations between the two countries. More important than the tomato war in this last respect is the U.S. point of view on the need for opening up the Mexican economy, the motives behind such views, and the alternatives available in the future.

For several years the subject of Mexican protectionism had not been important to U.S. leaders. True, on the one hand, this protectionism hindered the sale of a wide range of products, but on the other hand, it provided the conditions under which U.S. companies could establish themselves in Mexico and produce for the domestic market there. The matter of Mexico's commercial policies took on new dimensions in the mid-1970s when new goals were outlined for the U.S. economic policy toward the more-advanced members of the underdeveloped countries of the world. This policy was inspired, to a certain degree, by the need to confront the serious inbalances in U.S. foreign commerce since 1973.

In accordance with the new strategy, it was highly desirable to fully incorporate countries like Brazil, India, and Mexico into the game plan of international capitalistic economy. The plan espoused the removal of trade barriers in the way used by organizations like GATT. Since then, U.S. leaders have expressed an ever-increasing interest in changing Mexico's commercial policy. In their opinion, only in this way can arguments be presented to oppose the protectionist tendencies that are appearing in the United States due to increased Mexican exports.

The economic crisis in Mexico in 1976 and the prospects for the Mexican economy with the presence of petroleum confirm the previous ideas. On the one hand, the crisis was interpreted in the United States as a symptom of the failure of a model for industrialization that was exaggeratedly based on protectionist policies and that had led to an inefficient industrial plan that had few possibilities of conquering external markets. On the other hand, the United States noted that the reappearance of oil in Mexican exports would alter the traditional behavior of the commercial balance between Mexico and the United States, dangerously tipping the scale in favor of Mexico. This danger, and the belief that an important amount of currency will be available south of the border, precipitated the search for conditions that would permit greater participation of U.S. sales in the Mexican market.

Thus, the opening of the Mexican economy has become a priority in U.S. policy toward Mexico. Statements made by high-level officials in the Department of State and the importance given to this subject during President Carter's visit to Mexico are proof of this priority.[20]

The decrease in obstacles to commercial exchange between the two countries is seen as a precursor to the possibility of creating a common market including Canada, the United States, and Mexico. The ideas on this subject that have been presented to some members of Congress and in semiofficial documents made by academic institutions and in the private sector are still preliminary in character. They are sketchy outlines mostly destined to exalt the so-called benefits of this type of integration.[21] Nevertheless, serious research into this possibility if being done by both academic and official institutions. Furthermore, this idea is well accepted among government officials and business groups that have gone to Mexico to find out just how the Mexican political and business elite feel about such a project.

Although projects for economic integration probably will not progress easily, they provide a point of reference that expresses the aspirations of powerful sectors in the United States with respect to commercial relations with Mexico.

## Conclusions

Mexico's experiences in dealing with the United States during the late 1970s do not bear out the optimism of the people who saw in Mexican oil a new bargaining strength. Indeed, where the huge U.S. market is the only one open to Mexican exports—as is the case for natural gas going through a pipeline—price setting is dominated by a domestic situation in the United States that does not respond easily to the needs and interests of Third-World countries. The only way out of this problem is the collective bargaining of producers through an organization like OPEC. Negotiating by itself, Mexico has little chance of resisting the tendencies of international trade that have always benefitted the more-powerful countries.

True, Mexico's new-found oil wealth is setting a new tone for the U.S. handling of both the migratory problem and the conflicts generated by competing domestic producers' opposition to Mexican exports. Nevertheless, it would not really be possible for the State Department, or for the powers behind the throne of *Wall Street Journal* editorials, to carry through a genuinely conciliatory line that would respect Mexican interests. Statements on how useful the migratory workers are for the U.S. economy will hardly convince those who seek in the foreign workers a scapegoat for the drop in their standard of living that the last decade's crisis in the capitalistic system has brought about nor will telling them how good and cheap the Mexican tomatoes are placate those who fight to exclude Mexican products from the U.S. market.

In the United States, and in fact in most industrialized countries, a good deal of hostility exists toward foreign workers and of protectionist feeling toward competing foreign goods, and solid economic factors are found behind both of these tendencies. This makes it somewhat surprising that a common U.S.-Mexican market should have been proposed and that the proposal should have been so well received by various U.S. groups. In reality, there is good reason to believe that this idea is intended not so much to open up the U.S. market to agricultural and other goods from Mexico. Its aim rather is to obtain more-direct access to Mexican oil and to help the penetration of U.S. products in Mexico, even if this means that some smaller industries south of the border will be forced out and that Mexico will have to import even more foodstuffs. This being so, Mexico's oil wealth will hardly open the door to an ear of understanding and genuine interdependence between Mexico and the United States. Much more probable is that years of conflict will exist between the two countries, the final outcome of which is hard to foresee.

## Notes

1. For example, Richard Fagen, "El petróleo y la seguridad nacional de los Estados Unidos" in *Foro internacional* 74 (October-December 1978).

2. The most-dangerous effect of a rapid increase in oil exports would be the distortion of the production apparatus and inflation, doubly feared for its effect on the economy and the discontent of the worker. The World Bank has been against the rapid expansion of the oil industry. Summary of a document prepared on Mexico that appeared in *Proceso,* 17 July 1978.

3. The first part of the negotiations is amply covered in Richard Fagen and Henry Nau, "Mexican Gas: The Northern Connection," in *Capitalism and the State in U.S.-Latin American Relations* ed. Richard Fagen (Stanford: Stanford University Press, 1979).

4. *Los Angeles Times*, 2 August 1979.

5. The agreement was presented by the U.S. advocates as an authentic triumph of U.S. diplomacy. It is interesting to note that some advocates mentioned the possibility that the volume of gas would soon be increased. See *Excélsior*, 22 September 1979.

6. Fagen, "El petróleo," pp. 417-18.

7. Commentary on Wayne Cornelius' project, "Undocumented Immigration: A Critique of the Carter Administration Policy Proposals," *Migration Today* 5, no. 4 (October 1977).

8. See "Controversy over Proposed Amnesty to Illegal Aliens," *Congressional Digest* (October 1977).

9. *Wall Street Journal*, 14 February 1979.

10. *Washington Post*, 10 December 1978.

11. U.S., Congress, Senate, *S. 1427*, 96th Cong., 1st sess., 27 June 1979 (legislative day 21 June 1979).

12. *Excélsior*, 21 October 1971.

13. Jorge Bustamante, "Los parches migratorios," *Uno más uno*, 22 October 1979.

14. Jorge Bustamante, "Estado legal de indefensión" *Uno más uno*, June 1979.

15. Wayne Cornelius, "Americans in the Era of Limits: The Nation of Immigrants Turns Nativist Again," (Paper presented at the Meeting on Mexican Immigration at La Jolla, the University of California at San Diego, 10-12 June 1979).

16. *Wall Street Journal*, 2 July 1979.

17. *Wall Street Journal*, 1 November 1979.

18. *Miami Herald*, 19 July 1978.

19. *The New York Times*, 4 November 1979.

20. *Excélsior*, 17 February 1979; *Excélsior*, 23 September 1979; *Excélsior*, 15 November 1979.

21. See, for example, the testimony presented to the Subcommittee on International Commerce of the Finance Committee of the U.S. Senate, 6 June 1979, Kenneth E. Hill, "North American Energy: A Proposal for a Common Market Between Canada, Mexico and the United States," mimeographed (Blyth Eastman Dillon Investment Research, February 1979).

# 11

# The Negotiating Power of Oil: The Mexican Case

*Mario Ojeda*

## Theoretical Considerations

Analysts of the modern world agree that oil is a powerful element in international negotiations. This interpretation has gained credibility especially since the Arab-oil embargo of 1973. The industrialized Western world was then held in check economically, and various industrial powers were forced to modify their external politics, as in the case of Japan with relation to the Arab-Israeli conflict.

The analysts also agree that because of oil, a new type of international stratification can be projected for the future, a stratification that could have enormous repercussions on the traditional division of world power. Until quite recently, countries were classified according to an evaluation of their military and/or economic power, either of which determined their influence on the modern international community. Militarily, they were classified as superpowers (nuclear powers); conventional powers (nonnuclear); intermediary powers; and weak countries. Economically, various nations were classified as developed, moderately developed, and in the process of developing. A third classification could be developed that delineates nations by the level of economic production and the size of the market in each.

Today emphasis is being placed upon energy resources as a basic element for the classification of countries in terms of their international power as well as their political and economic viability. With respect to this new element, the countries that form the modern world can be divided into three groups: (1) oil-producing countries, (2) countries that do not produce oil but that have the financial resources to acquire it, and (3) countries that have neither oil nor the financial resources to acquire it from without.

According to observers of the international scene, this new element of international stratification has begun to revolutionize the political structures of all the industrialized powers, with the exception of the USSR but including the United States. The latter is included because of its dependence upon the importation of hydrocarbons to some degree to supply internal demands. In the case of the many underdeveloped nations, the problem is pathetic. They do not have an adequate natural-resource

---

Adapted with permission of the publisher from Mario Ojeda, "El poder negociador del petróleo: el caso de México," *Foro internacional* 21, no. 1 (July-September 1980).

base or adequate financial resources to import oil. At the same time, they must import great quantities of basic life-supporting necessities including food.

## Export and Politics

Countries export goods in order to be able to acquire abroad those goods they cannot produce internally. Moreover, some countries need to trade to a larger degree than do others. Usually, the degree to which a country is vulnerable to the fluctuations of an international market is related directly to its dependence on trade. Quantitatively, this dependence can be measured by calculating the proportion of imports and exports in relation to the GNP of the country. Countries such as Japan depend on trade and face the dilemma of either trading or succumbing, at least partially, as an economic power.

The importance of trade for many countries also depends upon qualitative elements. The qualitative importance of external commerce depends on the structure of trade—that is, the composition of the imports and exports. Thus, the strengths or weaknesses of a bargaining position depend upon the type of products that are being imported and exported. In turn, this depends both upon whether the products are essential or nonessential and their price. The degree of availability, which has an important impact on price, is influenced by the existence, and the number, of competitors as well as by the ease with which certain products may be substituted by similar or synthetic products.

Theoretically, this point of view places on one end of the scale those countries with great bargaining strength derived from their exports of capital goods or other essential goods, such as fuel and basic foodstuffs, in exchange for the import of so-called soft goods or luxury items. At the other end of the scale are those countries with the opposite balance of trade, such as importers of fuels and basic foodstuffs and exporters of luxury items and soft goods. Between these two extremes, a whole range of possible gradations of commercial dependency exists. For example, the width and breadth of the margin of negotiation of some countries clearly can be seen as related to the degree to which nonessential products are exported because essential products would have to be imported in exchange for such goods.

Theoretically, the commercial-negotiating position of these countries could be estimated by the degree of concentration or diversification of their exports in one or several markets. The same can be said with respect to their imports with relation to the concentration or diversification of their source of supply. Consequently, on the theoretical scale described earlier, the most-vulnerable country is one that must depend upon one export product and that must sell that product in only one market. Obviously this would seem to make that country extremely dependent upon importing countries, particularly if the exported product may be classified as nonessential. With this extreme case as an example, it is possible to conceive of a descending scale based upon the degree of diversification of products and markets as well as source of supply.

## The Unique Character of Oil

Oil is a special case in many respects. Its uniqueness can be ascertained in so many ways that it has been classified as the hardest of the so-called hard goods.[1] First, oil is a nonrenewable resource that could be totally and fatally exhausted. Second, its degree of availability is dependent upon proved reserves and estimated potential reserves. Third, it has double strategic importance—that is, both economic and military.

Oil derives its importance from its great versatility as a raw material. Oil can be used as the basic material in the transformation of other products or, by itself, as a fuel. As a raw material, oil is the base for a multitude of articles including fertilizers and primary and secondary industrial oil-based chemicals. As a fuel, oil or hydrocarbons display great versatility. They are important in industry, transportation, and many domestic uses. This is not the case with other conventional sources of energy such as electricity and coal, which cannot practically be used to power airplanes or the internal-combustion engine. More important is the fact that hydrocarbons can be used to generate other sources of energy. For example, electricity may be produced by thermoelectric plants powered by the combustion of oil or gas by-products.

Especially noteworthy is the value of hydrocarbons compared with other conventional fuels. First, compared with wind and water, hydrocarbons represent greater fuel power. Second, they are much cleaner than bituminous or soft coal. Third, compared with nuclear energy in its present state of technological development, hydrocarbons have the advantage of a lesser degree of danger of contamination. Fourth, solar energy still lacks the technology to be useful on an industrial scale or for transportation. None of the conventional sources of energy other than hydrocarbons is applicable to modern transportation, with the exception of electricity, whose application is limited to railroads and is in part generated by hydrocarbons.

Finally, it is important to emphasize that oil derives its strategic importance not so much from its considerable economic value but more from its military value—that is, the majority of armaments of modern warfare are based on combustibles derived from petroleum. Consequently, the negotiating power of oil is not merely commercial but also military and political.

## Effective Power of Oil

In the preceeding section the negotiating power of oil was analyzed on a theoretical level, and the conclusion was drawn that its power is derived in large part from its unique character. Nevertheless, obviously oil's effective power as a weapon of commercial and political negotiation has its limits. These limitations depend on a variety of factors that have either a structural or complicating nature.

## Structural Factors

The first structural factor is the influence that an exporting country wields in the international market. OPEC is a unique case among the international organizations of commodity producers because, in spite of its internal differences, it has had great success in fixing the price of oil and therefore controlling the bulk of the international oil market. For example, if OPEC is compared with the Organization of Copper Exporting Countries (OCEC), which has goals similar to OPEC's, a notable difference is evident in the degree of success of the organizations.[2] Based on available data for 1976-1977, OPEC controlled 95 percent of the world oil markets, whereas OCEC only controlled 60 percent of the world copper market. Several explantations for this can be offered. Finding a substitute for oil is difficult, a number of other metals such as iron and aluminum often can be substituted for copper. Oil is nonrenewable, whereas copper can be recycled in a process of recasting scrap metals and industrial by-products. Oil is a product for generalized consumption and with multiple applications. In contrast, copper consumption is more-highly specialized and useful only in certain types of industries. Finally, the majority of the countries that form OPEC have strong economies, or at least international financial solvency, and many copper-producing countries are confronted with deficits in balance of payments and figure importantly among those countries that have outstanding foreign debts.

The explanation of the success of OPEC in fixing the price of oil in the world market rests upon the fact that one of its members, Saudi Arabia, the world's largest producer of oil, is capable of controlling the balance between supply and demand. By virtue of its small population and underdeveloped and undiversified economy, Saudi Arabia does not need to produce at the level of its enormous potential and can readily close the production valves. This action reduces the world oil supply and maintains the price set by OPEC without internal political, economic, or social costs to the nation.

Much of the Saudi Arabian oil income has been sent abroad in the form of investments in enterprises and bank deposits. Consequently, it would not suit Saudi Arabia economically if the price of oil were to rise drastically. A sudden price increase would create excessive imbalances in those countries in which Saudi Arabia has invested its petrodollars, causing its investments to be harmed. This may explain, in part, why Saudi Arabia has followed a more-conservative line with regard to the price of oil than have most other OPEC members. This investment abroad also gives Saudi Arabia additional negotiating power because it could be suddenly withdrawn, although the Iran case indicates that the investments could also be frozen in the host country. The same circumstances that give Saudi Arabia the ability to control the price of oil without grave internal costs also explain why it has been able to impose its own criteria for the price of fuels above the criteria of the other members of the organization.

The rest of the OPEC members do not enjoy the same flexibility as do Saudi Arabia and Kuwait. In effect, the other countries have linked their profits from the exportation of oil with ambitious plans for industrial and economic development. Consequently they have remained prisoners of their own policies without the degree of production flexibility enjoyed by Saudi Arabia and Kuwait, and they cannot reduce the level of their exports arbitrarily without endangering their plans for industrialization and development and, consequently, the employment rate. Such development plans often require these countries to enter into contracts for the acquisition of parts and equipment that cannot be broken without penalties. For this reason, economists have always been in agreement that the greatest danger of a crack in the united front presented by OPEC, with regard to its prices and production quotas, would come from Iran and not from Saudi Arabia. This is because of Iran's urgent need for industrialization and its long association with the United States.[3]

A second structural factor related to the power of oil as a negotiating weapon is the specific influence the exporting country has in supplying the importing country. Saudi Arabia and Iran have enjoyed great influence in the United States becaues they have been (in the case of Iran before the revolution) the principal suppliers of imported oil to the U.S. market in recent years, at 20 and 15 percent respectively. Countries such as Libya, which supplied a smaller portion of imported oil to the United States in 1977, were able to exert much-less influence on Washington, independent of their own political and ideological problems at the time.

A third structural factor is the position of the exporting country in terms of its level of international economic solvency. The case of Saudi

Arabia compared with that of Mexico makes the point. While Mexico clearly occupies a position of debtor in the international economy—chronic trade deficit, high external debts—Saudi Arabia is a creditor country, and even if it is the captive of investments in the West, the persistent fact of being a creditor country makes Saudi Arabia able to withhold exports of oil without feeling significant repercussions in the balance of payments. The reason for this is that Saudi Arabia has the ability to fill the void with part of the capital deposited in foreign countries.

A fourth structural factor is the balance of power that exists between the importer and the exporter. Obviously, there is a great difference between selling to a small, weak country than to a superpower. For example, Mexico can exert more power over Costa Rica by exporting 7,000 barrels of oil a day than it can exert over the United States while exporting 4 or 5 million barrels a day to that country. Independent of the specific influence that these figures can have on the internal demands of those countries, obviously the United States as a superpower has much-more negotiating ability for the exchange of oil than has a country like Costa Rica.[4]

A fifth factor is that the geopolitical situation of the oil-producing nation is an important structural element in considering the negotiating power of oil. From a strategic point of view, Iran and Saudi Arabia are located in a no-man's-land zone. In contrast, other oil exporters such as Venezuela, Canada, and Mexico are located directly within the sphere of influence of the United States. This allows Washington to act with greater political and military freedom in the region without the inhibitions that are placed upon its actions in the Middle East, where a risk of a confrontation with the USSR exists.

*Complicating Factors*

Apart from structural factors, other factors of a complicating nature exist, which at any moment could affect the effective negotiating power of oil. Complicating factors have nothing to do with the fluctuations of supply and demand of oil in the world market but are derived from crises and political changes. The revolution in Iran, for example, affected the sale of oil in the world market and automatically raised the bargaining power of the other exporting nations. Moreover, the new Iranian government changed its international energy policy and decided to cancel its shipments of oil to Israel when it had been supplying 60 or 70 percent of that country's entire consumption. This change not only affected relations between Iran and Israel but also all the politics of the Middle East, and it had extraregional implications as well. Because of the void created by Iran and the influence this had on the attitude of the entire Muslim bloc toward Israel, Tel Aviv was forced to seek suppliers outside the Middle East in countries such as Mexico. This, as we shall see shortly, gave Mexico greater influence in its dealing with Israel.

The recent case of Mexico also illustrates the effect that complicating factors can have on the bargaining power of oil. Had it not been for the economic crisis that the country confronted in 1976 and 1977, the Mexican government perhaps would not have decided to convert to an exporter of oil. This crisis made it necessary for Mexico to break the bottleneck created by a trade deficit and by the imposed limitation on external indebtedness by the International Monetary Fund. It also caused Mexico to have to bargain with its oil reserves, although the country's bargaining power was greatly limited by the other financial circumstances of the time. The conclusion from this experience is that even if oil is a powerful weapon in the arsenal of international negotiations, it has clearly defined limitations that are derived as much from structural causes as from complicating factors.

**Mexico and the Power of Oil**

The following three sections represent concrete instances that describe Mexico's bargaining power as a result of oil. The first section discusses the large margin of internal and external bargaining power that oil gave to the López Portillo government when it was in the throes of a severe crisis. The second section discusses the impact of oil on Mexican-Israeli relations, which had been deteriorating since 1975 because of the Mexican vote in favor of the United Nations resolution that equated Zionism with racism. The third section discusses the prominent example of the role that oil is presently playing in relations between Mexico and the United States.

*Oil and the Mexican Internal Crisis*

The decisive factor in the Mexican government's decision to accelerate the exploitation of oil and natural gas and to convert the country into an important exporter was provoked by the economic crisis that threatened the country during the last third of 1976. Quite probably, had it not been for this crisis, the Mexican government would not have made its decision with such force and rapidity. Since that date, resource exploitation in Mexico cannot be isolated from the political, economic, and social reality of the country. All of these factors must be analyzed in order to shed light on the economic crisis.

It is important to recall that never has a Mexican government had to begin its regime while confronting such a profound crisis. The López Portillo government found itself facing a triple crisis: economic, political, and social. Never before had a president had to begin his administration with such limited freedom for maneuvering and such weak bargaining power in domestic and foreign spheres. López Portillo began his regime in an atmosphere of public mistrust of the capacity of the revolutionary governments to govern coupled with a disbelief in official declarations. From the first day of its administration, the new government was confronted with a public treasury that was in bankruptcy, a national debt and accumulated trade deficits that were the highest in the nation's history, a mounting lack of self-sufficiency in the production of basic foods, rampant inflation, and the withdrawal of private investments. To make matters worse, there was a severe economic recession that brought with it a notorious raise in the already chronic rate of underemployment and unemployment. Any one of these problems would have been enough to weaken a new government, but the combination of them all resulted in a crisis such as no government has ever had to face before. Not only was the viability of the new government at stake but also the entire political system.

The combination of these problems drastically reduced the foreign and domestic negotiating capacity of Mexico and explains, but does not necessarily justify, the oil policy of the current government. Clearly the government suffered a great setback in its ability to negotiate with internal power groups such as business and commercial agriculture, which had to be given many concessions in order to maintain the high rates of investment. In foreign affairs, the government's bargaining power was so drastically reduced that it had to seek an extension and reorganization of its foreign debt and accept a program of stabilization from the International Monetary Fund. Mexico's weak international position was further aggravated by a crisis in the balance of payments due to the hardening of the U.S. policy toward Mexican laborers. As a consequence of all these problems, the new government quickly turned to its natural resources as the only alternative left to reestablish both its domestic and foreign power.

The first task that the Mexican government confronted was to persuade domestic and foreign public opinion of the magnitude of its natural resources. For this reason, the search for new veins was intensified, and contracts were made with the best specialty firms in the oil industry to certify the magnitude of Mexico's natural resources. In spite of these public-relations efforts and a production of crude that increased from 293 million barrels a day to 358 million barrels in 1976, in 1977 an international aura of doubt still surrounded the size of the new finds.[5] Nevertheless, the increased value of the exports, which went from $436 million to $1 billion between 1976 and 1977, relieved the pressure on the balance of payments and helped national and foreign investors, as well as the public, to regain their confidence in the national economy.[6] The value of these exports continued to rise and by the end of 1978 had reached a total of 1.7 billion.[7]

By the time of his address on the state of the union in September 1978, President López Portillo was able to declare:

We have designed three successive steps in our plan for national development to be implemented in three two-year phases; the first two years, an
alleviation of the crisis; the next two years, a consolidation of the economy;
and the last two years, enormous economic growth. The first phase, alleviation of the crisis, is about to be concluded. . . . In the first phase, we have
alleviated the danger of bankruptcy, the withdrawal of capital investments
has ceased, and some have been returned. This has lessened our outstanding debt and improved the balance of payments. In the last half of the year,
industrial production has increased rapidly and agriculture has recovered,
the process of dollarization has ceased and even begun to reverse itself—a
sign that we have assimilated the floating of the peso with respect to the
dollar, which is also floating—with difficulty at times—in respect to other
stronger currencies. Now we know that our destiny as a nation is not
dependent upon foreign money but upon what we do or leave undone in
that nation.

Because of what we have done, for the first time in the last three years, actual growth is greater than the cost of living at 5 percent. Our first modest,
but realistic, proposals have been fulfilled.[8]

After this point Mexico could state that the worst of the crisis—inflation combined with recession—had been left behind. Inflation would continue but along with a rapidly growing economy. Effectively, for 1979 the
country's economy attained a growth rate of 7.5 percent, which was an increase of four times more than in 1976.[9] The surplus oil reserves also served
to increase the financial capacity of the country, which was limited by the
ceiling imposed on the agreement with the International Monetary Fund
and by the Mexican fiscal year. This financial self-sufficiency, as President
López Portillo termed it, increased the bargaining power of Mexico both
in foreign and domestic markets. Most important, the surplus reserves gave
Mexico the basic instrument to reactivate and redirect its economy and the
ability to increase and finance a large portion of public spending. In
September 1979, President López Portillo informed his country that:

Oil is the potential to make us self-sufficient because it makes us less dependent upon foreign investments and improves our international economic
relations. But not only this. Oil can help us increase our possibilities for expansion, transformation, persuasion, and association. It allows us to
develop a solid fuel strategy. It allows us to solidify our demand for capital
goods and, as a result, to develop industry and transportation along with
human acomplishments such as education, social development, and above
all, agriculture.[10]

Because of oil, the government recovered its negotiating power with
private enterprise that had been severely weakened because of the economic
crisis and direct confrontations with President Echeverría in 1975 and
1976. Indirectly, oil increased the maneuverability of the government with

regard to big business by allowing an increase in public spending and by reducing the dependency of the recovering economy on private investment.

The oil-induced economic recovery was a second indirect form in which hydrocarbons augmented Mexico's maneuverability with regard to the business community. Negotiating under the pressure and urgency of an economic crisis is far different from negotiating from a base of economic strength. Hydrocarbons gave Mexico a concrete and powerful bargaining weapon with which to negotiate with the business community. The government could offer the purchase of inexpensive fuels as an incentive. The gas pipeline to Cadereyta illustrates this point because it allowed the industries in Monterrey, which were out of natural gas, to buy it in large quantities and to substitute a cleaner and more-powerful fuel for the one they had been using.

*Impact of Oil on Mexican-Israeli Relations*

On 10 November 1975, Mexico, along with seventy-one member nations, cast its vote in the General Assembly of the United Nations in favor of a declaration that defined Zionism as a form of racism. The reaction was immediate. Toward the end of that same month, *The New York Times* published a plea to U.S. Jews to abstain from traveling to Mexico and from doing business that involved the import or export of Mexican goods. The Mexican vote in the United Nations was purported to be ample justification for such a boycott.

The insistence for the boycott by the U.S. leaders of Jewish groups rapidly attained success. A few days after the publication of the document, the president of the Mexican Association of Hotels announced to the press that 30,000 reservations had been canceled. It also made known that several conventions scheduled to take place in Mexico had been canceled for the same reason.

At the same time speculation arose over whether the withdrawal of large sums of money from Mexico on the part of the Mexican Jews was due to the United Nations vote. Such conjecture is difficult to verify, but equally difficult to believe, given that the Mexican Jews were made innocent victims as a result of the actions of their U.S. and Canadian coreligionists. The Mexican Jews also became victims of internal reprisals. However, during that time the removal of Mexican capital to positions outside the country clearly was on the rise because of the critical situation in the balance of payments and the fear of devaluation of the peso. Nevertheless, it still remains to be seen whether this withdrawal of capital, which accelerated during the first half of the following year and caused the devaluation of the peso in August 1976, was caused by purely economic circumstances or motivations or by, at least in part, deliberate pressures against the Echever-ría regime due to its economic policy and to its other policies.

U.S.-Jewish irritation seems exaggerated if one considers it the result of one declaration, but apparently the Jews considered this as one in a series of grievances against Israel on the part of the Mexican government. In an-ticipation of the United Nations vote, President Echeverría had conferred with the leader of the Palestine Liberation Organization (PLO), and the government of Mexico had announced that that organization could open an information office in Mexico. In accordance with international practices, this action was equivalent to a tacit recognition of the PLO by the Mexican government.

The U.S.-Jewish reaction also seems exaggerated because of the seventy-one other countries that voted as Mexico did. Nevertheless, the same leader of the group that authored *The New York Times* protest clarified the issue by stating that Mexico, because of its high degree of dependence on U.S. tourism, was vulnerable to a boycott. Therefore, it seems clear that Mexico, because of its vulnerability, was blackmailed. Moreover, Mexico was not an importer of Arab oil, which in the case of Brazil could justify a vote in favor of the resolution.

Justified or not, the U.S.-Jewish boycott had the desired effect and demonstrated the limited scope of an independent foreign policy when that policy is economically vulnerable. A short time after the call to boycott was published, the chancellor of Mexico was obliged to travel to Tel Aviv to discuss "whatever bad feeling has recently come between us."[11] According to newspaper accounts of 5 December 1975, the Israeli vice-premier replied: "We surely have the possibility of clearing up this misunderstand-ing. . . "[12] He added that "There is no discrimination in Zion . . . [thus] there can be no racism."[13] The very same declaration was reiterated by President Echeverria a short while later before a group of Jewish leaders from the United States and Canada that had been invited by the Mexican government expressly for the interview. Echeverría said that in no way was Zionism to be equated with racism and that the vote of his country at the United Nations had not been intended to give that impres-sion.[14]

A short while later, as a reaction to these exchanges, voices were heard within Mexico that severely criticized what seemed a swift reversal of Mex-ican foreign policy. Criticism was leveled against the manner in which the government had sought a reconciliation with Israel and Jewish-American political circles as it seemed to undermine Mexico's national dignity.

This reaction was an important factor in causing the Mexican govern-ment to find a forceful solution to the problem. As a result, at the end of December 1975, the secretary of foreign relations, who had been elevated to that position after scant diplomatic experience, resigned from his post. A diplomat of long-standing service was selected to replace him, and the office of subsecretary of business affairs and special studies was created. Observers interpreted this move as an admission of guilt for the United Nations vote on the part of the government. The admission apparently was due to the extreme vulnerability of the Mexican economy and as an intent to return to the cautiousness of traditional Mexican diplomacy.

Nevertheless, no sooner had the boycott begun to dissipate due to the previously mentioned negotiations when it was reinstated because of criticism leveled by the Mexican government at the expedition of Israeli commandos in the airport at Entebbe, an incident designed to rescue the passengers and crew of an El Al aircraft that had been hijacked by the PLO in conjunction with some members of a German terrorist organization. With respect to this issue, an editorial published in the U.S.-Jewish publication *Moment* said that, although the magazine had recently run an advertisement by the Mexican National Tourism Office it would not accept any more such advertisements ". . . until there is a substantial indication of certain changes in their attitude."[15]

Relations between Mexico and Israel and North American-Jewish political groups began to improve a short time after the change of governments in Mexico that took place in December 1976. A year and a half after the publication of the article quoted here, relations had changed substantially, due in large measure to oil. According to one newspaper account, Mexico had signed an agreement (of a standby nature) in which it made the commitment to supply to Israel all the oil it might need in the case of an emergency.

The report added that the agreement was important due to certain declarations made by the Shah of Iran that intimated that Iran could use its shipments of oil to Israel as a means of applying political pressure. Finally, the report stated that Mexican shipments of oil to Israel "continued to be below 50 percent."[16] The agreement materialized a short while later, not thanks to the Shah but to Ayatollah Khomeini. Indeed, one of the first steps taken by the revolutionary government of Iran with regard to foreign policy was to totally cancel its exports to Israel.

By the middle of 1979, Mexican-Israeli relations were much improved, due in large measure to the increasing shipments (see table 11-1) of Mexican oil, which amounted to 33,000 barrels a day. This increase had allowed Israel to recover from the Iranian boycott. The Israeli minister of energy declared that the Israeli government and people ". . . consider Mexico not only as a friendly nation but as a future potential world power."[17]

More important than even the Mexican-Israeli reconciliation was the reaction of the U.S.-Jewish political groups that further proves our contention that oil is a negotiating weapon with distinct advantages. During his visit to New York in September 1979 to attend a session of the United Nations

**Table 11-1**
**Destination of Mexican Oil Exports**
*(average barrels per day exported)*

| Destination | 1977 | | 1978 | | 1979 (first week) | |
|---|---|---|---|---|---|---|
| | *Barrels per Day* | *Percentage* | *Barrels per Day* | *Percentage* | *Barrels per Day* | *Percentage* |
| United States | 175,134 | 86.7 | 323,843 | 88.7 | 420,675 | 83.6 |
| Israel | 20,200 | 10 | 22,272 | 6.1 | 33,715 | 6.7 |
| Spain | 2,424 | 1.2 | 11,318 | 3.1 | 45,288 | 9 |
| Other | 4,242 | 2.1 | 7,667 | 2.1 | 3,522 | 0.7 |
| Total | 202,000 | 100 | 365,099 | 100 | 503,200 | 100 |

Sources: The figures for 1977 were collected in a series of interviews with Mexican government officials. For other years, see *Comercio exterior* 11(September 1979):1043.

Note: Beginning on 9 December 1979, Mexico began to export about 7,000 barrels a day. In 1980, exports will begin to Brazil, France, and Japan without jeopardizing the quotas already assigned to previous clients.

General Assembly, President López Portillo received a delegation from the American Jewish Committee. The purpose of the visit was to thank him for the changed Mexican policy toward Israel and the offers of friendship, especially in the area of energy. Furthermore, the delegates offered to intervene in the name of the committee on behalf of Mexican laborers in the United States, documented or not. They offered, if this interested the Mexican government, to lobby in favor of increased entry quotas to regulate the situation of those laborers who wished to obtain citizenship, to offer amnesty to undocumented laborers who had lived in the United States for a length of time, and to insure the rights of those undocumented laborers under the Constitution of the United States in spite of their legal status.[18]

## Impact of Oil on U.S.-Mexican Relations

In order to better understand the impact of the new, oil-based Mexican wealth on relations between Mexico and the United States, it is necessary to analyze the framework of their relationship and the threshold over which they both are passing and to distinguish between structure and process. On the one hand exists a framework within which economic and political reality control these relations, and on the other hand the questions and problems resulting from these relations have to be dealt with. From the Mexican point of view, the structure is the principal concern in relations with the United States. The structure of their relationship is precisely what prevents Mexico from being able to negotiate with the United States on equal terms. In addition, this same structure has frequently obligated Mexico to accept unilateral decisions made in Washington.

The structure of relations between Mexico and the United States has the following principal characteristics:

Territorial contiguity, which has strategic military implications and limits Mexico's autonomy;

Asymmetrical power, which means that Mexico is the weaker partner in the relationship;

Economic and technological dependency, which indicates a great vulnerability in Mexico to decisions made by the U.S. government and in business transactions between the two nations;

Cultural influence, which implies the penetration of the values and consumption patterns of an extremely wealthy society as well as the weakening of Mexican national identity.

This asymmetrical structure of relations implies that historically Mexico has negotiated with the United States on something other than equal footing.

One notable exception occurred during World War II when, for strategic military reasons, Mexico saw its bargaining power increased.

One must keep in mind that Mexico turned a new chapter in its history when it began to export hydrocarbons to the United States. Oil-based wealth gave Mexico a concrete instrument of negotiation with the United States. The change in attitude between President López Portillo's first and second meetings with President Carter is sufficient proof. Another indicator of this change would be the increase of U.S.-press coverage of both the undocumented-labor issue and the hydrocarbon issue from 1976 to 1979. A few concrete examples of intergovernment negotiations are useful to illustrate the altered relations.

The first example concerns undocumented immigrants. No doubt exists that the amnesty bill that President Carter presented to the U.S. Congress in 1977, in spite of its limited favorability to the immigrants, was a great improvement over the drastic measures proposed in previous legislation. It is noteworthy that such changes in attitudes occurred at a time when the export of hydrocarbons from Mexico to the United States increased significantly. Even more important is the fact that the U.S. government is convinced today that in order to develop an adequate policy toward the undocumented immigrants, it must be remembered that this is a bilateral issue and not an internal problem of the United States. Therefore, it is first necessary to examine the influx of immigrants, their length of stay in the United States, and other related factors. This attitude might never have come about without the increased importance oil has given Mexico in the eyes of the United States.

Another important example is the negotiations with the International Monetary Fund. In 1977 Mexico contracted with the fund for a line of credit fixed at $3 billion. In that year the Mexican government decided to build a gas pipeline that would connect its new fields on the northern border with the United States. However, the construction of this pipeline was estimated at $1.5 billion, or half the amount of the loan. If the loan were used it would have meant sacrificing other important projects—a most-difficult decision taking into account the recession that was crippling the economy. The problem was resolved when the International Monetary Fund gave its approval to the financing of the pipeline outside of the $3-billion loan agreement because it considered the pipeline to be a healthy project for the economy in that it was oriented toward exportation and could rapidly increase foreign spending.[19]

## Conclusions

The importance of Mexican oil for the United States does not lie in the 400,000 barrels of oil it is exporting at the moment, nor in the 300 million cubic feet of natural gas it also exports, but rather in its enormous potential as a future supplier for the United States and for the markets of the Western world. Until now the interests of both countries have coincided. The problem will arise when Mexico reaches its estimated production level of 2.25 million barrels a day, half of which are destined for exportation. The United States will likely exert pressure on Mexico to increase its production and, therefore, its exportation. The force of such pressures will depend upon circumstances. Due to the crisis in Iran, the indications are that these pressures will be greater than what might have been expected in 1978.

The outlook for oil as a factor in international relations presents at least two alternatives. First, it can be used as a negotiating tool. Second, it can be an element of discord that leads to pressures from the superpowers on oil-producing nations, including the possibility of military intervention. In the case of Mexico and the United States, the asymmetrical balances of power and economic relations give the United States a superior position that could be used to try to cause Mexico to increase its production by means of incentives as well as reprisals.

On the one hand, the United States can offer incentives to Mexico for increased production by lowering duties on Mexican exports and by offering preferences for U.S. tourism in Mexico. On the other hand, reprisals could be made through multiple channels of finance, commerce, tourism, and technology such as is being observed in U.S.-Iranian relations in 1979. However, according to some analysts, the United States would not even have to apply pressure because PEMEX's need for financing and equipment could in itself force Mexico to increase its production.

The big test for Mexico and the other exporters in the Western world will come if the Arab producers cancel or severely limit their exports. Knowing that this is not an impossible eventuality, Mexico has presented a proposal to the United Nations to ration the world oil market in a multilateral form. In the event of a worldwide energy crisis, the superpowers, particularly the United States, could resort to drastic methods of pressure such as destabilization, subversion, and even open armed intervention. In that event, the producing countries would have no recourse but to threaten to blow up their wells. If such a threat were carried out, both the producers and the consumers would suffer a heavy loss.

**Notes**

1. According to a pamphlet published by the U.S. government, the other minerals considered "critical" aside from oil are the following: aluminum-bauxite, chromium, minerals from the platinum group, iron, nickel, rubber, magnesium, zinc, tin, titanium, cobalt, mercury, tungsten,

lead, niobium, vanadium, flourite, copper, and phosphates. Council on International Economic Policy, *Critical Imported Materials, Special Report* (Washington, D.C.: Government Printing Office, December 1974); and Heraldo Muñoz, "Dependencia estratégica y no estratégica: materias petrolera," *Estudios internacionales* 33 (January-March 1976):82. To this list would have to be added other minerals more-closely related to the production of sophisticated weapons, such as barium, zirconium, lithium, and uranium, which are indispensable for the building of atomic reactors and for the atomic industry in general. Quoted by the same author, pp. 82-83.

2. OCEC is composed of Chile, Peru, Zambia, and Zaire.

3. John M. Blair, *The Control of Oil* (New York: Vintage Books, 1978), p. 284.

4. Beginning in December 1979, Mexico began to export to Costa Rica a shipment of 7,000 barrels a day of crude oil according to the facts given out by the secretary of state in San José, Costa Rica, on 8 December. That quantity constitutes an estimated one-third of the consumption of Costa Rica. During the first half of 1979, Mexico exported 420,000 barrels a day to the United States, which is approximately 6 percent of its imports and 3 percent of its consumption.

5. PEMEX, *Memorias de labores, 1977.*

6. Ibid.

7. Dirección General de Estadistica, *Anuario estadístico del comercio exterior* (Mexico: 1970 to 1978).

8. José López Portillo, *Segundo informe de gobierno* (Mexico: September 1978).

9. Ibid.

10. José López Portillo, *Tercer informe de gobierno* (Mexico: September 1979).

11. *Excélsior*, 25 November 1975, p. 4-A; and *Excélsior*, 29 November 1975, p. 4-A.

12. *Excélsior*, 5 December 1975, p. 1.

13. *Excélsior*, 8 December 1975, p. 1; and *Excélsior*, 11 December 1975, p. 1.

14. El Día, 13 December 1975, p. 1.

15. *Moment, The New Magazine for American Jews*, no. 1 (September 1976):3.

16. *The New York Times*, 11 March 1978.

17. *Excélsior*, 10 August 1979.

18. *Excélsior*, 28 September 1979.

19. See Richard R. Fagen and Henry R. Nau, "Mexican Gas: The Northern Connection," in *Capitalism and the State in U.S.-Latin American Relations* ed. Richard R. Fagen (Stanford, Calif.: Stanford University Press, 1979), pp. 400-01.

# Comments

*Robert L. Ayres*

## Observations

The principal question that seems to underlie the theme of this book is: What will be the overall effects of the discovery of fabulous reserves of petroleum in Mexico and in a broader sense, on U.S.-Mexican relations? There appears to be, moveover, a vague sense that this discovery will vastly complicate these relations, probably for the worse. Taken with other recent developments in U.S.-Mexican relations—the celebrated natural-gas deal, the tomato war, and the occasional rumors of the construction of a "Tortilla curtain" to eliminate Mexican illegal migrants to the United States—the exacerbation of some of the most-unpleasant aspects of U.S.-Mexican relations likely to be occasioned by petroleum politics could easily lead to yet another crisis in the relations between these countries. In this writer's judgment, the scenario based on these assumptions is incorrect for the following reasons.

First, at present no crisis exists in U.S.-Mexican relations, nor will one likely exist in the reasonably foreseeable future.

Second, whatever crisis exists is in most respects a creation of academic and intellectual elites in both countries who have a large stake in such crises.

Third, the reasons why no validity appears in the crisis scenario are briefly discussed later, but the principal reason is this: Mexican development strategy in the 1980s, with the specific development policies derivative from it, are unlikely to be significantly at variance with U.S. interests or values. Boiled down to its basics, this argument states that an elaboration and implementation of a distinctively Mexican path to development is not likely to occur. Rather, much-more likely is that strategy and policies will be broadly congruent with U.S. interests in capitalism, internationalism, interdependence, incremental reformist change, and so forth. One suspects that this prospect galls intellectual elites of a leftist persuasion in both countries, as well it should. Their disappointments aside, Mexico is highly unlikely to become another Cuba as a result of the complex antagonisms engendered by petroleum revenues. Even less likely is its becoming another Iran, the specter of which was raised by a number of the Mexican authors in this book. In Mexico the analogs of the Iranian situation of the moral absolutism of Islam, or the alleged torture and systematic persecution under a shah or the religious authority of an ayatollah, simply do not exist.

Fourth, in terms of the international context in which U.S.-Mexican relations are likely to evolve, it appears that Mexico's petroleum wealth will cement its status as an advanced developing, or newly industrializing, country. This is another factor likely to mitigate an alleged crisis in U.S.-Mexican relations. The most-likely prospect is that Mexico, in common with other advanced developing or newly industrializing countries, will be increasingly integrated into the international system of economic relations in its capitalistic variant. Its interests will be tied up even more with the advanced industrial countries, and even less with the poorest countries of the Fourth World, than they are today. A consistent Third-World nationalism or rhetorical flourish about dependency will be increasingly difficult to sustain. The nonoil-producing Fourth-World countries will continue to be relegated to the ash can of history as they have increasingly been relegated by oil-price increases since 1973. The emergence of Mexico as an oil power will heighten its rhetorical, and lessen its actual, concern for the poorest countries. Conversely, it will lessen its rhetorical, but heighten its actual, concern for the future of the wealthiest countries, with which its own future will be even more-inextricably linked than it is at present. This is another prospect that cannot be looked upon with favor by leftist elites in either country.

Fifth, if the foregoing generalizations and prognostications are even approximately accurate, they should not be interpreted as a recipe for complacency. The United States is fully capable of bungling this sensitive bilateral relationship as it has so badly bungled others. In this sense, the way in which the gas deal was conducted was a pure disaster. Some of the activities of the U.S. Immigration and Naturalization Service are an outrage to common canons of human decency as well as to the future of U.S. bilateral relations with Mexico. Tariff and nontariff barriers to trade also are a constant irritant and are likely to be more so as Mexico industrializes and increases its potential for exporting nontraditional products to the United States. It would be counterproductive to lean heavily on Mexico to produce vast annual amounts of petroleum and to export it to the United States. U.S. investment in Mexico is insufficiently attentive to employment creation among the Mexican masses. Agribusiness investment may in fact exacerbate rural income disparities and contribute little or nothing to Mexican rural development. The list could be expanded. However, complacency clearly cannot be recommended as an approach for U.S.-Mexican relations in the 1980s.

Sixth, despite this last point, the central generalization holds that for various reasons, the discovery, exploitation, export, and revenue generation of Mexican hydrocarbon reserves are unlikely to significantly alter in any way what might be labeled the basic parameters of U.S.-Mexican relations.

### Reactions

Some of the authors, particularly from Mexico, objected that insufficient or no evidence is available for the preceding assertions. In reply, the author asserted that the evidence was at least as good or better than that generally used to support arguments about crisis scenarios. The following points were made in defense of this contention.

A basic harmony of interests exists between the private elites of the two countries. Principal emphasis here was placed on the respective business and financial communities, and reference was made to the U.S.-Mexico Business Committee, the recently formed Quadripartite Commission, the U.S. Chamber of Commerce of Mexico, and the U.S.-Mexico Chamber of Commerce. Moreover, U.S. investment in Mexico is up after the traumas of the mid-1970s, and investment relations seem to be amicable.

More broadly, a basic harmony of interests was alleged between the middle classes of the two countries. Thousands of private interactions on a daily basis lead, in many long-term and indirect ways, to substantial congruence in values, interests, and perspectives, although some of this congruence is perhaps on things of dubious value such as the marked consumptionistic and materialistic orientations of the middle class. The evidence for this is admittedly less, but apparently the Mexican mass public does not harbor profound anti-American sentiments. A plausible hypothesis may be that there is a lack of latent, but exploitable anti-Americanism in the Mexican popular sectors. Even more certain is that there is a decided lack of mobilizers of whatever such sentiment exists compared to what has occurred in Castro's Cuba, Allende's Chile, or Khomeini's Iran.

The Mexican-American population in the United States is extremely unlikely to identify with the home country over its new country of residence. Even less likely is the ultimate fear of some—namely, Chicano—irrendentism. Tendencies in the opposite direction—that is, identification of Mexican-Americans with the official Mexican point of view on salient bilateral issues and, at the extreme, the development of separatist tendencies—would place almost intolerable strains on the bilateral relationship. Such tendencies, however, simply do not appear on the horizon, thereby also mitigating the possibility of a crisis scenario.

These secondary propositions about U.S.-Mexican relations met several heated objections from a number of the Mexican authors. Chief among them was the assertion that the views presented completely overlooked the forces of modern Mexican nationalism.

The only response to this contention must be the distinction between what might be called *rhetorical* and *operational* nationalism. Much, indeed most, Mexican nationalism has clearly been of the former variety. Mexico has developed a reputation as a highly nationalistic country, while at the same time accommodating itself quite well to foreign investors, foreign-trading interests, transferrers of science and technology, and dispensers of U.S. popular culture. How this apparent discrepancy has evolved, and what implications it poses for the operation of the Mexican political system, are highly interesting subjects but beyond the scope of these comments.

**Conclusions**

The major point, at the risk of the gross oversimplification of national identity, is this: Mexico desires to become a modern, developed country and to do so in a basically capitalistic, Western, and reformist manner. Important elements within Mexico also aspire to a greater measure of democratization in the country's political and social institutions. The exploitation of vast petroleum reserves, and the intelligent employment of the proceeds therefrom, can greatly facilitate these transcendent objectives. Recent petroleum developments in Mexico need not, therefore, inevitably mean a deterioration in U.S.-Mexican relations. The United States has a huge stake in an economically mature and politically stable southern neighbor. Petroleum proceeds have the capacity to produce economic maturity and, perhaps indirectly, to facilitate political stability. This can be accomplished by making income distribution less of a "zero-sum" game—that is, the petroleum proceeds have the capacity to improve U.S.-Mexican relations even as they make such relations less asymmetrical and more complex. The U.S. response will be crucial to the elaboration of a mutuality of interest that, despite the often incredibly ill-informed U.S. attitudes toward Mexico and the often harsh statements about the United States that make headlines in the Mexico City dailies, to a surprising degree already exists.

# Discussion Summary

The comments of discussant Robert Ayres provoked substantial discussion related to the conception of crisis as a depiction of the U.S.-Mexican relationship. Ayres noted that individuals had suggested that the U.S.-Mexican energy negotiations were in a crisis state. He disagreed with this perception of circumstances and indicated that, contrarily, he perceived share interests for the two countries. The discussion that followed explored the appropriateness of the depiction of crisis, analyzed the meaning of crisis given the U.S.-Mexican context, and speculated on characterizations other than the one of crisis.

Wionczek opened the discussion with a critique of the Ayres comments on both contextual and methodological grounds. The topical references that Wionczek extracted for response included Ayres's inferences that first, some oil-producing nations were not assisting developing nations as they might, and second, U.S. and Mexican interests coincided so that no crisis in the relationship existed. The former reference, he responded, was not an accurate characterization insofar as the OPEC countries have contributed 18 percent more of their GNP in foreign assistance to developing countries than the GNP-percentage contribution of the United States. The second inference was based on a view of Mexican society that was too narrowly conceived. He argued that a more-appropriate basis for speculation would be a recognition of the heterogeneity of Mexican society, particularly the expansive public sector. The reason for this inclusion, he implied, is because the forces of nationalism become more-readily apparent in public-sector discussion than they do in private-sector discussion. "The subjective concepts of survival, security, and power, for instance, take on different perspectives given this understanding."

Pellicer added that the private sectors of each country may very well share some values and interests, but this may not be true for other groups within each country. An analysis of each issue from the perspective of multiple groups would be the only way to determine a consensus of values and interests. For example, Mexican intellectuals and policymakers are searching for alternative models for determining levels of oil production and policies for the sale of natural gas. Some of these models do not appear to be in conjunction with U.S. policy, while others may be. She concluded, "A concert of opinion should not be taken for granted . . . these questions are very complex."

Ayres explained that he was not implying that no conflicts of interest exist between Mexico and the United States. However, he wanted to introduce a counterweight that might mitigate hypothetical fears detrimental to an energy agreement beneficial for both countries. Ayres' opinion is that

Mexico will implement an oil policy that will be congruent with U.S. interests, if the United States cares to view it in this way.

Ronfeldt observed that the concept of crisis needed elaboration before it could be appropriately used. His impression was that two different crises were being discussed. The first he termed a crisis of success. When PEMEX successfully reaches its determined oil-production platform level in 1980-1981, Mexico will face two major decisions: (1) how to alter or maintain the oil-production level and (2) how to invest the revenues that will accrue beyond the recirculation level. He remarked that these decisions will probably be affected by the next presidential-election period in Mexico, in addition to internal and external issues being raised in energy negotiations.

The second crisis he termed as one of symbolic realities. "World realities are being looked at differently—not empirically, but symbolically." Petroleum issues appear to be an acute manifestation of these differing realities, and this may be so because petroleum and PEMEX represent almost a mystical reality for Mexican nationalism. "What happens to Mexican petroleum and PEMEX affects what Mexico's leaders and the man in the street thinks about what is happening to Mexico's independence, dignity, sovereignty, and development as a nation." Mexico is facing the need to transform its nationalism in order to find a new role for itself in the world. Ronfeldt concluded, "Nationalism is at stake, not economic rationality."

Villarreal remarked that the focus on trade agreements was important for future delineation of the Mexican role. Furthermore he suggested that it is in this arena that Mexico and the United States need to explore positive conclusions and a variety of frameworks. "The main problem confronting this relationship is not one of energy and oil, but one of investment and trade." Mexican nationalism for Villarreal must be pragmatic. "Oil in Mexico is not just energy. It is not just an instrument with which to accumulate foreign exchange. It is an instrument of economic policy, and it is very important." According to Villarreal, Mexico does not want to become just an oil-exporting country but a country with a diversified trade and investment policy. Energy negotiations must recognize this goal if they are to move forward.

Sepúlveda underscored Villarreal's comments and closed the session by emphasizing the need for an even broader perspective. Instead of a discussion that gravitates toward U.S. energy needs and Mexican problems, it might be useful to discuss U.S. problems and Mexican needs. He emphasized his point by asking, "If Mexico is experiencing a symbolic crisis, what type of crisis is the United States experiencing?"

# Mexican Oil: A Guide to Source Materials

### Walter V. Brem, Jr.

The Mexican-oil discoveries in the early 1970s and the subsequent resurgence of the Mexican petroleum industry have stimulated a profusion of information and documentation concerning their potential impact on the United States and Mexico. Early international analysis was skeptical of the size of the reserves and the ability of PEMEX to tap the oil fields effectively. The official Mexican position was characterized by secrecy and guarded assessments. However, since 1977, as estimates of the size of the reserves have been revised significantly upward and as doubts about PEMEX's technical capabilities have been seemingly resolved, the literature has boomed with pronouncements celebrating Mexico's tremendous oil wealth. Simultaneously, questions of international- and domestic-policy implications have been raised. Diverse aspects of U.S.-Mexican relations; Mexican foreign policy toward the hemisphere and the world; and Mexican internal political-, economic-, and social-development processes are being analyzed, discussed, and debated vigorously. As these policies are further defined, the flow of information is likely to increase considerably.

Although a substantial corpus of literature on Mexican petroleum already exists, it is still a very recent phenomenon, and no single bibliography is available. Extensive bibliographies are appearing in new monographic studies such as that in Edward J. Williams's *Rebirth of the Mexican Petroleum Industry*. This guide does not pretend to replicate or supersede Williams's list. Rather, it is a complement, a pathfinder, through the disparate and diverse source materials on the subject. It is a highly selective, working guide to bibliographical tools and specific sources for the efficient and effective retrieval of current information. It is intended for a broad audience of researchers, teachers, businessmen, and laymen who want to anticipate those sources that will regularly, frequently, and substantively cover the subject of Mexican oil as the pace and volume of publication quickens and increases.

The burgeoning literature covers many aspects of Mexican petroleum—scientific and technical as well as political, social, and economic. This guide is limited specifically to U.S.-Mexican relations and to Mexican internal-developmental policies pertaining to petroleum and natural gas. Many foreign and domestic issues stemming from the oil boom are sharply drawn in Mexico, and these divergent policy, editorial, and ideological positions are liberally represented in the guide. In the case of the U.S. imprints, Mexican petroleum is often treated tangentially as a part of broader U.S. energy requirements and policies. Therefore, monographic publications, particularly government publications, are selected specifically for their focus on U.S.-Mexican oil and natural-gas dealings.

The fundamental bibliographical criteria for inclusion of materials in this guide were currency and accessibility. Indexes and abstracts are the cornerstones of the guide. Besides their frequency of updating and cumulation, indexes also provide the most-systematic and thorough coverage of the widest range of document types—books, articles in journals and newspapers, chapters in collected works, consultants' reports, government publications, and so forth. Several-dozen indexes and abstracts were tested for their coverage of Mexican oil and its policy ramifications. Those listed here yielded the best results.

Serial literature is the most-consistent source of current information. The newspapers and periodicals listed are the results of the analysis of the indexes and abstracts. Although indexed serials predominate, many Mexican newspapers and periodicals escape consistent or up-to-date indexing and had to be selected by intensive citation analysis to ascertain which sources were most-consistently used in contemporary research. In these cases, currency and frequency requirements were relaxed to allow for more time lag in publication. Therefore, more quarterly journals were listed. Mexican serial government publications were chosen the same way so annuals could be included. Last, for both U.S. and Mexican periodicals, popular weekly news magazines were essentially omitted in favor of more-specialized publications.

The last section on books, articles, and chapters deserves some explanation. Only the most-recent publications on Mexican oil were listed, although all available literature published since 1974 was evaluated. The criterion of currency was especially applied to authors who have been publishing related articles or who have published several articles culminating in a book. In all those cases the latest scholarship includes citations of earlier writings of the subject. For further brevity, collected works or journal issues devoted entirely to Mexican oil were listed only by the title, issue, and date. Annotations were kept to a minimum. Finally, only published and verified works were listed.

## Indexes, Abstracts, and Computerized Data Bases

*ABI/Inform.* Louisville, Ky.: Data Courier, 1971-     . On-line.
*ASI (American Statistics Index).* Washington, D.C.: Congressional Information Service, 1973-     . On-line and printed.
*Business Periodicals Index.* New York: H.W. Wilson, 1958-     . Printed.
*CIS/Index.* Washington, D.C.: Congressional Information Service, 1970-     . On-line and printed.

*CLASE: Citas latinoamericanas en sociología economía.* Mexico: Centro de Información Científica y Humanística, Universidad Nacional Autónoma de México, 1976-    . Printed.

*Economic Abstracts International.* The Hague: Ministry of Economic Affairs, 1974-    . On-line.

*Energy Data Base.* Washington, D.C.: Department of Energy, 1974-    . On-line.

*Energyline.* New York: Environment Information Center, 1971-    . On-line. Includes *Energy Index.* New York: Environment Information Center, 1973-    . (covers 1970-    ); and *Energy Information Abstracts.* New York: Environment Information Center, 1976-    . Printed.

*Management Contents.* Skokie, Il.: Management Contents, 1974-    . On-line and printed.

*P/E News.* New York: American Petroleum Institute, 1975-    . On-line Includes *Petroleum Energy Business News.* New York: American Petroleum Institute, 1975-    . Printed.

*Petroleum Abstracts.* Tulsa, Ok.: University of Tulsa, 1961-    . Printed. Public Affairs Information Service (PAIS). *PAIS International.* New York: 1972-    . Includes *Bulletin.* 1976-    ; and *Foreign Language Index.* 1972-    . On-line.

*Social Scisearch.* Philadelphia: Institute for Scientific Information, 1972-    . On-line. Includes *Social Science Citation Index.* Philadelphia: Institute of Scientific Information, 1972-    . Printed.

**Serials**

*Newspapers*

*Christian Science Monitor.* Boston, 1908-    .
*Excélsior.* Mexico, 1917-    .
*Financial Times.* London, 1888-    .
*Journal of Commerce.* New York, 1827-    .
*Los Angeles Times.* Los Angeles, 1881-    .
*The New York Times.* New York, 1851-    .
*Wall Street Journal.* New York, 1889-    .
*Washington Post.* Washington, D.C., 1877-    .

*Periodicals*

*Barron's.* New York, 1921-    . Weekly.
*Business Week.* New York, 1929-    . Weekly.

*Comercio exterior*. Mexico, 1951-    . Monthly. *Comercio exterior de México*, English-language edition. Mexico, 1955-    . Monthly.
*Economist*. London, 1843-    . Weekly.
*Estrategia*. Mexico, 1974/1975-    . Quarterly.
*Euromoney*. London, 1969-    . Monthly.
*Examen de la situación económica de méxico*. Mexico, 1925-    . Monthly. (*Review of the Economic Situation in Mexico*, English-language edition: Mexico, 1932-    . Monthly.)
*Forbes*. New York, 1917-    . Biweekly.
*Foro internacional*. Mexico, 1960-    . Quarterly.
*Fortune*. Chicago, 1930-    . Biweekly.
*Information Services on Latin America*. Oakland, Calif.: 1970-    . Monthly.
Instituto Mexicano del Petróleo. *Revista*. Mexico, 1969-    . Quarterly.
*Latin America Regional Report: Mexico*. London, 1979-    . 10 issues per year.
*Lloyd's Mexican Economic Report*. Guadalajara, 1963-    . Monthly.
*El mercado de valores*. Mexico, 1941-    . Weekly.
*Mexican Newsletter*. Mexico, 1971-    . Monthly.
*Oil and Gas Journal*. Tulsa, Ok.: 1902-    . Weekly.
*Oil Daily*. New York, 1951-    . Daily.
*Petróleo internacional*. Tulsa, Ok.: 1974-    . Monthly.
*Petroleum Economist*. London, 1934-    . Monthly.
*Problemas del desarrollo*. Mexico, 1969-    . Quarterly.
*Proceso*. Mexico, 1976-    . Weekly.
*El trimestre económico*. Mexico, 1934-    . Quarterly.
*World Oil*. Houston, 1916-    . 14 issues per year.


**Government Publications**

*Mexico*

Mexico. Secretaría de la Presidencia. *El gobierno mexicano*, 3a época. Mexico, 1976-    . Monthly.
_____ . Secretaría de Programación y Presupuesto. *Boletín mensual de información económica*. Mexico, 1977-    . Monthly.
Petróleos Mexicanos. *Informe del director general*. Mexico, 1938-    . Annual. (*Report of the Director General*, English-language edition. 1973-1981.)
_____ . *Memoria de labores*. Mexico, 1965-    . Annual.

*United States*

*Business America.* Washington, D.C.: Department of Commerce, 1978-    . Biweekly.

Moler, Elizabeth. *Mexico, the Promise and Problems of Petroleum.* Washington, D.C.: Government Printing Office, 1979.

*Monthly Energy Review.* Washington, D.C.: National Energy Information Center, 1974-    . Monthly.

U.S. Congress. House. Committee on Science and Technology. *U.S./Mexico Relations and Potentials Regarding Energy, Resources, National Economy.* Washington, D.C.: Government Printing Office, 1979.

_____. Subcommittee on Investigations and Oversight. *Mexican Oil and Technology Transfer.* Washington, D.C.: Government Printing Office, 1979.

_____. Foreign Broadcast Information Service. *Daily Report: Latin America.* Washington, D.C.: 1974-    . 5 issues per week.

_____. General Accounting Office. *Prospects for a Stronger United States-Mexico Energy Relationship.* Washington, D.C.: Government Printing Office, 1980.

_____. Library of Congress. Congressional Research Service. *Mexico's Oil and Gas Policy.* Washington, D.C.: Government Printing Office, 1979.

**Books, Articles, and Chapters**

Barrientos, Javier A., Jr. "Energy Development in Mexico: The Assessment of Its Implications." In *U.S.-Mexico Economic Relations.* Barry W. Poulson and T. Noel Osborn. Boulder, Colo.: Westview Press, 1979.

Bermudez, Antonio J. *La política petrolera mexicana.* Mexico: Editorial J. Mortiz, 1976.

Carlson, Sevinc. *Mexico's Oil: Trends and Prospects to 1985.* Washington, D.C.: Center for Strategic and International Studies, Georgetown University, 1978.

Carmona, Fernando. "El salvavidas del petróleo, La estrategia del regimen." *Estrategia*, no. 25 (January-February 1979), pp. 2-28.

*El economista mexicano* 12, no. 2 (March-April 1978).

El Mallakh, Ragaei. "Mexico, the United States, and OPEC: A Potential Energy Triangle," in *U.S.-Mexico Economic Relations.* Ed. Barry W. Poulson and T. Noel Osborn. Boulder, Colo.: Westview Press, 1979.

Estrada, José Luis, and Camacho, José Luis. *1979, La verdad Sobre el petróleo en México.* Mexico: Costa-Amic Editor, 1978.

Fagen, Richard R. "Mexican Petroleum and U.S. National Security." *International Security* 4, no. 1 (Summer 1979):39-53.

Fagen, Richard R., and Nau, Henry R. "Mexican Gas: The Northern Connection." In *Capitalism and the State in U.S.-Latin American Relations.* Ed. Richard R. Fagen. Stanford, Calif.: Stanford University Press, 1979.

Grayson, George W. "Oil and U.S.-Mexican Relations." *Journal of Interamerican Studies and World Affairs* 21, no. 4 (November 1979):427-56.

Lazar, A. von; Duersten, A.L.; and Dickson, M.T. "Development Planning in Mexico: Case Study of an Oil-Rich Economy." *Resources Policy* 5, no. 3 (September 1979):197-207.

Luis-Pineda, Octavio. "Impact of Economic Policymaking Regarding Energy Resources: The Mexican Case." In *U.S.-Mexico Economic Relations.* Ed. Barry W. Poulson and T. Noel Osborn. Boulder, Colo.: Westview Press, 1979.

Mancke, Richard B. *Mexican Oil and Natural Gas: Political, Strategic, and Economic Implications.* New York: Praeger, 1979.

Margulis, Mario. "Petróleo, indocumentados y maquiladores: teoría de la renta ya transferencia de valor." *Arte, sociedad, ideología,* no. 6 (April-May 1978), pp. 103-19.

Pazos, Luis. *Mitos y realidades del petróleo mexicano.* Mexico: Editorial Diana, 1979.

*Perspectivas del petróleo mexicano.* Mexico: Colegio de Mexico, 1979. Includes papers presented at a symposium sponsored by the Colegio de Mexico, 6-7 July 1978 and published in *Foro internacional* 72.

*Petróleo y soberanía: El gasoducto y el futuro de México.* Mexico: Editorial Posada, 1979.

*Problemas del desarrollo* 7, no. 27 (August-October 1976); and 10, no. 37 (February-April 1979).

Ramírez Heredia, Rafael. *La otra cara del petróleo: Mexico: Editorial Diana, 1979.*

*Tirado, Manlio. El problema del petróleo: Tabasco, Chapas y el gasoducto.* Mexico: Ediciones Quonto Sol, 1978.

Villar, Samuel I. del. "Estado y petróleo en México: experiencas y perspectivas." *Foro internacional* 20, no. 1 (July-September 1979):118-58.

Williams, Edward J. *Rebirth of the Mexican Petroleum Industry: Developmental Directions and Policy Implications.* Lexington, Mass.: Lexington Books, D.C. Heath and Company, 1979.

# Index

Abu Dhabi, area, 178
Administration and administrators, 45, 48, 59, 89
Advisors, economic and financial, 90, 96
Aerospace and air routes, 13, 156
Agriculture, 93, 95, 106, 152, 160, 195; commercial, 204; commodities, 13, 121, 125; development, 23-26; employment in, 192; exports of, 33; investment in, 108, 158; and irrigation, 156; modernization of, 136; production, 33; reform in 57; subsidy aids for, 101; subsistence, 164
Agriculture and Hydraulic Sector, Secretary of, 24
Alaska: North Slope area, 103; oil reserves in, 20
Alliance for Production, 163, 167
Alternative energy sources, 181
Ambiguity, concept themes of, 3, 5, 10, 14
American Jewish Committee, 210
Anarchy, forms of, 136
Anglo-Saxon Protestant countries, 4-5
Anti-: dumping laws, 192; inflation measures, 79, 126, 192; Yankeeism, 7-8
Antiquities, Mexican, 13
Arab countries, 17-19, 27, 197, 212
Arab-Israeli conflict, 197
Aramco (Arabian American Oil Company), 19
Argentina, 64
Arizona-Sonora border, 21
Arms race, fear of, 136
Assets: capital, 126, 165; foreign investments, 107; ownership, 161
Associated Press (AP), 20
Attitudes, 5, 140-141
Authority and authoritarianism; civil, 129; dispensing of, 48; military, 129; political system, 8, 45, 63; technocratic models, 64-65
Automotive industry, 98
Autonomy, 63, 210; and decision-making process, 50-51; loss of, 53; national, 162; and public enterprises, 45
Ayres, Robert L., 130, 215-219

Baja, California, 38, 91
Balance of payments, 22, 25-26, 73, 79, 118, 200, 202, 204, 206
Balance of power, 202, 210-212
Balance of trade, 55, 148-150, 198
Bank of America, 156

Bank of Mexico, 95, 104
Banks and banking system, 95, 156; credit, 108; deposits, 201; failures of, 54; international, 62; private, 11
Bargaining: collective, 126; political, 64; positions, 198; power of oil, 186-189, 193-194, 203-205, 211; weapons, 206
Barriers, trade, 94, 142, 193, 216
Bell System, 153
Bergman, Elihu, 129
Bermúdez, Antonio, 50, 53
Bids and bidding, competitive, 176
Bilateral relations, complexity of, 3-5, 9-14, 55, 171
Birthrate, factor of, 179
Blau, Thomas, 171-173
Boom times in oil, 8, 20, 23, 45, 91, 128-130, 162, 221
Borrowing, foreign, 70, 105, 155
Bottlenecks: existence of, 90-91, 127, 203; structural, 92-93, 95-96
Boycotts, 4, 206-208
Brazil, 7, 11, 57, 64-65, 129, 162, 178, 193, 207
Brem, Walter V., Jr., 221-226
Budgets and budgeting, 24, 47, 70, 119, 150
Bueño, Gerardo, 84
Bureaucracy and bureaucrats, 118
Burgos basin, 38
Business confidence, need for, 57, 87, 89

Cactus I well, 39
Caderyta, pipeline to, 206
California, 155-157, 159, 177
Campeche, Bay of, 8, 90; Gulf of, 61
Campeche Bank, 38-39, 42
Campeche Province, 43, 58, 60
Campeche Sound, 54
Canada, 7, 120, 143, 178, 187-188, 191, 202, 206-207
Capital: assets, 126, 165; availability, 58; budgets, 119; developmental, 13; flow of, 89; foreign, 56, 62, 69, 81-82; goods, 56-57, 61, 80, 82, 84, 95, 198; human, 164; imports, 80, 97; income, 161; insufficient, 136; intensive, 100, 102, 119; international, 56; investments, 56; private, 46, 104; requirements, 13, 155; return on, 163-164; stock, 166; technical, 84
Capitalism and capitalists: contradictions of, 163; criticisms of, 165; international, 57; market-oriented corporations, 47; national, 82; power, 186; system, 194, 215; transnational, 69, 82

227

# List of Contributors

**Robert L. Ayres**, Senior Fellow, Overseas Development Council, Washington, D.C.

**Thomas Blau**, Professional Staff, Research and Development Associates, Washington, D.C.

**Walter V. Brem, Jr.**, Latin American Area Specialist, Hayden Library, Arizona State University

**Olga Pellicer de Brody**, Professor of Political Science, Colegio de México

**John H. Christman**, Director, Economic and Investment Information, American Chamber of Commerce of Mexico, A.C., Mexico City

**Robert E. Ebel**, Vice-President of International Development, ENSERCH Corporation, Washington, D.C.

**Lawrence Goldmuntz**, President, Economics and Science Planning, Inc., Washington, D.C.

**Bernardo F. Grossling**, Natural Resources Advisor, Inter-American Development Bank, Washington, D.C.

**Sidney M. Leveson**, President, Leveson Associates, Inc., Marlboro, N.J.

**Jesús Puente Leyva**, Member, Energy Committee, Mexican Chamber of Deputies, 1976-1979. Currently Mexican Ambassador to Venezuela

**Bruce C. Netschert**, Vice-President, National Economic Research Associates, Inc., Washington, D.C.

**Mario Ojeda**, Professor of Political Science, Colegio de México

**Laura Randall**, Professor of Economics, Hunter College, City University of New York

**Clark W. Reynolds**, Professor of Economics, Food Research Institute, Stanford University

**Isidro Sepúlveda**, Professor of Political Science, Universidad Nacional Autónoma de México

**René Villarreal**, Sub-Director, Office of Planning, Mexican Ministry of Treasury

**Edward J. Williams**, Professor of Political Science, University of Arizona

# About the Editors

**Jerry R. Ladman,** professor of economics and director of the Center for Latin American Studies at Arizona State University, received the Ph.D. from Iowa State University. He has had a long-term research interest in Mexico, with emphasis on agricultural development, the border economy, the Border Industrialization Program, and internal migration. In Mexico, Dr. Ladman was in program management with the Mexico City office of the Ford Foundation and was twice visiting professor at the National Agricultural University in Chapingo. He has been a Fulbright Lecturer in Ecuador and a consultant to the World Bank, the U.S. Agency for International Development, the U.S. Department of State, the U.S. Department of Agriculture, the Ford Foundation, and the Central Bank of Ecuador. Dr. Ladman's current research emphasis is on Bolivian rural financial markets.

**Deborah J. Baldwin,** assistant professor of Latin American history at the University of Arkansas at Little Rock, received the Ph.D. from the University of Chicago. She is a specialist on twentieth-century Mexico and has taught classes on the subject at Arizona State University, University of Arizona, and the American Graduate School of International Management. Dr. Baldwin has traveled extensively in Mexico, has directed an on-site community-action project for the American Friends Service Committee in Chihuahua, and has been a consultant to several Hispanic agencies in the Southwest.

**Elihu Bergman**, executive director of Americans for Energy Independence, a national public-interest association based in Washington, D.C., received the Ph.D. in political science from the University of North Carolina at Chapel Hill. Dr. Bergman's career has involved government, private, and foundation experience in the planning and management of economic-development programs. These activities have included long-term assignments in Iran, Yugoslavia, and Mexico, and extensive travel in the Middle East, Africa, and Latin America with the U.S. Agency for International Development, the Ford Foundation, and Development and Resources Corporation. From 1971-1977 Dr. Bergman served as assistant director of the Center for Population Studies at Harvard University.

His publications on U.S. energy policy include *American Energy Choices Before the Year 2000*, coedited with Hans Bethe and Robert Marshak, Lexington Books, (1978); and *New Perspectives on the International Oil Supply* for which he was also a coeditor (Americans for Energy Independence Energy Policy Series, 1979).